INTERACTIONS

INTERACTIONS
Collaboration Skills
for
School Professionals

Marilyn Friend
Northern Illinois University

Lynne Cook
California State University, Northridge

Longman
New York & London

Interactions: Collaboration Skills for School Professionals

Longman, 10 Bank Street, White Plains, N.Y. 10606

Associated companies:
Longman Group Ltd., London
Longman Cheshire Pty., Melbourne
Longman Paul Pty., Auckland
Copp Clark Pitman, Toronto

Senior editor: Naomi Silverman
Production editor: Victoria Mifsud
Cover design: Tony Alberts
Text art: Fine Line Inc.
Production supervisor: Richard C. Bretan

Library of Congress Cataloging-in-Publication Data

Friend, Marilyn Penovich
    Interactions : collaboration skills for school professionals /
Marilyn Friend, Lynne Cook.
        p. cm.
    Includes bibliographical references and index.
    ISBN 0-8013-0297-8
    1. Special education teachers—Training of. 2. Interpersonal
relations. 3. Communication in education. I. Cook, Lynne.
II. Title.
LC3969.45.F75 1992
371.9—dc20   91-7686
                                                        CIP

    3 4 5 6 7 8 9 10-MA-959493

Contents

Foreword

Every year produces a new spate of advice books, so soon to be forgotten, on educational improvement. The only thing on which there is agreement is that schools are in for massive changes and these changes will require learning new collaborative processes if schools are to adapt and survive. This book is about collaboration; it offers a comprehensive treatment of collaboration in schools. This volume is on the creative edge because it can be used as a tool to learn skills that are of immediate necessity as well as those that have broad application and lasting value.

The authors eschew the two typical educational approaches to inducing educational change. One is to produce a "how to" book that resorts to specific rituals of very narrow application. The other is to emphasize the philosphy to such an extent that there is no room for the psychological substructure that is critical to understand. In this book, the authors have recognized the complex nature of the true task and emphasized generic *process* over ritual, and psychologically based understanding over ad hoc pronouncements. They help us to understand and use the principles and skills necessary for effective interpersonal collaboration in a time of change.

Because of the design the authors employed, they produced a book that can be used as a class text, a small-group in-service training manual, or a self-teaching skills book. They offer realistic, specific examples from their extensive practical field experience and foster direct application of the theory-embedded processes. There is no implication of a magic cure-all. It is designated hard work to facilitate collaborative behavior in ourselves and others. Plans do not always work out well. Although we are all supposedly well meaning, we still have our own egos to protect. The scholarly base is evident; the authors have studied and analyzed the literature woven into text.

So much depends on the veracity of the examples that are found throughout. Since the authors have "been there," they produce problems for analysis that we recognize and can identify as ours, often with names attached to a specific reminiscence. The authors imply no one simple resolution, or even that every conflict can be resolved. Difficulties and risks are matched with benefits. A very engaging aspect of this skill-teaching book is realism. The authors recognize from their extended experience in applied action settings that change is not a simple process and is not accomplished by edict.

There are many carefully crafted conceptual expositions in this book. For example, consultation is contrasted with collaboration and the importance of interpersonal style is examined in Chapter 2. The often neglected literature from group dynamics gives substance to the sections on collaboration in group settings. The pitfalls of unclear language are avoided by providing concrete definitions of terms throughout. This again sets their work apart in a field that often assumes as common technical terms that are in fact not common at all.

For the person wishing to develop skills in collaboration, Friend and Cook have produced an excellent source book. The applications are as broad as program implementation and as specific as how to ask useful questions. The context for this text reflects conditions we all face almost every day. Especially pertinent are discussions of resistance and conflict resolution. This is a book that will pay dividends to anyone, regardless of the specific educational role one has. Finally, it is a pleasure to read a book about a complex subject written in clear, direct English.

William C. Morse
University of Michigan/University of South Florida

Preface

At the annual convention of the Council for Exceptional Children in 1988, we met for the first time and shared with one another concerns we had about directions that the field of special education seemed to be taking regarding the issue of professionals working together to provide services to special education students. *Interactions* is the result of our concerns.

This book deals with the interpersonal working relationships among professionals in schools. It is a guide for students and professionals to help them understand and participate effectively in their interactions with other professionals and parents in schools. This book was written for a broad audience: preservice and inservice special education, general education, and related services personnel who educate students with disabilities. The examples and activities herein focus on special service providers but are not unique to that group. What we know clearly after writing this book is that the principles for effective interaction are not dependent on roles or settings—they are universal.

In our own undergraduate and graduate teaching, we have found that many textbooks rely too heavily on theory and abstraction; although the concepts they address may be intriguing, too little applied information is given to readers to enable them to implement the ideas to practice. The knowledge and skills presented in *Interactions* follow a specific sequence of development, and examples given in text as well as the activities and exercises provided at the end of each chapter provide opportunities to learn how the information is related to the interactions you may have tomorrow.

OVERVIEW OF THE BOOK

Chapters 1 and 2 present a conceptual foundation for understanding collaborative interactions and activities and settings that support them. A framework is established in Chapter 1 when we define collaboration and highlight its benfits and risks. Two widely accepted practices in schools—teaming and consultation—are examined in Chapter 2, and the application of collaborative principles within these activities is considered.

Chapter 3 connects the introductory chapters and the chapters that focus on interaction skills. Chapter 3 presents the concepts that underlie communication and interaction skills including understanding categories of information, recognizing diverse frames of reference, and preparing to listen.

Interpersonal problem solving—the first major interaction skill—is addressed in Chapter 4. It is the most central process for collaboration. All of the communication and interaction skills presented in Chapters 5 to 9 are used in problem-solving processes.

Chapters 5, 6, and 7 focus on communication skills. The principles of interpersonal communication, both verbal and nonverbal, are presented in Chapter 5. The discussion of verbal communication in Chapters 6 and 7 is structured around the use of statements in Chapter 6 and questions in Chapter 7. In Chapters 6 and 7, verbal strategies are considered according to their intent to provide, solicit, or clarify information.

A somewhat different direction is taken in Chapters 8 and 9, which deal with conflict and resistance. Strategies are emphasized that require the use of many of the interaction process and communication skills addressed earlier in the text. Strategies for program development are outlined in Chapter 10. Because so many schools are making programmatic changes that try to facilitate collaboration, professionals frequently ask us how they should go about setting up a program that emphasizes collaboration. For readers engaged in this process, Chapter 10 may be the most appropriate starting place.

TEXT FEATURES

Advance organizers.   Each chapter begins with a section "Keeping Perspective," which is designed to assist readers in understanding how the specific chapter context relates to the overall organization of the text.

Chapter objectives.   Each Keeping Perspective section is followed by objectives that inform the reader about the main purposes of the chapter. The objectives also help the reader to set expectations for what he or she will be able to do after studying the chapter.

Case descriptions.   Case descriptions are presented throughout the text to illustrate relevant concepts and principles.

Skill models.   Chapters 3 through 10 provide instructional formats that give concrete models or examples of specific skills. This feature is enhanced by contrasting poor examples and/or alternatives that help readers to discriminate multiple aspects of skills.

Application/practice.   Application times are given to involve the reader in analyzing and applying the principles described to actual interpersonal situations. These items are also found at the end of each chapter; they assess the readers' understanding of important information in the chapter and provide suggestions for skill development activities. These exercises may be used as part of organized training experiences or may be used independently.

Chapter summaries.   Each chapter concludes with a summary that briefly recaps the major points addressed in it.

Related readings.   A brief list of additional readings is included for each chapter. These references enable readers who want detailed information about a particular topic as a means of quickly accessing that information.

We hope you enjoy and find useful the information we have collected in *Interactions*.

ACKNOWLEDGMENTS

We are indebted to many people who assisted in the development of this text and the work that undergirds it. Many of our teachers, colleagues, students, family members, and friends have contributed in diverse and highly valuable ways to make this work a reality. Even though we cannot name them all, we hope they see their influence reflected in this volume and know of our appreciation.

We would like to specifically acknowledge several people whose contributions have been especially helpful: First, we thank Claire Cavallaro and Charles Hanson; several case descriptions and illustrations included in the text are variations of training activities they helped to design. Without the background provided by that work many of the examples in *Interactions* would not have been developed.

We would also like to thank our colleagues who provided professional reviews of the manuscript. Gaye McNutt, Mary Male, and Lani Florian read the first full draft of *Interactions* and provided insightful suggestions and guidance for improving it. Vicki Phillips, Cindy Geeza, Marty Kaufman, Kathy Hebbeler, Wendy Webster, and Marcia Hann read portions of the manuscript to assist us on specific parts of the material. In addition, Lynnette Farrell, Heather Weintraub, Judy Hill, Debbie Holderness, Cathy Lubbers, and Debbie Ching provided patient and skillful assistance in producing a technically sound manuscript across long distance using incompatible technologies.

Throughout the development of *Interactions* we received guidance, encouragement, and advice from the professional staff at Longman. We are particularly appreciative of Naomi Silverman who expertly guided us through the process.

We are especially indebted to Professor William Morse for his guidance in improving our work and this text. Professor Morse reviewed portions of the manuscript and the first complete manuscript. In all cases, he made invaluable suggestions for improving the substance and clarity of presentation. More importantly, his insightful, gentle, and yet penetrating critiques improved every aspect of our work and *Interactions*.

To our families and friends, we express heartfelt thanks for their continued support and encouragement to see this project through. They patiently tolerated our preoccupation with the book and lovingly made the accommodations and modifications in holiday and vacation plans necessary to allow us to work together during those times. Finally, we want to express our deepest appreciation to Fred Weintraub who tirelessly supported our efforts in every way. He critiqued drafts and challenged our ideas in ways that strengthened our material and its presentation. He brought humor, advice, encouragement, and wonderfully prepared meals to us throughout the highly rewarding collaboration that resulted in our writing *Interactions*. Thanks, Fred.

Marilyn Friend
Lynne Cook

CHAPTER 1

The Fundamentals
of Collaboration

Keeping Perspective

In Chapter 1, you will learn what collaboration is, how it relates to societal trends and trends in schools, and why it may sometimes be difficult for school professionals to engage in collaborative activities. This information introduces you to basic collaboration concepts that will be discussed in applied contexts in Chapter 2.

Learner Objectives

1. To give examples illustrating the current trend toward collaboration in public schools.
2. To define collaboration and describe its characteristics.
3. To outline societal and school trends contributing to the evolution of collaborative activities in schools.
4. To explain professional and pragmatic factors that sometimes make it difficult for school professionals to collaborate in providing services to special education and at-risk students.

INTRODUCTION

The roles and responsibilities of special education and related services professionals have changed tremendously over the past two decades. Increasingly, special education teachers who traditionally instructed students in a resource room or self-contained class now may provide learning assistance or share teaching responsibilities in their students' mainstream classrooms. School psychologists whose primary function used to be assessing students for possible special education placement now may work with teachers to design and manage curriculum-based measurement systems. Similarly, physical therapists who typically worked with special education students in a clinical setting now may spend considerable time assisting teachers to incorporate therapeutically beneficial activities throughout the school day. In addition, speech and language specialists who previously provided remediation to students in their offices now may offer integrative therapy in their students' classes.

The changes in professionals' roles are even more complex than they may first appear because they are so varied: If you visited schools across the country, you would find that no single model could describe all the different ways in which school professionals carry out their roles and responsibilities. Consider the following three school situations that could easily occur in neighboring districts in a single metropolitan area:

TAYLOR SCHOOL DISTRICT

After three years of limited trial, Ms. Gordon, the school counselor, has convinced the administrators in the Taylor School District that several of the students with whom she works show greater progress when she counsels them in small groups in their classrooms and when other students are included. She has developed working relationships with two teachers who meet with her each week to coordinate instructional plans and to agree on classroom-based follow-up activities that the teachers will implement to reinforce her weekly interventions. Ms. Gordon continues to provide traditional office-based counseling services to the remainder of her caseload, assist new students to adapt to school, and arrange class schedules for students with special programmatic needs.

One of the teachers with whom Ms. Gordon has worked is Mr. Chan, a special educator. Mr. Chan has been so pleased with the progress his students have made and with his own improved group counseling skills that he has established a similar relationship with the general education teacher of two of his students. He has reorganized his schedule to create time to provide math instruction to the students three times weekly in their general education classroom. After meeting with his teaching colleague, however, Mr. Chan becomes aware that he will also need to arrange opportunities for joint planning and consultation with this general education teacher.

FLATROCK SCHOOL DISTRICT

Mr. Powell is a special education teacher in the Flatrock Schools, a district that has a long tradition of providing exemplary services to students with disabilities. Mr. Powell's typical day involves delivering intensive small-group instruction for his students scheduled around their limited mainstream classes. The other teachers in the building know they can rely on Mr. Powell to give special education students the instruction they need. In fact, the teachers sometimes ask Mr. Powell about other students experiencing difficulties in their classes, and he frequently uses his preparation period to consult with them on strategies to help remedial or unmotivated learners.

Ms. Frere, the district's school psychologist, is Mr. Powell's colleague. Although Ms. Frere's hectic schedule of assessments, report preparation, and team meetings sometimes makes conferring difficult, the two professionals try to keep in touch concerning students' behavior problems and day-to-day issues such as changes in district special education record-keeping requirements, upcoming professional development activities, and parental concerns. Ms. Frere and Mr. Powell sometimes discuss how they might provide more systematic assistance to their general education colleagues who request it. Ms. Frere and Mr. Powell are considering starting a peer support group for interested teachers.

CANNON SCHOOL DISTRICT

With approval from the school board, vast changes have occurred in the Cannon School District's special education service delivery model over the past three years. For example, as a resource teacher in the district for 15 years, Ms. Harris has delivered instruction using a traditional tutorial approach until recently. Now, however, she complies with the district philosophy that this type of special education service is only justified if sustained efforts to keep students in their mainstream classes have not been successful. On a day-to-day basis, Ms. Harris spends nearly three-fourths of her time providing instruction to designated students in general education classrooms and meeting with teachers. She coordinates her services with those of Ms. Averitte, the speech and language specialist, who is similarly providing most of her services in the general education setting. For both professionals, scheduling is a challenge: Because their day-to-day work is greatly influenced by the immediate needs of their students and the classroom teachers, Ms. Harris' and Ms. Averitte's schedules must remain flexible enough to juggle the changing demands. Also, Ms. Harris and Ms. Averitte regularly coteach with general education teachers and find they must arrange planning time with all their teacher colleagues. Both specialists find that classroom teachers' attitudes toward the special education program approach range from enthusiasm and collegiality to resentment and resistance.

In each of the foregoing situations, adult–adult interactions are central features. In each school district, special services and general education professionals are currently engaged in, or attempting to engage in, joint planning and decision making. Likewise, special service professionals are providing consultation or technical assistance to classroom teachers. The professional interactions that occur in each of the districts illustrate three critical points for understanding the premise of this text:

First, regardless of the type of educational setting in which professionals work or plan to work, adult–adult interactions are an essential part of their responsibilities. In the Taylor School District, the service delivery approach and professional roles are somewhat innovative but strongly anchored in cautious change. In Flatrock, the programs are very traditional, but the two special service providers are actively promoting collaborative interactions without modifying services. In Cannon, program redesign is requiring significant role changes for professionals and significant changes in the delivery of special education. The amount of program or service change is not the critical factor; the contemporary demand for effective adult–adult interactions exists in the most innovative settings as well as in the most traditional ones. Therefore, it might be helpful for school professionals to think about the types of adult–adult interactions that they have or are likely to have, and to read this text with those interactions in mind.

Second, the case descriptions demonstrate that effective adult-adult interactions are not the focus for any one group of school professionals. General and special education teachers, speech and language specialists, school psychologists, and counselors are being affected by the trend toward increased interactions as are other special service professional groups such as occupational and physical therapists, social workers, and adaptive physical educators. All school professionals need to be able to interact successfully with other professionals and parents.

Finally, we hope that the case descriptions demonstrate that adult-adult interactions are not limited to specific program names, position descriptions, or role titles. For example, in some states the special education program in Cannon might be called a consultation program, and the teacher might be called a teacher consultant or a consulting teacher. Similarly, in some locales the counselor's work in Taylor might be considered a version of coteaching, in others it would be viewed as a systematic prevention program, while in still others it would be called counseling. Ultimately, we have abandoned the notion that we can present the concepts in this text in a way that meets the infinite array of terms being used to describe the implementation of programs and services focusing on adult-adult interactions. Instead, we will clearly define the technical terms we introduce, and we will rely on readers' ability to relate the concepts presented to the situations and settings with which they are familiar.

This book, then, is about effective interactions. It presents the generic concepts, principles, skills, and strategies that school professionals can use to enhance their shared efforts to educate their students.

COLLABORATION CONCEPTS

Whenever professional interactions or emerging special education service programs are discussed, the term "collaboration" is likely to be mentioned. You may hear colleagues talk about collaborating to develop an intervention, or your school district or agency may be promoting collaborative programs. Perhaps your professional role requires you to establish collaborative relationships with other professionals and parents. All the professionals in the Taylor, Flatrock, and Cannon school districts might label their interactions collaboration. Collaboration appears to have become the special services "buzzword" of the 1990s, often carelessly used and occasionally misapplied as suggested in Figure 1.1

Despite all the current discussion about collaboration, few clear definitions of it have been presented. In fact, some dictionary definitions of collaboration include reference to treason or working together for sinister purposes! In the human services, Pryzwansky (1977) has offered a somewhat more contemporary view by noting that collaboration includes joint responsibility and the mutual development of interventions. Others, including Glickman (1985), Kennedy (1980), and Scott and Smith (1987), have described the benefits of collaboration but have not defined it. Still others (e.g., Idol, Paolucci-Whitcomb, & Nevin, 1986; West, 1990) have mistakenly treated collaboration as a synonym for other concepts such as consultation and teams. What most authors do

"Hey, look. It's really simple. All we do is take everything
we were doing last year and call it 'collaboration.'"

Figure 1.1.

seem to agree on is that collaboration includes working together in a supportive and mutually beneficial relationship. What remains unclear is how collaboration relates to all these other terms and ideas. Later in this chapter and in Chapter 2 we address the latter issue; for now we begin by clearly defining collaboration.

Definition

For this text we begin our discussion of interpersonal collaboration with a more precise definition:

> *Interpersonal collaboration is a style for direct interaction between at least two coequal parties voluntarily engaged in shared decision making as they work toward a common goal.*

Notice that we call collaboration a *style*. In the same way that writers use various styles to convey information to readers so, too, do individuals use interpersonal styles or approaches to their interactions with one another. Some professionals may choose to be directive when they interact; others may choose to be accommodative; still others choose to be collaborative. At first glance, referring to collaboration as a style may appear to detract from its significance by equating it to something ephemeral and seemingly lacking in substance. However, using this term enables you to distinguish the nature of the interpersonal relationship, that is, collaboration, occurring during shared interactions from the activities themselves, for example, teaming or problem solving.

As just implied, because collaboration is a style of interaction it cannot exist in isolation. It can only occur when it is used by people who are engaged in a specific process, task, or activity. To clarify this point, consider the following: If colleagues mentioned to you they were collaborating, would you know what they were doing? Probably not. They could be collaboratively planning an educational program for a student, sharing the teaching responsibilities for an academic lesson, or arranging next year's textbook adoption timeline. What the term *collaboration* conveys is *how* the activity is occurring, that is, the nature of the interpersonal relationship occurring during the collaboration.

Defining Characteristics for Collaboration

Considered alone, the foregoing definition only hints at the subtleties of collaboration. Through our previous reviews of the literature (e.g., Cook & Friend, in press; Cook & Friend, 1990b; Friend & Cook, 1990), our own ongoing collaboration, and our experience facilitating the collaboration of others, we have identified several elements of collaboration that we call *defining characteristics* since they more fully explain the basic definition.

Collaboration Is Voluntary

It is not possible to force people to use a particular style in their interactions with others. States may pass legislation, school districts may adopt policy, and site administrators may implement programs, but unless school professionals and their colleagues choose to collaborate, they will not do so. Perhaps the best illustration of this notion is the current trend for schools to mandate that professionals collaborate in designing and implementing programs for mainstreamed or remedial students, as is occurring in the Cannon Schools. If you are familiar with such a situation, you are probably also aware that some individuals are unwilling to collaborate, regardless of the mandate. If those professionals attend meetings as required and give other superficial indications of being "team players," they do not truly have to collaborate in the sense outlined in this chapter. In essence, education agencies can mandate administrative arrangements that require staff to work in close proximity, but only the individuals involved can decide if a collaborative style will be used in their interactions. In our work in schools we frequently find ourselves emphasizing that there is no such thing as collaboration by coercion!

Does this mean that people *cannot* collaborate if programs are mandated? Not at all. Consider the Cannon School District's policy to promote in-class specialized services for students with disabilities. The adaptive physical education teacher may say, "That sounds like a good idea. Maybe I could get together with Sally's teacher and give it a try." In this example, voluntariness exists within the mandate, even though others may be voicing objections to or ignoring it.

Collaboration Requires Parity Among Participants

Parity is a situation in which each person's contribution to an interaction is equally valued, and each person has equal power in decision making. If one or several individuals are perceived by others as having greater decision-making power or more valuable knowledge or information, collaboration cannot occur. To illustrate, think about a principal's participation on a child study team. If the principal is considered to have equal, not disproportionately greater, power in the decision-making process, other team members may disagree with the principal's position and the team's ultimate decision may be one the principal did not support. Without parity, it is likely that some team members will acquiesce to the principal's preferences because of concern about repercussions for disagreeing.

It is important to understand that individuals may have parity as they work together on a specific collaborative activity even though they do not have parity in other situations. For example, you may have parity in interactions with a paraprofessional to plan a community-based activity, but may interact directively and with appropriately greater authority and decision-making power when giving instructions to the same paraprofessional about working with students. Administrators and staff on a curriculum committee may have parity; outside the committee, however, the relationship among the members may be markedly different.

Collaboration Is Based on Mutual Goals

Individuals who collaborate must share at least one goal. Imagine a meeting at which a decision must be reached about what specialized services a student should receive and how much time the student should spend in a mainstream setting. In one sense, the mutual goal of designing an appropriate educational program seems to be obvious. In reality, however, there may be at least two goals present. The parents, social worker, and principal might think that the student should be mainstreamed for most of the day, whereas the special education teacher, classroom teacher, and psychologist might believe that great care needs to be taken before any mainstreaming occurs. In this case, the goal of designing the program would have to be significant enough for all parties to commit their time and energy to collaboration.

Professionals do not have to share many or all goals in order to collaborate, just one that is specific and important enough to maintain their shared attention. They may differ in their opinions about a student's achievement potential but share the goal of arranging convenient transportation for the student. Their differences can be set aside as not being essential to the immediate issue.

Collaboration Depends on Shared Responsibility
for Participation and Decision Making

If you collaborate with a colleague, you are assuming the responsibility of actively engaging in the activity and the decision making it involves. We have found it useful to distinguish between responsibility for completing tasks associated with the collaborative activity and responsibility for the decision making involved in that activity. Shared participation in task completion does *not* imply that the individuals involved must divide tasks equally or participate fully in each task required to achieve their goal. In fact, participation in the activity often involves a convenient division of labor. For instance, as a speech and language therapist you might collaborate with a kindergarten teacher to plan a series of language lessons for all the students. You volunteer to outline the concepts that should be addressed and to prepare several activities related to each. The teacher agrees to locate needed materials and to plan student groupings and instructional schedules for the lessons. In this case, you and the teacher are both actively participating in accomplishing the task even though the division of labor may not be equal.

The second component of responsibility concerns *equal* participation in the *decision making* involved in the activity. In the example just described, you and the teacher had different responsibilities for the task, but to be collaborative both of you must equally participate in deciding the appropriateness and possible needed modifications in the material you prepare, and both of you are equally responsible for deciding if the grouping and proposed schedule are workable.

Individuals Who Collaborate Share Their Resources

It should be a given that each individual engaged in a collaborative activity has resources to contribute that are valuable for reaching the shared goal. The type of resources professionals have depends on their roles and the specific activity. Time and availability to carry out essential tasks may be the critical contribution that one person offers. Knowledge of a specialized technique may be another's resource. Access to other individuals or agencies that could assist in the collaborative activity may be a third person's contribution.

Sharing resources often occurs when parents and school professionals collaboratively plan home reward programs for students. The parent is likely to have access to reinforcers to which the student responds (e.g., video games, special meals, access to a bicycle or car). The special services providers may be able to recommend the number of positive behaviors the student should display, the frequency of rewards, and the plan for systematically phasing out the rewards once success has been achieved. The program would not be possible without the contributions that everyone makes.

You may have found that sharing resources is sometimes the key motivator for individuals to collaborate. In fact, pooling the available—but too-often scarce—resources in schools can lead to tremendously satisfying efforts on behalf of students; at the same time, it enhances the sense of ownership among the professionals. Unfortunately, the reverse may also occur: A scarcity of resources sometimes causes people to horde the resources they control. Collaboration becomes unlikely when that happens.

Individuals Who Collaborate Share Accountability for Outcomes

Whether the results of collaboration are positive or negative, all the participating individuals are accountable for outcomes. Suppose you and several colleagues plan a parent information meeting. One person arranges for a room, another orders coffee, and a third reserves a film and projector for the presentation. Shortly before the meeting is to begin, you realize that no one has remembered to pick up the film. In a collaborative effort, all the professionals share the resulting need to change the program at the last minute or to arrange to have someone dash to retrieve the film.

Emergent Characteristics

Several characteristics of collaboration can have multiple functions—they are mentioned both as prerequisites for as well as outcomes of collaboration and we refer to these as *emergent*. These characteristics must be present to some discernible degree at the outset of collaborative activity, but they typically emerge and grow from successful experience with collaboration.

Individuals Who Collaborate Value This Interpersonal Style

Collaboration is difficult but rewarding. Professionals who anticipate collaborating must believe that the results of their collaboration are likely to be more powerful and significant than the results of their individual efforts, or else they are unlikely to persevere. Typically, success in collaboration leads to increased commitment to future collaboration, and so beliefs and attitudes become increasingly positive. As a former graduate student once reported, "I used to work in a school where there was no collaboration. I worked very hard, but it was like beating my head against a wall. Now I work in a place where collaboration is the norm. I work even harder than I used to, but now it's fun."

An additional element of the value system that supports collaboration is the belief that two heads are better than one. Individuals who collaborate usually do not have the same expertise. If you are skilled in an area in which your colleague is not, the colleague can rely on your input and is not obliged to try to acquire mastery of it. For school professionals who address a seemingly never-ending list of complex student problems, building such a sense of expanded expertise through collaborative interactions can help to alleviate one source of ongoing professional stress.

Professionals Who Collaborate Trust One Another
Even if you firmly believe in the beneficial outcomes of collaboration, you cannot suddenly introduce it, fully developed, into your professional interactions. If you re-call your experiences as a new employee of a school district or agency, you probably remember experiencing a phase in which you learned about your colleagues, the norms of the school setting, and the manner in which to approach the other pro-fessionals with whom you worked most closely. And even though you interacted with other professionals during that time, the extent to which you could collaborate was limited. Only after a period of time in which trust, and subsequently respect, are established can school professionals feel relatively secure in fully exploring col-laborative relationships. Once begun, however, those relationships may be strength-ened until trust of colleagues becomes one of the most important benefits of col-laboration. This scenario describes the emergence of trust: At the outset, enough trust must be present for professionals to be willing to begin the activity, but with suc-cessful experiences the trust grows.

A Sense of Community Evolves from Collaboration
David and Frank Johnson (1987), in their work on the social psychology of groups, discuss the concept of interdependence. They describe it as a feeling of "we'll sink or swim together." For collaboration, a sense of community is similar. It is the perception that by interacting collaboratively, all participants' strengths can be maximized, their weaknesses can be minimized, and the result will be better for all. Perhaps you have experienced the sense of community in a church, social, or student group. The willing-ness to work toward a common goal is accompanied by a decrease in concern about individual differences.

Taken together, these emergent characteristics highlight the risks you take when you begin to collaborate. You may attempt to establish trust and be rebuffed; you may attempt to communicate an attitude supportive of collaboration but find that others do not share your beliefs. Collaboration is certainly not easily accomplished nor is it appropriate for every situation. At the same time, the emergent characteristics also summarize many of the powerful benefits of taking those risks. When collaborative efforts result in higher levels of trust and respect among colleagues, and working together results in more positive outcomes for both students and professionals, the risks taken seem small in comparison to the rewards.

COLLABORATION IN CONTEXT

Why has collaboration become so important in special services? Why are so many professionals advocating that special services staff work with each other and classroom teachers in order to design innovative programs for students? Answers to these questions can be found by pausing to examine collaboration in a broader context. That is, collaboration in special education is closely related to the significant societal trend toward collaboration as well as the reform efforts that have brought that trend into schools.

Societal Trends

Consider the world in which we now live. The vast majority of jobs available are in service industries in which individuals interact with clients or customers to meet their needs (e.g., retail sales, food services). This is a sharp contrast to preceding eras in which most workers toiled in isolation on assembly lines. Contemporary life is also characterized by an accelerated flow of information: People are inundated with it, whether through the deluge of unwanted mail that arrives each day or the stacks of publications that pile up, unread, in many homes, offices, and classrooms. Few individuals can hope to keep up with even the most crucial events occurring in their communities and their professions, much less throughout the world. News highlights and abridged books often have to suffice.

One response to the pressures of contemporary society's changing labor needs and its information explosion is an increasing reliance on collaboration. For example, in business, managers are involving employees in decision making as a strategy for improving organizational effectiveness (Tjosvold, 1987). Furthermore, employees report they find their jobs more satisfying if they participate in such activity. Researchers agree that a sense of ownership and commitment appears to evolve through participation in decision making. All of these ideas, coming not from education but from business and industry, are directly related to collaboration.

Another example of the broad trend toward collaboration is found in the current use of quality circles in business. This approach for increasing participation emphasizes shared responsibility for product quality and group problem solving, as well as the efficient and effective management of available resources (Ross & Ross, 1982).

A final example of the growing importance of collaboration from a societal perspective comes from the futurists (e.g., Toffler, 1980). For example, when this country was settled, the notion of rugged individualism was important. The concept alluded to individuals' willingness to risk going into unknown territory and facing dangers in order to settle the frontier. However, this individualism included reliance on others as clearing fields and raising barns, for example, could not physically be accomplished by one person. As society industrialized and individuals began to rely on machines and technology, reliance on others as part of individualism declined, and an era of sole responsibility emerged. Now, the original concept of rugged individualism seems once again to be needed: Because society has become so complex, it is no longer possible for individuals to know everything they need to know and act on everything demanding their attention. As a psychological support, we are turning as did the pioneers to collaboration and reliance on others to accomplish our goals.

School Collaboration

If we begin with the premise that schools are a reflection of larger society, the current trend toward collaboration in our nation and around the world makes it quickly apparent why collaboration is such a prominent trend in schools. Some innovations that affect schools are fads that fade nearly as soon as they appear. Two examples are the new math of the early 1960s and the open classrooms of the early 1970s. Phenomena such as these have no permanence because there is no ongoing societal demand for them. On the other hand, when societal needs lead to changes in schools, the impact is likely to be long lasting. One current example of a societally mandated school innovation is the infusion of computer instruction, even for young students. Collaboration is another example.

One of the ways that collaboration is emerging in schools is through various aspects of school reform (e.g., Goodlad, 1984). *Empowerment* refers to enabling educators to increase their participation in educational decision making so that they are more respected (Maeroff, 1988). *Participatory management* requires that teachers work with each other as well as with other decision makers. *Site-based decision making* is an extension of empowerment. It refers to teachers' power to participate in making a wide range of decisions about their schools, sometimes including budgetary matters as well as curricular issues. All these reform efforts attempt to incorporate many of the characteristics of collaboration we have already discussed.

Another example of collaboration in schools—cooperative learning—has students as its primary focus. Cooperative learning is used increasingly for teaching children how to interact effectively. The method appears to have gained popularity because it allows students to learn alternatives to competition and because it helps them acquire the interpersonal skills employers have identified as essential for today's job market (Johnson & Johnson, 1990). In cooperative learning, small groups of students work together to master specified curricular material. The learning activities typically are structured in such a way that students are encouraged to help all group members to learn. Unless team members collaborate, they are unlikely to succeed at the task.

THE DILEMMAS OF COLLABORATION

Although the concept of collaboration is gaining prominence and collaborative efforts seem to be beneficial for school professionals, a number of issues arise when they attempt to establish collaborative relationships. First, several aspects of school structure and the way school professionals are socialized are not particularly conducive to a collaborative style of professional interaction. In addition, a number of pragmatic issues may affect the feasibility of collaborative endeavors.

School Structure and Professional Socialization

It has long been recognized that professionals in schools typically do their substantive work in isolation from others (e.g., Goodlad, 1984; Lortie, 1975; Sarason, 1982). Each teacher is assigned to a classroom and each specialist to an office or room (or at least a desk!). And although staff members are friendly to one another and may socialize in the lounge (Little, 1982), when it is time to get on with teaching or otherwise serving students—the primary business of schools—everyone literally or figuratively shuts their doors. This structure of physical isolation is contrary to the concept of collaboration.

Within this physical isolation from other adults, each school professional sets about working with students. How do they accomplish this? Essentially, they take charge. In their classrooms or offices, they are the experts who hold authority and power over students, and so they typically use a directive style to promote student learning, which is appropriate. However, constant use of this style with students may interfere with professionals' ability to switch to a collaborative style for interactions with colleagues and parents.

Physical isolation and the use of a directive style with students are part of what contributes to the lack of emphasis in schools on collegial relationships, that is, the norm of isolation. You begin to learn about this in your professional preparation program. As you complete your student teaching, practicum, or internship experiences, you discover that if you are mastering the skills needed in your planned role, your supervisor leaves you alone to work with students. This socialization continues as you enter your profession and gain experience. What evolves is a belief that you should handle your professional problems yourself. If you seek help, it is often only after you have decided that whatever is occurring is no longer your problem; your goal becomes seeking another to take ownership of it.

Essentially, then, most school professionals have been trained to function individually as expert problem solvers (Friend & Cook, 1990). Whether you are a classroom teacher, special education teacher, psychologist, occupational or physical therapist, speech/language specialist, counselor, or administrator, you learned the same four clinical problem-solving steps to guide your professional behavior:

1. Assess the student or situation.
2. Diagnose the problem and plan action to address it.
3. Carry out the planned intervention.
4. Evaluate the success of the intervention.

These steps are carried out repeatedly and individually by all professionals in schools, usually so automatically that they are not even aware of the specific steps they use. However, when school professionals engage in collaboration, their carefully nurtured, individualistic problem-solving skills are disrupted. Each step of a collaborative activity is discussed and negotiated until mutual understanding and agreement is reached. As a result, specialists may feel both inefficient because this collaborative process is costly in terms of time and awkward about what they may perceive as a breakdown in their professional skills.

This discussion of structural isolation and individualistic professional characteristics found in schools may leave the impression that collaboration is seldom likely in school settings. That certainly is not true all the time. We raise it only to increase your awareness of the difficulties in collaborating. We also want to convey some of the challenges that you will undoubtedly experience as you attempt to collaborate. These challenges that are not unique to your specific school setting or professional relationships; they result from many factors that are part of all school professionals' experiences.

Ultimately, these dilemmas provide the rationale for exploring the skills described later in the text because it is those skills that can enable special service providers to complement their other professional skills with collaborative ones.

Pragmatic Issues

When we described the defining characteristics of collaboration, we noted that resource sharing is essential. We consider the topic further here because the availability of resources may pose serious pragmatic dilemmas for school collaboration.

Time
Collaborative activities require time—often more time than would be needed if the activity were being completed by one person. And because time is always a scarce commodity in schools, it may be the most crucial resource for collaboration.

    Three time-related issues are critical: First, each school professional typically has a full workload, whether it be related to teaching, assessing, counseling, providing therapy, or administering. Simply arranging for time to interact with others may be problematic. Second, if time can be found, the difficulty of finding *shared* time may be an issue. It is obviously essential for all the professionals who are going to engage in a collaborative activity to be available at the same time! Finally, professionals who collaborate need time to reflect on their work (Pugach & Johnson, 1988). If you can recall instances when you have had a flash of insight *after* a meeting and wished you could meet again to use it, you can understand why time for reflective thought is so necessary.

Space
Individuals who collaborate need appropriate space in which to work. Sometimes this is a matter of finding a neutral location such as a conference room or another space that does not "belong" to any of the participants. At other times, this involves locating appropriate space: For example, if you and a colleague need to hold an intense discussion of an issue related to your collaborative decision making, the lounge, cafeteria, or learning center may be too public a place. And in some school settings, the critical space issue may be finding *any* space. When professionals experience the stress that accompanies overcrowded buildings with little or no space for interactions, collaboration will no doubt be limited.

Other Resources
Depending on the school or educational agency in which you work, other resources may also affect opportunities for collaboration. For example, budgetary issues may lead to increased workloads and overcrowding and may exacerbate the time and space problems just mentioned. Access to materials and equipment may also be a concern: If you cannot locate alternative books or specific adaptive equipment, you may be frustrated in a collaborative effort. And, finally, sometimes access to ancillary personnel such as paraprofessionals or parent volunteers can affect the extent to which collaboration is feasible. You may be able to enumerate other resource issues unique to your workplace that function as dilemmas for your collaborative activities.

This entire discussion of the dilemmas of collaboration may have a somewhat sobering effect on your enthusiasm for it. In part, we hope this is so. Collaboration can be a powerful vehicle for accomplishing professionals' goals of educating students, but we believe it can also be overused and misused. Collaboration efforts should be espoused only with a realistic understanding of their complexities and difficulties because such understanding will lead to careful consideration of the extent to which collaborative efforts are feasible and recommended.

SUMMARY

Collaboration is an interpersonal style that professionals may use in their interactions with colleagues, parents, and others. It can only exist voluntarily in situations in which individuals with parity have identified a mutual goal and are willing to share responsibilities, resources, and accountability. Several characteristics of collaboration both contribute to its development and are potentially its outcomes: attitudes and beliefs supportive of a collaborative approach, mutual trust, and a sense of community. Collaboration in the realm of special services is critical as a reflection of societal trends that are, in turn, being mirrored in schools. The dilemmas special service providers face in their collaborative efforts are those related to the structural and professional isolation of schools, professional socialization emphasizing individualism, and pragmatic issues in the allocation of resources.

ACTIVITIES AND ASSIGNMENTS

1. In your professional setting, identify two different situations in which you work with one or more other people to provide services to a student with special needs. Select one in which you believe collaboration is possible and one in which collaboration is unlikely. Complete an analysis of the extent to which the defining characteristics of collaboration are present or could be established in each situation. Which characteristics can most easily be met? Which may pose significant barriers to developing effective collaborative relationships?

2. Peruse recent issues of popular news magazines. What examples of societal collaboration are addressed?

3. Discuss the following question with colleagues: How should a professional respond when all the individuals on a team are attempting to collaborate, but one individual undermines their attempts?

4. Discuss the issue of parity with a group of classroom teachers. To what extent do they perceive that they have equal status with special services providers? How could issues related to parity be addressed?

5. Repeat your discussion of parity with others who have roles similar to yours. How do their views about teachers' and special services providers' parity compare to those of the classroom teachers?

6. If you have worked in a setting in which collaboration was valued and encouraged, write a summary of your experience. Use this as the basis for a discussion with others to generate specific examples of the characteristics of collaboration.

7. Generate a list of behaviors you learned as a clinician that may not be appropriate in collaborative interactions. Compare your list with those of others in different professional roles. How are they similar? How are they different?

RELATED READINGS

Barth, R. S. (1990). *Improving schools from within.* San Francisco: Jossey-Bass.

Glickman, C. D. (1985). *Supervision of instruction: A developmental approach* (pp. 14–25). Boston: Allyn & Bacon.

Hord, S. M. (1986). A synthesis of research on organizational collaboration. *Educational Leadership, 43*(5), 22–26.

Little, J. W. (1982). Norms of collegiality and experimentation: Workplace conditions of school success. *American Educational Research Journal, 19*, 325–340.

Maeroff, G. I. (1988). *The empowerment of teachers: Overcoming the crisis of confidence.* New York: Teachers College Press.

CHAPTER 2

Applications of Collaboration in Special Services

Keeping Perspective

Using the introductory information presented in Chapter 1, Chapter 2 describes how collaboration applies to two common activities for special service providers: consultation and teaming. The chapters that follow present interaction processes and interpersonal communication skills that assist you to carry out these activities collaboratively.

Learner Objectives

1. To define consultation and outline the characteristics of consulting relationships.
2. To describe models of consultation frequently used in special services.
3. To describe the relationship between consultation and collaboration.
4. To define teams and describe their characteristics.
5. To describe different types of teams in schools and delineate their importance to special service providers.
6. To identify barriers to effective team functioning in special services and describe strategies for promoting team effectiveness.
7. To describe the relationship between teams and collaboration.

We explained in Chapter 1 that nearly any adult–adult activity in schools can be conducted collaboratively just as it can be conducted using a directive, authoritarian, or other style of interaction. We also noted that consultation and teams are two specific topics very frequently and often carelessly linked with the term *collaboration*. In this chapter, for each of these two topics we first outline their structural components or requirements; we then sketch their development and use among special service providers. Second, we discuss the relationship between the structure or application and its emphasis on using a collaborative style. By separating the discussion of the team structure and the consultation process from examples of how collaboration is used within these illustrative applications, we hope to clarify further the ways in which collaboration is used in schools.

CONSULTATION IN SCHOOLS

Many definitions have been offered for consultation. For example, Conoley and Conoley (1982) call it a "voluntary, nonsupervisory relationship between professionals from differing fields established to aid one in his or her professional functioning" (p. 3). Brown, Pryzwansky, and Schulte (1987) define consultation as a "voluntary problem solving process that can be initiated and terminated by either the consultant or consultee" (p. 8). Gallessich (1982) adds the dimension of the client by describing consultation as "tripartite interactions in human service agencies [in which] the consultant (a specialized professional) assists consultees (agency employees who are also professionals) with work-related concerns (the third component) (p. 6). From our perspective, key elements of these definitions as well as those proposed by others (e.g., Parsons & Meyers, 1984; Rosenfield, 1987; Zins, Curtis, Graden, & Ponti, 1988; Zischka & Fox, 1985) can be summarized as follows:

> *School consultation is a voluntary process in which one professional assists another to address a problem concerning a third party.*

Characteristics of Consultation

The essential characteristics of school consultation have been widely described in the school psychology, counseling psychology, special education, and other special services literature (e.g., Conoley & Conoley, 1982; Heron & Harris, 1987; Idol & West, 1987; Rosenfield, 1987). Generally, the characteristics seen as most central for successful consultation are the following.

Consultation Is Triadic and Indirect
Although consultation in other disciplines (e.g., law, business) may occur between two individuals and not relate to a third party, in schools it is typically triadic, involving three parties and an indirect relationship. The consultant and the consultee (whether an individual or a group) together design services that the consultee provides to the client (most often a student). The latter is not a direct participant in the interaction but is the beneficiary of the process nonetheless. Thus, a psychologist who acts as a consultant may

meet with a teacher to plan classroom based interventions for students, but in this event the psychologist's relationship to the students is indirect.

Consultation Is Voluntary

A consultee may be puzzled by a situation and seek the assistance of a consultant, or a consultant may notice some difficulty and offer insight to a consultee for remedying it. In each case, both the consultant and consultee have the prerogative of entering or terminating the relationship at any time. This characteristic of voluntariness establishes the principle that consultation cannot be a coerced process (Alpert, 1976; Gutkin & Curtis, 1982). Both professionals choose to participate, and the process can only be implemented for as long as their participation is voluntary.

Consultation Is Typically an Expert Relationship

Most individuals who study consultation emphasize that consultants and consultees mutually influence each other and that consultants do not have authority over consultees. They also recommend that consultants be facilitative, empathic, and collegial (e.g., Gallessich, 1982; Rosenfield, 1987). Regardless of its egalitarian nature, however, the consulting relationship only exists because it is perceived that the consultee, not consultant, has a work-related problem. Thus, the primary reason for the interaction is the consultee's perception of a problem that cannot be solved without another's expertise. In fact, it is difficult to imagine why consultees would participate in consultation unless they were relatively certain a consultant had expert knowledge and could provide insight on the matters they had been unable to alleviate themselves.

Consultation Is a Problem-solving Process with Steps or Stages

The number of steps in the consultation process varies according to the author outlining them and typically include: (1) entry, the physical and psychological beginning of a series of interactions, (2) problem identification, the establishment of a goal for the interaction, (3) planning and intervention, the actual "work" of deciding how to address the problem and carrying out the plan, (4) evaluation, the determination of intervention success, and (5) exit, the termination of the consulting relationship. Knowing the precise steps or stages is not as critical as recognizing that consultation is a process that is comprised of such steps.

Participants in Consultative Interactions Have Shared but Differentiate Responsibilities and Accountability

Consultants and consultees do not share the same responsibility and accountability. If you are a consultant, your primary responsibility and areas of accountability are to ensure that the consulting process is appropriately followed and to offer feasible assistance that is responsive to your consultee's needs (Rosenfield, 1987). Because consultants do not control consultees' decisions about whether to accept and implement the specific strategies or interventions, in the strictest sense they cannot be accountable for the success or failure of the outcomes of the interventions. On the other hand, if you are a consultee, you have the responsibility to participate in good faith in the consultation process and to seriously consider the assistance being offered (Conoley & Conoley, 1982). If you agree to use a strategy, you are responsible for doing so appropriately. Furthermore, because consultees determine whether a strategy is actually employed, your accountability includes a judgment about whether the problem has been resolved or whether another intervention is needed and desired.

Consultation Models

The practice of consultation is based on varying theoretical perspectives that have led to the development of distinct consultation models. These models prescribe the approach used throughout a series of consultative interactions. Several models are particularly important to understanding the types of consultation that occur in school settings, either because they are directly applicable to schools (behavioral and clinical consultation), or because they contain components that are useful for facilitating school consultation (mental health and organizational consultation).

Behavioral Consultation

Tharp and Wetzel's (1969) text on using applied behavior analysis in naturalistic settings established behavioral consultation as a distinct model to guide the consulting process. In this model, behavioral consultants combine their knowledge of behavioral psychology and the indirect service delivery model as they apply operant and social learning principles in their consultation with others (Bergan, 1977).

Behavioral consultants rely on two major types of skills: First, they must possess a thorough understanding of behavioral interventions that can be used to change the behavior of the consultee and to propose interventions for the student. Second, consultants need to understand the steps in a behavioral problem-solving sequence (see Chapter 4 for a list of problem-solving steps similar to those used in behavioral consultation).

Behavioral consultation has been widely used in school settings by special service providers in a variety of roles. Its popularity seems to be due to its reliance on well-researched strategies that often result in successful outcomes. In addition, behavioral consultants emphasize data collection, and thus part of behavioral consultation's appeal is that its procedures provide documentation of its effectiveness. However, several issues and concerns may arise if behavioral consultation is used. For example, some consultees, including parents and classroom teachers, may object to seemingly coercive behavioral principles and may resist the use of this approach. They may lack the understanding of behavioral principles necessary to systematically carry out proposed interventions. Finally, behavioral consultants must always be aware of the ethical dilemma of using behavioral technology to change student behavior rather than assisting the student in making self-identified changes.

Clinical Consultation

Clinical consultation is a diagnostic model that traditionally has been used by school and counseling psychologists, diagnosticians, speech and language specialists, and, to a lesser degree, by social workers and occupational and physical therapists. In this model, the consultant is concerned with identifying a consultee's problem with a client and prescribing strategies for resolving it (Bell & Nadler, 1985; Conoley, 1981). However, the consultant is not actually involved in the ongoing implementation of the intervention or monitoring of it. As a clinical consultant, you might meet with a teacher to learn about a student's apparent problem, and you would assess the specific problem by interacting temporarily with the student, conducting observations, administering appropriate diagnostic tests, and the like. You would then analyze the student's strengths and needs and suggest recommendations, approaches, or interventions that might be successful. You would not be involved in the implementation of the intervention, but at a later date you might follow up to determine whether the suggested approaches were successful.

Because consultant involvement is generally confined to the diagnostic stage only, clinical consultation may be preferred when consultants have limited time in which to offer assistance to consultees or when a complex problem situation needs clarification that can be offered by an expert diagnostician. However, this consultation model generally assumes that the problem exists primarily in the client and that the consultee has the professional skills needed to act on the consultant's recommendations. If these conditions do not exist, the model has limited utility.

Mental Health Consultation

This model of consultation derives from the work of Caplan (1970). Its primary focus is psychodynamic, but it also takes into account interpersonal and organizational factors. Mental health consultants engage in the complex process of weighing the importance of those factors in isolating and resolving problems presented by consultees. If you consulted using a mental health model, a typical situation would require that you first decide whether the problem being described by the consultee was a result of a lack of knowledge, skills, or confidence, or whether it was caused by the consultee's lack of objectivity about the problem situation. In this model, the latter is viewed as the most frequent source of problems. Based on that determination, you would then assist the consultee to resolve the problem by employing a complex set of therapeutic techniques which might include discussion, use of parables, confrontation, and exploration of feelings.

One major contribution this model has made to the knowledge base about consultation for special service providers is clarification of the different levels at which consultation may occur. These levels may focus on the client (even though assistance is offered through the consultee), on helping the consultee to function more effectively, on assisting an administrator to manage human resources more productively, or on enhancing an entire program's functioning. As suggested by our previous example of a consultative situation, mental health consultation most often targets assistance that improves consultee interpersonal functioning.

Some of the techniques used by mental health consultants require highly specialized training and supervised practice that many special service providers have not had. However, its advantages are its fundamental concepts that may be applicable outside the mental health framework (e.g., levels for consultation and the importance of establishing trusting, empathic relationships) and its emphasis on prevention instead of crisis intervention. Issues related to the model include the lack of empirical data that support its effectiveness and the limited value of psychodynamic interventions for school professionals.

Organizational Consultation

Concern in the business community about worker morale led to the study of entire organizations and the factors that make them effective (Bennis, 1969; Huse, 1980). Organizational consultation is an outgrowth of this area of inquiry. In organizational consultation, it is assumed that individuals in a work setting can only be assisted by examining the entire environment in which they work. Thus, the job of an organizational consultant is to assess the physical, interpersonal, and organizational environment and to assist employees to resolve a broad range of identified concerns that may affect their job functioning. If you worked from this framework, you would probably first complete an assessment of the school setting by gathering pencil-and-paper needs assessment information, observing teachers and others in their work, and interviewing school staff in many different roles. You would then analyze and prioritize the major issues interfering with effective organizational functioning and work with staff to address these issues. Your work would probably emphasize the interpersonal relationships among the staff members, including techniques such as survey feedback, communication exercises, and role playing. In this type of consultation, then, the consultee is the staff, and the client is the entire school organization.

Although special service providers seldom have the skills or opportunity to systematically implement the entire organizational consultation process, they may find information about this model helpful in several ways. First, the model considers the importance of interpersonal relationships and offers specific ideas and techniques for managing these. Second, an organizational perspective helps sharpen the idea that in many cases, individuals alone cannot necessarily make consultation or any other service effective; the many complex and interconnecting subsystems of the school organization must be supportive.

The primary concerns about the use of organizational consultation models in schools are the pragmatic matters of time and expense. Used systematically, the entire consulting process may take a year or more to complete, and many school budgets simply cannot support this type of consultation. Even if resources are available, the time required of staff may be prohibitive.

Consultation and Collaboration

For the past several years, the terms *collaboration* and *consultation* have come to be used in ways that probably create confusion. Sometimes they are used as synonyms, sometimes each is also equated with other concepts such as teaming or teaching, and sometimes they are combined and addressed as a single entity (i.e., collaborative consultation).

The emphasis on relating collaboration and consultation can be traced to the early 1970s, particularly in the fields of school and counseling psychology (e.g., Kurpius & Brubaker, 1976; Pryzwansky, 1974). Concern was expressed that consultative interactions were more likely to be successful if they were facilitative and supportive rather than prescriptive and directive (e.g., Parker, 1975). By the end of the 1970s, it was clear that for psychologists and counselors in schools, a collaborative approach to consultation was generally preferable to other approaches.

Consultation as a role responsibility for special education teachers was rapidly evolving during the same time period (Friend, 1988). The Vermont Consulting Teacher Program (Christie, McKenzie, & Burdett, 1972), begun in the late 1960s, was setting a precedent for the systematic use of teacher consultation. It was implemented by highly trained consulting teachers who held postmaster's degrees and adjunct faculty appointments at the University of Vermont. As these consultants (trainers) worked with, trained, and offered course credit to classroom teachers and others (trainees), their status as trainers and university faculty reinforced the notion of consultant as expert. Later, an additional issue arose in this model: Although in the original Vermont model the consultative relationship was voluntary, as this approach spread to other geographic areas the participation of teachers became less voluntary—students with disabilities were mainstreamed and special education teachers or other special service providers were assigned to consult with their general education teachers often without any preparation for the consultation role. General education teachers began to make it clear by their reactions that it was inappropriate for special education to assume responsibility for "fixing" general education; they did not need special educators to serve as experts who would tell them what to do. By the early 1980s, then, the special education teacher consultation literature was stressing the need for collegial relationships (Evans, 1980; Friend, 1984) and collaborative approaches to consultation were being advocated (Idol, Paolucci-Whitcomb, & Nevin, 1986; McClellan & Wheatley, 1985).

Using our definitions, the distinction between consultation and collaboration can be clearly delineated so that special service providers can base their practice on an understanding of each. Because collaboration is a style or an approach to interaction, it can be attached to the consultation process, just as it can be attached to problem solving, assessing, and teaching. Moreover, a collaborative approach can be used at some consultation stages and not others just as it can be used with some consultees and not others.

However, ascribing collaboration to the consultation process does not make it a unique model (Conoley & Conoley, 1988). Any model of consultation can be implemented collaboratively. For example, consider the brief description presented earlier for behavioral consultation: As a model, it has clear guidelines and principles that give it conceptual integrity and prescribe its practice. Whether or not behavorial consultation is carried out collaboratively is an issue that is distinct from the model. Behavioral consultation can be conducted collaboratively within a relationship characterized by parity, mutual goals, shared decision making, and all the additional characteristics of collaboration. However, behavioral consultation may also be conducted by someone who, using a directive style, retains much of the decision-making responsibility, prescribes interventions, and offers expert advice and explanations to consultees. This same analogy could be made for each model of consultation mentioned earlier: Each has a theoretical framework, and each could be implemented by a consultant who may or may not use a collaborative style of interaction.

Distinguishing the model of consultation used from the interactional style of the consultant is one way to clarify the distinction between consultation and collaboration. As you observe and participate in consultative interactions, however, you will notice that successful consultants use different styles of interaction under different circumstances and in different consultation situations. Sometimes the nature of the consultation situation or the needs of the consultee require the consultant to use an authoritative or directive style. For example, you may receive an isolated request for assistance in interpreting a student's assessment results from a colleague. Your caseload, available time, and knowledge of your colleague's other resources and sources of collegial support, among other considerations, may lead you to simply offer your expert opinion of the assessment results. Similarly, you may occasionally find in a generally collaborative, ongoing consultation relationship that specific situations are more appropriately addressed using an alternative style.

Consider a consultation situation in which you and your colleague, Jane, have been working together collaboratively for several weeks to design and evaluate a systematic reinforcement schedule for use with Henry, a student in her class. Increasing district demands, the inclusion of new students, and a number of other events have created significant and competing demands for Jane. Henry, the student who is your shared responsibility, is no longer responding satisfactorily to your jointly planned intervention and has begun to display his originally problematic and disruptive behaviors. You and Jane both recognize that you have a problem that must be addressed, but Jane does not currently have the emotional, physical, or logistical resources to participate in any significant way in a joint problem-solving effort. Under these circumstances, attempting to maintain a collaborative relationship by meeting all the defining characteristics described in Chapter 1 may well be counterproductive. Rather, you may need to use a directive style to solve a pressing problem (e.g., making an immediate adjustment in the implementation of the intervention with Henry). Depending on the situation and your assessment of it, you may decide that neither a directive nor a collaborative approach is appropriate. If Henry's lack of progress appears to be only temporary and Jane's stress seems to be the most salient issue, you may determine that a nondirective, supportive, or empathic style is most appropriate. You may use a collaborative style with any model of consultation. So, too, may you choose to use or not to use a collaborative style at various stages within a given situation.

If you develop an understanding of how collaboration and consultation can be distinguished from one another and how they work in tandem, it will assist you greatly in clarifying the meaning of the terms you read and hear. Each term has a precise definition. To the extent that you adhere to these definitions, your descriptions of school activities, services, and programs will be accurate, distinguished from one another, and clearly communicated to others.

PROFESSIONAL TEAMS

You were born into a social group and have become increasingly involved in a wide range of groups as you have become an adult and a professional. Consider the various groups to which you belong: You are probably a member of a family group, and you may belong to a neighborhood or community group, staff group, sports group, recreational or fitness club, professional association, political party, or civic group. If you conduct an inventory of the groups to which you belong and examine the extent of your involvement with each one you might be surprised to discover that your participation in these groups accounts for nearly all of your social activities. Although social scientists describe many different types of groups, they identify the three most important types of groups relative to daily interaction as family, friendship, and work groups (Argyle, 1983; Hargie, Saunders & Dickson, 1987). The focus for the remainder of this chapter is on work groups, or teams.

Team or group approaches have long been a valued part of the special service professions and have become increasingly popular structures for addressing highly diverse issues in schools. We will consider the development of several different types of school based teams, examine their current status, and consider the relationship of collaboration to these structures.

The social sciences, including special education, have often tried to define the terms *team* or *group* and have, thus, contributed to the development of a profusion of definitions (e.g., see Johnson & Johnson, 1983 for a review). Collectively, these definitions stress that

> A team is a relatively small set of interdependent individuals who work and interact directly in a coordinated manner to achieve a common purpose.

Characteristics of Teams

Different defining characteristics of teams highlighted in the social sciences literature can be used to further clarify the definition of a team.

Team Members Are Aware of Their Own and Others' Membership on the Team

Individuals cannot be part of a team unless they perceive themselves to be. Extending the notion, team members must also be perceived by others as forming a team (Feldman, 1985).

The Direct Interaction of Team Members Is Regulated by Shared Norms

The team is an organized system of individuals whose behavior is regulated by a common set of norms or values (Sherif & Sherif, 1956). These individuals are motivated to participate in team activities and to jointly establish a set of role relationships and norms that regulate individual members' behaviors and team functioning (Abelson & Woodman, 1983).

Team Members Are Interdependent

Members of work teams are highly interdependent because their organizational roles are functionally interrelated. An event that affects one member is likely to affect the rest of the team, and team results will affect each individual member (Fiedler, 1967; Lewin, 1951).

Teams in Schools

Enthusiasm for changing the way schools are organized emerged from the wave of educational reform reports and studies of the 1980s. The recommendations of these reports frequently emphasized restructuring schools to allow for greater teacher empowerment through participation in shared decision making. And teams, of the widest variety, are the most frequently advocated structures for making these changes as illustrated by the continuing attention to site-based management teams, interdisciplinary teaching teams, planning teams, professional development teams, school improvement teams, and so on. As we noted in Chapter 1, increased emphasis on team structures and team decision making is frequently equated with collaboration thereby intensifying an already confusing situation.

As a school-based special service provider you may find the current fervor about teams puzzling for several reasons. First, much of the attention focuses on teams as a feature of the restructuring and reform themes that occupy a significant position in contemporary educational thought. As Pugach (1988) and others have noted, these themes are being articulated without serious regard for the special service needs of students with disabilities. This conspicuous absence of concern for special education and related services in the general education reform literature may make it difficult to understand how the team structures that are so visible in that context will affect special services and special service providers.

Second, concurrent with the general education reform movement, is an ongoing debate in the special service disciplines about alternative futures for educational and related services to students with disabilities and those at risk for school failure. And although the terminology and arguments share similarities, the relationship of proposed special services reforms and general educational reforms is unclear. It is not our purpose to try to sort out the numerous reform proposals or to examine how proposed organizational structures may influence particular services. Instead, we want to acknowledge these as potential sources of confusion and offer a framework that you may wish to apply to discussions of teams in various contexts. In presenting this framework we will consider the development of teams in special services, review some of the types of teams in which special service providers participate, examine elements that influence team effectiveness, and consider the relationship of teams structures to collaborative relationships.

Multidisciplinary Teams

Special service providers may wonder at the notion in educational reform literature that team structures are new or innovative since they have held a prominent place in special services fields for some time (Newman, 1974; Rettke, 1968). If you completed a traditional professional preparation program you probably agree that the long-established professional values of the interdisciplinary process and the case-centered team structures that support it are integral components of effective services. Long before a team structure was *required* in special education, examples of case-centered teams such as school-based child study teams (Armer & Thomas, 1978), psychological service delivery approaches (Menninger, 1950), and similar approaches were established as elements of effective service delivery.

The passage of P. L. 94–142 established as a federal requirement that multidisciplinary teams implement evaluation and placement procedures for exceptional children. This landmark legislation requires that special education evaluation and placement decisions be made by a team that includes school professionals, parents, and the student when appropriate. With this mandate, multidisciplinary assessment and group decision making regarding classification, placement, and the development of an individualized educational program (IEP) are now formally part of special education procedures. These case-centered teams are, in fact, the primary structures for planning and coordinating the delivery of special education and related services in the public schools.

The apparent rationale for requiring a multidisciplinary team is the belief that a group decision provides safeguards against individual errors in judgment and ensures greater adherence to the law's due process requirements (Pfeiffer, 1980). Research in behavioral sciences supports the use of teams to improve decision-making effectiveness and quality. Abelson and Woodman (1983) summarize several widely accepted reasons for this: (1) a group offers a greater amount of knowledge and experience; (2) a greater number of possible approaches to a problem exist within a group; (3) participation in decision making increases acceptance of the decision; and (4) problem solving in a group involves greater communication and understanding of the decision.

P. L. 94-142 did not prescribe the composition of the team or the specific procedures it would follow but left those decisions to the states. States interpreted the federal law differently and mandated different composition requirements and operational procedures for teams. Not surprisingly, the titles of teams also vary widely from state to state: child study team, school assessment team, placement team, planning team, and multidisciplinary team are among the names used.

Regardless of the team's title, the intent was to limit the decision-making authority of any one professional, ensure the incorporation of different educational perspectives, and involve parents in the decision making about their children. The legislative and professional expectations for multidisciplinary teams were summarized by Reynolds, Gutkin, Elliott, and Witt (1984):

> ...multidisciplinary teams have been expected to provide a number of functional benefits beyond those provided by any single individual. These benefits include: greater accuracy in assessment, classification, and placement decisions; a forum for sharing different views; provision for specialized consultative services to school personnel, parents, and community agencies; and, the resource for developing and evaluating individualized educational programs for exceptional students. (p. 63)

Even though the multidisciplinary team had been envisioned as having the potential to enhance school-based services to students with disabilities, early research demonstrated many problems with multidisciplinary teams. For example, team functioning is adversely affected by several problem areas including (1) use of unsystematic approaches to collecting and analyzing diagnostic information, (2) minimal parent or regular educator participation on the teams, (3) use of a loosely construed decision-making/planning process, (4) lack of interdisciplinary collaboration and trust, (5) territoriality, (6) ambiguous role definition and accountability, and (7) lack of experience and training for professionals to work together (Fenton, Yoshida, Maxwell, & Kaufman, 1979; Kaiser & Woodman, 1985; Pfeiffer, 1981).

As the field recognized the shortcomings of the multidisciplinary team concept, various implementation analyses and proposals for corrective action were advanced. Among the problems most frequently cited as needing corrective action was the lack of preparation in effective collaboration and team participation skills (Fleming & Fleming, 1983). Fortunately, training programs and resources such as this text and other resources listed at the end of this chapter are being developed in response to this preparation need.

The emerging training is addressing many of the previously noted problem areas identified in the early and continuing research.

Another serious barrier to effective team decision making, as noted by Pryzwansky and Rzepski (1983), may stem from the fact that it is mandatory. These authors suggest that this characteristic of multidisciplinary team decision making is the reason that teams have defined their purpose so narrowly and have seldom taken the opportunity to define their conceptual base. Without a clearly understood conceptual foundation, teams lack the grounding on which to construct their structure. At the same time, organizational variables, such as lack of program options and no opportunity for follow-up, also interfere with establishing a broader structure.

Other Case-centered Teams

While acknowledging the problems encountered in the implementation of multidisciplinary teams, special service providers have continued to pursue the potential for team decision making. In response to the limitations of multidisciplinary teams as they were initially implemented, special service providers have proposed functional and structural improvements and they have advocated, developed, and implemented alternative models for operationalizing the team concept.

One significant response to some of the practical barriers associated with multidisciplinary teams was the development of building-level, problem-solving teams to assist teachers in accommodating students with behavioral or learning difficulties in their classrooms. These teams evolved, in part, to augment the formal referral and evaluation processes in special education. Often known as *prereferral teams* or *prereferral intervention teams*, they are meant to provide prereferral screening for special education services and immediate support for teachers trying to develop appropriate in-class interventions.

A variety of prereferral intervention programs have been established in schools and described in the literature. Use of the term *prereferral* has been criticized, however, because it implies that these programs are simply the first step in referral for special education evaluation (Hayek, 1987). Because these teams were designed to reduce inappropriate referrals to special education and to prevent the escalation of students' learning and behavior disorders, the implication of subsequent referral and evaluation seems contradictory.

Various intervention assistance approaches are growing in popularity, but some important structural and conceptual differences among them may affect their impact. Although evidence supports the effectiveness of several approaches to early intervention or prevention, limited comparative data have established the efficacy of specific team approaches (see Phillips, McCullough, Nelson, & Walker, 1990). Variations in structures and implementation decisions may be necessary in different school ecologies and schools must select appropriate criteria for discriminating and selecting among program structures. Examples of some variations in intervention assistance team structures include the following:

Teacher Assistance Team (TAT). The TAT was one of the earliest examples of a prereferral intervention assistance model. As originally developed by Chalfant, Pysh, and Moultrie (1979), this teacher support system or peer problem-solving group consists of three elected teachers and the referring teacher. Parents are invited to become members and, when appropriate, specialists are also invited; the latter, however, are not regular members. The team provides teachers with the support needed to accommodate students with learning and behavior disorders in their classrooms. The referring teacher defines the problem, develops alternative interventions jointly with other TAT members, and then selects the favored intervention. The TAT functions on the assumption that general education teachers have the knowledge and talent to individually or jointly resolve a great number of the problems they encounter in teaching students with learning and behavior problems. TATs support the assumption of the superiority of group decision making that underlies the multidisciplinary team structure, but they differ from multidisciplinary teams by not including specialists as team members unless the specialists' unique expertise is needed for a particular case. The TAT either provides direct assistance to the referring teacher or helps the teacher to obtain follow-up from special education personnel.

Prereferral Intervention System. A TAT variation developed by Graden, Casey, and Bonstrom (1985) uses a multidisciplinary building-based team and combines teacher consultant and team formats in a six stage process. The first four stages are prereferral processes and the final two are formal referral, assessment, and eligibility determination processes.

Stage 1—request for consultation—is the referring teachers' initial contact with the system. This stage usually involves informal contact with a consultant (generally a special educator, psychologist, or social worker) although some districts may require a building-based team review and subsequent assignment to a consultant.

Stage 2—consultation—follows the standard steps of behavioral consultation.

Stage 3—observation—entails observation in the classroom by the consultant, feedback regarding the observation to the referring teacher, and collaborative development, implementation, and evaluation of interventions based on observations.

Stage 4—conference—is where a child review team meets to share information and make a decision regarding the continuation, modification, or termination of the intervention.

Stage 5 and Stage 6 encompass the formal referral and program planning meetings.

This prereferral intervention system is an alternative to a formal, special education decision-making team. It is similar to the TAT in its emphasis on teacher support and prevention. It is also similar to multidisciplinary teams in its reliance on special service providers as key players in the process. By including a consultation component, the system also incorporates elements of the consultative structure that was discussed in the beginning of the chapter.

Additional Decision-making Teams

As we noted earlier, many building-based organizational structures and procedures facilitate group or team approaches to planning, decision making, and problem solving. You may be familiar with examples such as teaching teams, grade-level teams, and schoolwide teams. These teams address a full range of school management, curricular, and instructional issues and are not necessarily case centered or focused on individual students' problems.

Teaching Teams. The variations of team teaching and their implications for special service providers have been discussed in the special education literature (see Bauwens, Hourcade, & Friend, 1989). Considerable attention recently has been given to team teaching in general education as well, and its use seems to be increasing significantly. For example, in a recent study of middle schools, MacIver (1990) reported that about 42% of early adolescents in a sample of 2400 public schools that enroll seventh graders received instruction from interdisciplinary teams of teachers at some time between grades 5 and 9. In this study, the interdisciplinary teams of teachers, with each member teaching a different subject to the same group of students, produced a wide range of benefits particularly if they had a designated leader, adequate planning time, and a commitment to the interdisciplinary team concept demonstrated through their willingness to use planning time for team participation. Specifically,

> These teams were seen to increase the effectiveness of instruction, to provide teachers with a much-needed support system, to help insure that students' problems will be recognized and solved, to improve students' work and attitudes, and to have a positive impact on the school's overall program for the middle grades. (p. 464)

Grade-level Teams. This team structure is very similar to that of the teaching team. Grade-level or departmental teams are constructed around members with highly similar interests and expertise (i.e., the grade level or subject matter they teach). The nature of the decisions these groups make may focus on curriculum, schedule, budget, or other matters of group interest or concern. These teams do not exist for the purpose of case consultation or conferencing, but they may elect to discuss and jointly solve problems about student-related issues. The probability of grade-level or departmental teams focusing the resources of the decision-making team on a particular case or student increases greatly if more than one team member has contact with the same student. Depending on the nature of the team's activity and the range of expertise among team members, the team may request that additional staff serve on the team on an ad hoc basis.

Schoolwide Teams. The case-centered teams previously discussed are often schoolwide teams, but here we use the term to describe organizational team structures that address schoolwide issues such as curriculum, school image, governance, professional development, and resource management. As part of the school reform movement that seeks to empower school personnel, increased emphasis has been placed on involving all school professionals in school-based, decision-making teams (Glickman, 1989).

This emphasis has led to a demand for new structures in schools to facilitate increased professional decision making and shared leadership (Passow, 1986). Different approaches to schoolwide decision making have been established by an array of groups including professional associations, teacher unions, parent and community groups, and creative educational leaders. Changes have been made in school schedules, curriculum structure, budgeting priorities, staff development designs, as well as personnel roles and responsibilities through the innumerable variations in structures that have emerged in response to the call for restructuring (Lieberman & Miller, 1990). Because of space limitations we will not discuss these variations here. We simply point out that diverse team structures and configurations are being developed to address these macrolevel issues at the building level. The opportunities for and barriers to effective team functioning are highly similar for these and the other types of teams previously described.

Team Effectiveness

The effectiveness of a team can be evaluated in terms of its goal attainment because, as we defined earlier, the team's purpose for existence is to achieve the common goal of its members. Another criterion for judging team effectiveness is its *output*. Abelson and Woodman (1983) note that a team is effective when its productive output exceeds or meets the organization's standards of quality and quantity. In schools, teams would be considered effective when their output meets the standards of their profession and the expectations of the various constituencies including administrators, parents, and peers.

A model of work team effectiveness advanced by Nadler, Hachman, and Lawler (1978) suggests that the ultimate effectiveness of a team depends on (1) the level of effort team members devote to the team's task, (2) the level of knowledge and skills within the team, and (3) the strategies the team uses to accomplish its work. Furthermore, these factors are affected by the design of the task, the composition of the team, and the appropriateness of the strategies used by the team. In combination, these factors and design elements are critical in developing effective teams and they are included in the following list of characteristics of effective teams:

The Team's Goals Are Clear
The goals of an effective team are clearly understood by all of the team's members. Effective teams will have many goals. Mutual goals represent the team's primary purposes, but each activity the team pursues to achieve its purposes will also have goals. Members of effective teams have clear understanding of both the central goals and activity or process goals.

Members' Needs Are Met
In effective teams, the personal needs of team members are satisfied more than frustrated by the group experience. The interpersonal needs of being included, respected, and valued can be met through active participation in a team. Teams in schools are not likely to be effective in achieving their common goals if the team relationship prevents individuals from meeting these interpersonal needs or attaining their individual professional goals.

Members Have Individual Accountability
Team members should clearly understand their roles as well as those of other members. Earlier, we identified role interdependence as a defining characteristic of teams because work teams are constructed with members who have complementary and interconnected

roles. Each member has responsibility for something the group needs in order to function. The structure of an effective team provides for individual accountability that increases the tendency of team members to devote adequate effort to meeting their responsibilities to the team. Individual accountability is achieved by conducting assessments of the performance of group members to determine the quality and quantity of their contribution. Conducting such assessment serves many purposes including clearly identifying contributions, reducing duplication of effort, reinforcing and clarifying responsibilities, identifying needs for assistance, and minimizing the likelihood of freeloading by non-contributing members.

Group Processes Maintain the Team

The group processes used in effective teams serve to increase, or at least maintain, the team's capacity to work collaboratively on future endeavors. Specifically, these group processes ensure that team leadership and participation are distributed throughout the team. Leadership skills, such as initiating discussion, setting standards, encouraging, summarizing, and gaining consensus, can be used by different members of the team. A team that wants to make maximum use of the diverse experience, expertise, and information of its members will distribute leadership roles. Team members recognize that leadership is a shared responsibility and will assume the role of leader when necessary to support the functioning of the group.

Collaboration and Teams

In the first part of the chapter we discussed consultation and considered the relationship between the process of consultation and the interaction style of collaboration. Now, after examining variations in school teams, we examine the relationship of the team structure to the use of a collaborative style of interaction.

The distinctions among elements of a collaborative style and team structure are far less clear than the earlier distinctions among elements of the consultation process and a collaborative style of interaction. This is partly because the defining characteristics of a team are those that define the relationship among team members just as the defining characteristics of collaboration are those that define the relationship among participants in a collaborative activity. Moreover, the defining characteristics of a team are very similar to those of collaboration because it is these elements of collaboration that distinguish a team from a loosely constructed group or a committee.

Teams are characterized by collaborative relationships among members. Team members share parity, have a common goal, share responsibility for decision making, and share accountability for outcomes. Teams have common norms and shared beliefs and values, and team members trust one another. Collaboration's emergent characteristic of interdependence is a critical defining characteristic of a team. Two essential, defining characteristics of collaboration—voluntariness and shared resources—will enhance the functioning of teams, but they are not essential characteristics of teams. The relationship between teams and collaboration is simple: An effective team is a collaborative group.

SUMMARY

Consultation and teams are two topics frequently linked with the term collaboration in schools. This chapter discussed both topics and clarified their relationship to collaboration.

Consultation is a voluntary process in which one professional assists another to address a problem concerning a third party. The characteristics of consultation are that it is (1) triadic and indirect, (2) voluntary, (3) an expert relationship, (4) a problem-solving process, and (5) a process that involves shared but differentiated responsibilities for decisions and accountability for outcomes. Consultation has several different theoretical models including behavioral, clinical, mental health, and organizational. Collaboration is a style of interaction that may be used within the consultation process, but consultation may be conducted without collaboration as well.

A team is a relatively small set of interdependent individuals who work and interact directly in a coordinated manner to achieve a common purpose. The defining characteristics of teams include: (1) shared norms, (2) structured role relationships, and (3) interdependence. Effective teams are further characterized by clear goals, individual accountability, and shared responsibility. Multidisciplinary teams have long been important structures in special service disciplines and are significant structures in schools. Other types of teams in schools are variations of case-centered teams (e.g., teacher assistance teams, prereferral intervention teams), teaching teams, schoolwide teams, and grade-level teams. Teams, by definition, share many characteristics with collaboration. In fact, teams may be described simply as collaborative work groups.

ACTIVITIES AND ASSIGNMENTS

1. Think about the position titles and descriptions that special service providers have in your school setting or in a school with which you are familiar. Do those who are called consultants have responsibilities consonant with the description of consultation provided in this chapter? How would you write a position description to maximize a consultant's effectiveness?

2. Which model(s) of consultation might be useful for you in your current or anticipated professional role? Which would you not use? Why?

3. In Chapters 1 and 2, the concepts of collaboration and consultation were distinguished. If someone now asked you to define collaborative consultation, how would you respond? Why is it inappropriate to refer to collaborative consultation as a unique model of consultation?

4. List the teams with which you have been involved and consider which ones were most effective. Identify the characteristics of the effective and ineffective teams you have experienced.

5. Consider the organization and dynamics of your school or one with which you are familiar. Design a problem-solving structure that you think would be most effective in assisting classroom teachers to meet the educational needs of all students. Your design may include any combination of the elements of structures described in this chapter and may include multiple formats (e.g., consultation, teams, and peer dyads).

6. Identify one consultation and one team experience that you have had or observed that was not as successful as you would have wanted it to be. Using the characteristics of collaboration

presented in Chapter 1 and the issues raised in this chapter, analyze each situation and describe how these factors may have contributed to the problems encountered in the consultation and/or the team.

RELATED READINGS

Brown, D., Pryzwansky, W. B., & Schulte, A. C. (1987). *Psychological consultation: Introduction to theory and practice*. Boston: Allyn & Bacon.

Dyer, W. G. (1977). *Team building: Issues and alternatives*. Reading, MA: Addison-Wesley.

Kerr, M. M., & Nelson, C. M. (1989). *Strategies for managing behavior problems in the classroom* (2nd ed.). Columbus, OH: Charles E. Merrill.

Menlo, A. (1986). Consultant beliefs which make a significant difference in consultation. In C. L Warger & L. Aldinger (Eds.), *Preparing special educators for teacher consultation*. Toledo, OH: Preservice Consultation Project, College of Education and Allied Professions, University of Toledo.

Moore, K. J., Fifield, M. B., Spira, D. A., & Scarlato, M. (1989). Child study team decision making in special education: Improving the process. *Remedial and Special Education, 10*(4), 50–58.

Phillips, V., & McCullough, L. (1990). Consultation-based programming: Instituting the collaborative ethic in schools. *Exceptional Children, 56*, 291–304.

Phillips, V., McCullough, L., Nelson, C. M., & Walker, H. M. (1991). Teamwork among teachers: Promoting a statewide agenda for students at risk for school failure. *Special Services in the Schools, 6* (3–4).

Reynolds, C., & Salend, S. J. (1989). Cooperative learning in special education teacher preparation programs. *Teacher Education and Special Education, 12*(3), 91–95.

Rosenfield, S. (1987). *Instructional consultation*. Hillsdale, NJ: Erlbaum.

West, J. F., & Idol, L. (1990). Collaborative consultation in the education of mildly handicapped and at-risk students. *Remedial and Special Education, 11*(1), 22–31.

Zins, J. E., Curtis, M. J., Graden, J. L. & Ponti, C. R. (1988). *Helping students succeed in the regular classroom*. San Francisco: Jossey-Bass.

CHAPTER 3

Prerequisites for Effective Interactions

Keeping Perspective

Regardless of the setting or activity in which collaboration occurs, it depends on effective interaction among participating individuals. Chapter 3 begins the discussion of how to interact effectively. It overviews three topics: frame of reference, the types of information required for clear communication in interactions, and listening—the basis for communication.

Learner Objectives

1. To define frame of reference.
2. To propose alternative meanings for statements made by colleagues and parents.
3. To describe the types of information that may be needed in each of three dimensions for effective collaborative decision making.
4. To identify the types of information conveyed in statements and questions of colleagues and parents.
5. To define listening and explain why it is so essential in collaboration.
6. To use cognitive rehearsal, categorization, and note taking as strategies to enhance listening.

Once you have decided to collaborate with a colleague or parent, how do you assure your personal readiness to begin? Collaborative relationships require much more than just initiating interactions and hoping that the characteristics described in Chapter 1 fall into place. There are important prerequisites to effective collaborative interactions that involve your self-awareness and your ability to understand others.

FRAME OF REFERENCE

Every individual enters each life experience with a unique perspective. Your past experiences, acquired attitudes and beliefs, personal qualities, past and present feelings, and expectations for others affect what and how you observe and perceive, and ultimately how you respond and act. What you bring to the situation, independent of the situation itself, is called your *frame of reference*. It is your predisposition to respond in some particular manner to a particular situation.

Frame of Reference and Your Role

Your professional socialization contributes to your frame of reference. We discussed several of the common elements in the professional socialization of all school personnel, including individualistic performance and expert problem solving, in Chapter 1. At the same time, however, the discipline into which you were socialized (e.g., special education, school psychology, counseling, math, reading) and through which you prepared for a particular professional role (e.g., classroom teacher, occupational therapist, speech and language specialist, school psychologist) also contributes elements to your frame of reference. The latter component of your frame of reference may be considerably different from that of colleagues in other disciplines.

For example, general education teachers and special service providers may have pronounced differences in their perceived levels of responsibility for facilitating student learning (Pugach & Johnson, 1988). Consistent with their disciplinary preparation in general education, classroom teachers are likely to view their primary responsibilities as facilitating the progress of a group of students through a prescribed curriculum. Their professional studies emphasized curriculum, its scope and sequence, instructional methodology, techniques for group management, and strategies for delivering specific subject matter content. Their frames of reference tend to emphasize group instructional tasks and issues.

On the other hand, the professional preparation and socialization you experienced as a special service provider probably emphasized individual variations in human development and learning, procedures for assessing individual differences and learning needs, and a variety of instructional or therapeutic strategies to respond to unique needs of individual students. Not surprisingly, you probably believe your primary responsibilities are to identify a student's current level of functioning and to design and deliver services tailored to meet those needs. Your professional background, a major component of your frame of reference, leads you to focus on various aspects of *individual* students.

These differences in classroom teachers' and special service providers' frames of reference may have a profound impact on how they interact with one another. For you to successfully undertake collaborative activities, you will no doubt find that awareness of these variations and sensitivity to their influences is essential.

Substantial differences characterize the frames of reference held by the various disciplines that comprise special services. Some of these differences reflect the diverse philosophical and theoretical orientations within these fields (e.g., a preference for psychoeducational versus behavioral approaches), some reflect variations in the nature of the special services provided (e.g., specialized instruction, therapy, or diagnostic evaluation), and still others relate to the specific knowledge bases of the disciplines. For example, it is easy to understand how a speech and language specialist with responsibility for a student's articulation therapy might have a very different frame of reference from the specialist who provides the student's adaptive physical education. The former works individually with students, diagnosing the speech disability, designing interventions to remediate it, and perhaps delivering services in a one-to-one situation. However, the adaptive physical education specialist may focus on assessing a student's general physical deficits in the context of the student's strengths. This specialist will then design a program to maximize the strengths and reduce the deficits of the student, often delivering services by individualizing for the particular student within the group of students served. In a similar way, reading specialists are likely to have frames of reference that differ in several significant ways from those of occupational and physical therapists, administrators that differ from special education teachers, and so on.

We hope that by including these examples of variations in frames of reference among different professionals here, we can help you to focus on how your frame of reference, unique because of your personal and professional history, is both similar to and different from those of others with whom you may want to collaborate. What is most important to understand is that no two people experience a single interaction in the same way.

Selective Perception

Everyone uses selective perception. They choose, either consciously or unconsciously, to focus on some information while largely ignoring others. Selective perception is often necessary in professional interactions because such communication is quite complex (Wilson & Hanna, 1990). Often, too much information is transmitted for anyone to assimilate it all. Your frame of reference is the mechanism that guides your selective perception, that serves to filter or obscure some information and focus your attention on other information. Generally, you are most likely to perceive those elements of a message or situation that have the greatest relevance to your frame of reference. The biases your frame of reference contains can enhance or inhibit your perception and thus your understanding of another's situation.

Consider the following exchange at a team meeting.

Mr. Swanson, the tenth-grade English teacher, has come to a child study team meeting to discuss Susan, a student in his class who has a learning disability. He reports:

"Susan is having an extremely hard time with our writing program. She can *tell* me all of her ideas in a very organized fashion, but she can't *write* them because her spelling is outrageous. Her written work is simply unacceptable. I'm an English teacher not a spelling teacher! There's no way Susan can succeed in my class. It must be hard on her to continue to fail so often; she really should be in a special education class. I tried that peer tutoring you suggested. The papers she turns in are good, but it's probably because her tutor spells so well. Susan just dictates her compositions. She couldn't possibly write them. I have very high standards, and I won't lower them for one student. It wouldn't be fair to the other students and certainly wouldn't be fair to Susan."

One team member at the meeting thinks:

"Here we go again! It's another version of 'I can't stand having this kid in my class, and I won't adapt the program. Just get the kid out of my class, but let's agree it's for her benefit.' I can't let this guy push Susan out of his class. I'll have to stand firm on this."

Another team member says to herself:

"It's always difficult for secondary teachers when they first start to have LD kids integrated into their classes. He's completed both his BA and MA in English literature and wants to teach English, not spelling. I could discuss differential standards with him. Maybe he'd see that Susan is benefiting from the writing program. She's learning to structure her ideas and she feels good about herself for being in his class."

In the example just presented both professionals picked up on information presented by Mr. Swanson, but they each attended to different aspects of his report based on their roles and previous experiences. You can easily understand the thoughts of the two team members in response to Mr. Swanson if you are aware of the different strongly held biases of each: The first team member believes that classroom teachers do not care about special education students and that they want to minimize their work. The second team member believes that all teachers want to teach well and feel that their teaching benefits their students. Both professionals identified and selectively perceived something in Mr. Swanson's statements that corresponded with critical elements in their own frames of reference.

The message for professionals who engage in collaborative activities is clear: Your own frame of reference may prevent you from understanding someone else's. You can become more aware of your frame of reference and learn to consider multiple frames of reference by constantly challenging yourself to develop alternative explanations for others' statements. For example, what might a classroom teacher mean who says, "I'm not sure this student will *ever* learn how to divide!"? The teacher might be conveying general frustration at the student's difficulties, a "statement of fact" that the rest of the class is ready to learn a new skill while the student in question has not mastered the division concept, or the teacher might be expressing frustration and doubts about his or her own teaching abilities. You can probably generate several additional meanings for this simple statement. Continuing to remind yourself to think divergently and consider alternative meanings will help you to suspend judgment of others, avoid making premature decisions or conclusions, and more accurately comprehend multiple elements of complex situations.

INFORMATION NEEDS

Two of the several significant defining characteristics of collaboration, as we discussed in Chapter 1, are that it is shared decision making in a style of interaction. These characteristics help to highlight the two different aspects of all professional collaboration: (1) the task or problem being addressed and (2) the collaborative working relationship. Within all interactions both aspects—task and relationship—must be viewed simultaneously (Hersey & Blanchard, 1988). Although they may be labeled with other terms (e.g., content and process, or task and maintenance) the importance of both dimensions is raised during the professional preparation of most special service providers (Friend & Cook, 1988).

Effective shared decision making requires that those involved have access to and understanding of the pertinent information related to both the tasks they are pursuing and their relationship. To emphasize the importance of attending to elements of both the task and relationship, we refer to *task information needs* and *relationship information needs*. Because information related to both contexts is exchanged in all interactions, ongoing assessment and sorting out of these two types of information needs can contribute measurably to the success of collaborative efforts. The relationship information needs are essentially the same regardless of the tasks being undertaken, whereas the task information needs may be different for each discrete task comprising the collaborative effort.

DIMENSIONS OF INFORMATION

Both the collaborative relationship and the task you are collaborating to accomplish require exchange of and attention to the same categories of information. We identify three dimensions that can be used to organize these categories (Fig. 3.1): locus, domain, and detail. Each instance of communication will focus on at least one dimension and may simultaneously address all three. When you work collaboratively with others, you will need to determine what dimensions of information you should address as you plan and implement efforts to achieve your specific relationship and task goals. The success of both the task and relationship will rely to some degree on your ability to identify, gather, and exchange the appropriate dimensions and amount of information.

In this section we consider the three dimensions and the categories they contain. You probably will notice that our discussion of information needs is similar to others you have heard relative to other aspects of your professional functioning. That is, you consider these same dimensions when you prepare to carry out activities such as assessment and behavior management. As you progress in this text and practice the skills and activities in later chapters, you will learn to judge what information is needed and appropriate in different situations.

The information needed for collaborative activities may be gathered in many ways and from many different sources. It may be obtained by review of permanent products (e.g., cumulative files, assessment protocols), through direct observation, and through discussion. Similarly, you may express information verbally or nonverbally and receive it auditorily or visually. These different types of communication are the topics of

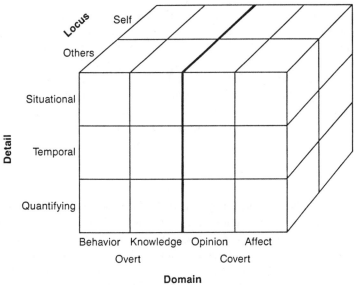

Figure 3.1. Dimensions of Information

Chapters 5, 6, and 7. To illustrate our discussion of the general concept of information needs in this chapter, however, we rely almost exclusively on verbal communication examples.

Locus

One critical dimension of information important in collaborative activities is its *locus* indicating whether the information refers to the locus of self (information located within the sender) or the locus of other (information located within the receiver, a third party, or other topics). The information exchange may focus on either the self or other locus, or simultaneously on both as these sentences illustrate:

1. How can I get appointed to that committee?
2. I enjoy committee work.
3. Do you have any influence over committee assignments?
4. Jack could suggest appointing new members to the committee.
5. Do you think Harold could help me to get an appointment to the committee?
6. You could nominate me for an appointment on the committee.

Each statement or question above can be classified as to the locus of its verbal content. The locus of the first two items is self as they refer only to the speaker. The locus for Items 3 and 4 is other as they refer to someone other than the speaker. Items 5 and 6 each refer to both self and other(s). You may get the sense that all six items refer primarily to the locus of self when you read them as a single group because the speaker is so clearly interested in becoming a member of the committee. In this context, Item 3 ("Do you have any influence over committee assignments?") may be viewed as a question that is actually focused on self because the speaker's primary interest appears to be self-serving (e.g., "I'm interested in your influence only to the extent that it may help me").

If you examine that question separately and out of context, it may be easier to identify the exact locus of the specific item. In fact, you can probably imagine several other scenarios where the same question would suggest very different motivations on the part of the speaker. As you apply these principles, keep in mind that it is important to understand that analyses of information dimensions should be based on the actual words used, not on inferences or opinions drawn from what was stated.

Domain

All information can be categorized by a second dimension, its *domain*, which is either covert or overt. As illustrated in Figure 3.1, if information is in the *overt domain* it refers to something that is observable (e.g., event, situation, or behavior) or something that can be reliably accessed by more than one person (e.g., knowledge or permanent product). Overt material is public. If several people objectively observe the same behaviors or examine the same factual information, they are likely to glean the same or highly similar information from it.

Examine the following examples and identify those that contain informational content in the overt domain:

1. I have her art project here.
2. Does she know that material?
3. I thought I'd die I was so embarrassed!
4. He threw the glass on the floor, yelled "No!", and ran from the room.
5. I feel like the third period would be better.
6. When was the field trip?

Three of the six items contain overt statements. The art project in Item 1 is a permanent product available for more than one person to see. Item 4 describes three overt behaviors that could be independently observed. Certainly you can infer that the person who displayed those behaviors was expressing feeling, but precisely what was the feeling? Anger? Frustration? Fear? In terms of the actual verbal content of Item 4, only overt behaviors are included. Item 6 refers to an event, the field trip, which is the final example of content in the overt domain.

Information in the *covert domain*, such as one's opinion or affect, is private and idiosyncratic. This type of content is capable of being seen or experienced by only one person. Although you and a colleague may share a similar situation, you are likely to have your own unique opinions and feelings about it. Before reading further, return to the preceding list of examples and try to classify each item with covert content and indicate why it is covert.

Did you identify Item 2 as covert? It refers to "knowing material" which suggests that knowledge (overt domain) is the content. Or if you made an assumption about observable performance that would demonstrate her knowledge you may have classified the item in the overt domain. However, the item is in the covert domain because it asks for an opinion and makes no reference to public or observable information. Item 3 uses "thought" which refers to the feeling of embarrassment and is covert. Item 5, although it contains the words "I feel," is covert because it expresses an opinion (a preference for third period). Further discussion and illustration of different purposes and approaches to communication of information content in these domains is presented in greater detail in Chapters 5 and 6.

Detail

The third dimension of information, shown on the left side of the diagram, is a modification of Cook and Cavallaro's (1985) structure for analyzing interactions. It specifies three types of detail: situational, temporal, and quantifying.

Situational Detail
Often, you will deal with information similar to that commonly found in leads to newspaper articles: who, what, where, when, and how. This information clarifies the parameters of the interpersonal relationship and helps to delineate the tasks required within the collaborative activity.

Temporal Detail
Examining pertinent time-related elements of collaborative activities is critical to understanding and successfully completing the tasks. Sometimes this category includes the amount of time needed; sometimes it pertains to analyzing the antecedents and consequences of events being addressed as part of the collaborative activity; and occasionally it involves establishing a chronology for either tasks to be accomplished or the various events that describe a specific situation that should be understood by everyone in a collaborative activity. Attending to the temporal detail of the task and understanding others' time needs can have very powerful effects on relationships as well.

Quantifying Detail
Having a strategy for assessing the quantifying detail of both the collaborative relationship and the tasks being addressed within the activity, is usually helpful. In some collaborative activities (e.g., intervening in a student problem), you may wish to gather data on the frequency of the problem or issue, and its duration, intensity, and/or latency. In other activities you may be concerned with quantifying detail such as the number of meetings required or the amount of space available.

To illustrate how the three categories of information detail are present in a wide variety of school collaborative activities, examine the following examples.

> The schedule in an elementary school has become a problem for a number of reasons. Teachers complain that too many special programs and activities take their students out of class and special service providers are concerned that students are missing assistance they need. A team has been formed to address the issue with representatives from the teachers, special services, "specials" (e.g., art, music), and an administrator.

Illustrative questions from a partial information needs analysis for this situation are included in Table 3.1. Although the table highlights the detail dimension, the content of

TABLE 3.1. ASSESSMENT OF DETAIL FOR DEVELOPING A SCHOOL SCHEDULE: SAMPLE ITEMS

Relationship Information Needs

Situational Detail

Who will be on the team? Are any additional participants needed?
Who has the most knowledge about the issues?
For what aspects of the schedule is the team responsible?
What is the team's role? Is it advisory or regulatory?
What role do I want to play on the team?
How will the team function to make decisions?
What are the attitudes of team members toward the team activity?
Where will the team meet?

Temporal Detail

When will the team meet?
When must the schedule be set?
How much of my preparation time will this require?

Quantifying Detail

How frequent and how long will meetings need to be?
How strongly are the special service providers committed to team decision making?
How invested am I in participating with the others?
How much involvement is required of team members?

Task Information Needs

Situational Detail

Who are the primary stakeholders?
What are teachers' preferences for restructuring the schedule?
What concerns might the special services staff have regarding the configuration of the schedule?
What are the restrictions on class size or student–teacher ratio?

Temporal Detail

What issues have to be resolved regarding the sequencing of courses?
How long will my consultation periods be?
How long must classes be?
What courses may need to be scheduled first?

Quantifying Detail

How much instruction is required for which subjects?
How many students need special physical accommodations?
How many periods will I have for collaborating with others?
How strongly committed to pullout programs are the special service providers?

---

each item also could be classified according to the locus and domain dimensions. Notice that the team has several tasks, but the first two require team members to analyze the parameters of their relationship and the activity they are pursuing. In analyzing the relationship parameters team members will attempt to clarify the purpose of the interactions, delineate operating procedures, determine needs for expanded membership, and establish timelines and responsibilities.

Establishing and clarifying the task parameters requires analysis of detail needed to fully understand the problem or situation to be addressed. For this task the team needs to consider which people are concerned about which aspects of the schedule; relevant sequencing issues in the schedule; and requirements regarding the amount, length, and frequency of instruction.

A second example involves Susan, a student with a disability who has been exhibiting temper tantrums. Her parents are very concerned about this behavior. The primary task of the special service providers is to work with other school professionals and the parents to eliminate the tantrums.

Table 3.2 lists the types of questions that would be addressed in a partial information needs analysis for this collaborative activity.

The relationship information needs are essentially the same as those in the first example. For the initial task, situational detail includes a description of the presenting problem, and temporal includes an analysis of specific events that precede and follow the tantrums. Quantifying detail entails consideration of the frequency, duration, and intensity of the problem behavior. Notice, too, that information in the locus and domain dimensions is also included in this analysis.

The locus, domain, and detail dimensions of information you will need for the tasks and relationships of collaboration may appear dauntingly complex. However this should not deter you from consciously monitoring their role in your interactions. Our experience suggests that practice related to these concepts enables professionals and students to assimilate them. The following strategies also may assist you.

Suggestions for Assessing Dimensions of Information

Identifying Information Needs

An awareness of the three dimensions and various categories within each should help you to identify the information needed in your collaborative activities. Note, however, that you will not consider each type of information in every situation. In fact, too much information can hinder, rather than help, a collaborative interaction. We suggest that you view the dimensions of information as a sort of mental checklist that you periodically use to assess the relationship and tasks in a collaborative endeavor. You can use this checklist to ensure that you examine all dimensions and categories in deciding which are most necessary to share and which should be eliminated.

Attending to Task and Relationship

Because both the task and relationship are important in collaborative endeavors, you will analyze the information you have and need in both contexts simultaneously. At various stages in any collaborative activity either the task or the relationship may seem to have greater importance, but both are critical to the success of your collaboration.

TABLE 3.2. ASSESSMENT OF DETAIL CONCERNING
SUSAN'S BEHAVIOR: SAMPLE ITEMS

Relationship Information Needs

Relationship Information Needs for this example are essentially the same as those in the preceding one. See information in Table 3.1.

Task Information Needs

Situational Detail

What does Susan do when she has a tantrum?
Where do the tantrums generally occur?
What are professionals' roles when she has tantrums?
Does the teacher think that action should be taken to
    stop the tantrums?
Who is present when she has a tantrum?

Temporal Detail

When does Susan have a tantrum?
What happens immediately before a tantrum?
What is Susan's affect immediately before a tantrum?
How long does the tantrum last?
What happens immediately after a tantrum?
What do I say to Susan after she has a tantrum with me?

Quantifying Detail

How often does Susan have a tantrum?
How much do the parents know about behavior
    modification?
How do I feel about Susan after she has a tantrum with me?
For how long does a tantrum last?
How serious do Susan's parents believe the tantrum problem is?
How intense are her tantrums?

Developing Shared Meanings through Concrete and Specific Communication

Even when focusing on only a few of the many types of information presented here, you may need to find ways to make the information more specific in order to assure that everyone participating shares a common understanding. For example, imagine that a teacher tells you, "That schedule option would make my class size too large." The description is too general and does not provide you with adequate information to understand the situation. To clarify, you might try to answer questions such as these:

- How large would the class size be under this option?
- What class size is allowed by regulation?
- How large should this class be for appropriate instruction and learning?

Ultimately, it is not enough simply to exchange vital information. Effective collaborative decision making requires participants to have a similar understanding of the essential facts. Specific and concrete rather than general information should be sought.

LISTENING

A final prerequisite for collaborative interactions is effective listening. Listening is essential in all aspects of life. People listen for pleasure at concerts and movies, they listen for learning in courses and meetings, and they listen for understanding in day-to-day interactions with families and friends. You may best understand the importance of listening if you recall experiences of *not* being listened to—whether at a party, in a work setting, or at home. In all these settings, you may have participated in "parallel conversations," much like the parallel play of children, in which individuals, either simultaneously or alternately, talk about the thing that most interests them without much regard for others. The speakers appear to have agreed to take turns speaking and acting as an audience for each other without responding in any meaningful way to what the other person says. If you have been part of such adult parallel play, you no doubt realize that dissatisfaction and feelings of being misunderstood usually result.

In collaboration, listening is especially critical. It is a complex and difficult-to-measure process for attending to and accurately comprehending what another person is saying and then demonstrating that this has occurred (Brammer, 1985). It is a primary means for gaining information, but it is also a means of conveying interest in the messages communicated by colleagues and parents. Effective interpersonal relationships are only possible when participants continually work to hone their listening skills.

Rationale for Listening

One of the primary reasons for listening to another person is to establish rapport (Danziger, 1976). In collaborative interactions, listening can help to establish and build rapport in two major ways: First, when you listen you show concern and a desire to understand both the other person and the situation. By listening you communicate concern for the speaker as an individual as well as the intent to understand what that person has to say. You also demonstrate that you are sensitive to the situation and to the person's perception of the situation. Second, listening can help you build rapport when it allows you to demonstrate accurate understanding. Attention, willingness to listen, and desire to understand are important elements in establishing rapport, but accurate understanding is required to build and maintain a relationship. When you demonstrate precise understanding of what the person has said about a particular situation, you are perceived as being both competent and a worthy collaborator.

Another major reason for developing effective listening skills is that good listening is essential for obtaining adequate and accurate information (of the type outlined in the preceding section) necessary for continuing the collaborative activity. Too frequently, professionals assume they understand an inadequately articulated comment or concern and begin acting on it only as they perceive it. This is a dangerous practice for several reasons. First, it is quite improbable that anyone can accurately understand an inadequately articulated situation. Without accurate understanding, appropriate actions are rare. Second, a "kneejerk" response may give others the impression that they are incompetent. Have you ever had the following happen? People listened haphazardly as you described a problem, responded quickly, and left you thinking, "If it was so easy, why couldn't I think of an answer? I'm embarrassed to have thought it was such a problem! But I'm not sure anyone even heard what the real issue is." This kind of situation does nothing to establish parity. Finally, and perhaps most threatening to the collaborative relationship, a rapid and inaccurate response to a person's comments suggests little concern for the person's perception of the issue, and even less for the person as a significant individual.

Factors That Interfere with Effective Listening

Have you ever found that despite good intentions to listen carefully to what a colleague was describing, by the time the other person finished providing a rather clear and precise description you were not at all sure of what had been said? This experience is common, and it illustrates how difficult it is to listen. Recall a recent experience when you listened ineffectively. Can you identify what it was that interfered with your listening in that situation? DeVito (1986) identified several obstacles to effective listening that may be the culprits.

Rehearsing a Response
Perhaps while your colleague was talking you caught the "drift" of what was being said and proceeded to work on framing what you would say when you had the opportunity to speak. Similarly, at a team meeting perhaps you were anticipating that it would soon be your turn to report, and so you were reviewing your notes—and missed what someone else said.

Daydreaming
When you listen, you are engaged in an inefficient process. You are capable of receiving information more rapidly through listening than an average speaker can convey, even a speaker who talks at an unusually high rate of speed. The result is that you have available spare time to think, even while you listen. Unfortunately, you may use this time to mentally prepare a shopping list, plan next week's vacation, develop an instructional unit, or prepare how you are going to address a family problem this evening. You suddenly may find that daydreaming is receiving the proportion of attention that should be for listening, and you have lost understanding of the speaker's message.

Stumbling on "Hot" Words
To what words do you respond strongly? Inclusion? Merit pay? Aversives? Sometimes when a speaker to whom you are listening uses a "hot" word, you may begin to think about the meaning of the word and its implications for you. This special category of daydreaming has the same impact: You temporarily halt effective listening while you cognitively address other matters.

Filtering Messages
Occasionally you may simply not want to listen to a particular message. For example, think about times you have attended a staff meeting on a topic about which you were already knowledgeable. Did you listen while the topic was announced and then "tune out?" If so, you were filtering the message. You might have done the same thing if the information seemed to have little relevance to your situation. Finally, your frame of

reference may cause you to filter messages. As we noted earlier, your frame of reference may cause you to selectively attend to specific parts of a message and ignore others, thereby causing you to inaccurately perceive the message.

Being Distracted by Extraneous Details

Most people have had the experience of finding listening difficult because their attention is drawn to a detail that is extraneous to the message being conveyed. For example, have you ever spent so much time wondering where a colleague or parent got such an unusual haircut that you could not attend to what was being said? Perhaps you have interacted with someone who had a minor speech impairment and you discovered it was especially difficult to attend to the words instead of the impediment. Any distractions—physical, verbal, gestural, environmental—may cause your attention to be drawn from the message and interfere with effective listening.

Suggestions for Improving Your Listening Skills

Because listening has a powerful metacognitive component, refining your listening skills requires addressing your ability to sustain attention and monitor your comprehension of the verbal message. And although there are no simple solutions for becoming a more effective listener, you can improve your skills by trying the following strategies.

Rehearse the Information Being Conveyed to You

One strategy for improving listening skills is to practice mentally repeating the information being conveyed. Challenge yourself to assess whether you have truly "gotten" everything that was said. Later, in Chapter 5, we discuss paraphrasing as one means of sharing this mentally rehearsed information with the other person. But even if you do not repeat information aloud, trying to repeat it mentally can be a strategy for determining how well you understand it and whether you should interrupt the communication to seek clarification.

Categorize the Information Being Received

Another strategy closely related to mental rehearsal is to categorize information as it is shared. For example, as a parent explains to you concerns about a child's development, group these according to whether they are academic, behavioral, emotional, or developmental. As you develop a categorization scheme and actively sort information and revise the system, you are acting on the information and ensuring that you comprehend what is being said. In addition, when you begin speaking you have a structure through which to address the topics being raised, one that includes all the essential elements of the parent's comments.

Jot Notes for Details

Although note taking can interfere with listening if it distracts your attention from the information being conveyed, in some instances it is the strategy of choice. Note taking is one way that may help you comprehend when a large amount of information being presented and you have inadequate time to sort it cognitively. Notes can also be a strategy for you to cut off the habit of rehearsing your response. You can jot down the point you want to make and then devote your attention to using other strategies to aid your listening.

Select and Use a Signal to Hold Your Responses

Sometimes you may not be able to write down an idea you want to share, or a concern you need to express. In that case, you can develop an unobtrusive signal to yourself that enables you to "store" the information until it is time to use it. This strategy is the equivalent of tying a string around your finger. For example, when you want to remember a point but listen more effectively, try bending and holding down your little finger or turning a ring you wear so that the stone is toward your palm. Then attend to the speaker's message. When the person is finished, your signal will remind you of the point you wanted to make. With a little practice, you may find this strategy nearly as effective as note taking!

SUMMARY

In preparing for collaborative interactions, it is important for you to understand your own and others' perceptions of situations and how these have been shaped by past experiences. This is called frame of reference. No two individuals have the same frame of reference. Differences in frames of reference occur between special service providers and general educators because of differences in their preparation and professional socialization. However, differences also exist in the frames of references among and within the disciplines in special services. Another element preparatory to collaboration is recognizing the complexity of the information about the collaborative task to be accomplished as well as the collaborative relationship. The information that needs to be exchanged and understood in collaborative activities can be classified in one of three dimensions. Information in the first dimension addresses the locus of self or the locus of other. The second dimension, domain, includes either covert or overt information. The third dimension, informational detail, falls into three categories: situational, temporal, and quantifying. A final means of preparing for collaboration is to refine your listening skills. Listening is a complex process that may be impeded by various internal and external events. However, listening skills can be improved by using metacognitive and other strategies.

ACTIVITIES AND ASSIGNMENTS

1. Think of two or three statements or remarks heard in your professional setting that bother you (e.g., "They're special education students, not mine"). What is it that disturbs you about each statement? What does each imply that bothers you? Now consider each statement separately and imagine the possible different frames of reference someone who makes such a statement may have. Try to generate four or five different frames that may underlie each statement. Discuss this exercise with a colleague.

2. Consider a student-related problem you have recently heard someone else mention. Imagine yourself planning to help the other person understand and respond to the problem. Identify the

widest range of task information needs and relationship information needs using the dimensions presented in Figure 3.1, and generate a list of these. Review the information needs to determine which are truly necessary and which are likely to result in too much information.

3. To open yourself to considering alternative meanings and frames of reference, try to generate four distinctly different possible meanings for the statements below. Get additional practice by doing the same for statements made by others in the course of conversations during the next few days.

   Practice statements:

   a. Teacher: I really don't know what to do to help her. I desperately need your help.
   b. Parent: He's been in special education for three years now. Isn't he caught up yet?
   c. Speech and Language Specialists: If I'm going to work in classrooms with students, shouldn't I take courses in how to be a teacher?

4. Conduct information needs analyses attending to both the relationship and task involved in the following situation:

   A colleague with whom you've not collaborated previously recognizes that one of his or her students needs more intensive programming. This colleague has asked you to discuss ways you can help in providing a better program for the student.

5. To practice your listening skills, proclaim a "Listen to My Colleague Week." Select one colleague with whom you interact frequently. Using the strategies mentioned in this chapter, practice effective listening with the person for one week. Write a description of the experience. Discuss it with others.

RELATED READINGS

Egan, G. (1982). *The skilled helper: Model, skills, and methods for effective helping* (2nd ed.). Monterey, CA: Brooks/Cole.

Jobes, N. K., & Hawthorne, L. W. (1977). Informal assessment for the classroom. *Focus on Exceptional Children, 9*(4), 1–13.

McKay, M., Davis, M., & Fanning, P. (1983). *Messages: The communication book.* Oakland, CA: New Harbinger.

Mastropieri, M. A., & Scruggs, T. E. (1987). *Effective instruction for special education.* Boston: Little Brown.

Schmuck, R. A., & Runkel, P. J. (1985). *The handbook of organization development in schools* (3rd ed.), 91–149. Palo Alto, CA: Mayfield.

Wilson, G. L., & Hanna, M. S. (1990). *Groups in context: Leadership and participation in small groups* (2nd ed.). New York: McGraw-Hill.

Wolvin, A., & Coakley, C. G. (1988). *Listening* (3rd ed.). Dubuque, IA: William C. Brown.

CHAPTER 4

Interpersonal Problem Solving

Keeping Perspective

In Chapter 4, interpersonal problem solving is presented as the most commonly used interaction process through which school professionals collaborate. This chapter also marks the beginning of those that directly address collaboration skills. Chapters 5, 6, and 7 provide information on interpersonal communication skills (e.g., making statements and asking questions) that you may find helpful for carrying out the problem solving steps outlined here.

Learner Objectives

1. To describe why problem solving is so fundamental for collaboration among school professionals.
2. To define three types of problems you may encounter in your professional roles that would be appropriate for interpersonal problem solving.
3. To assess whether a problem is appropriately addressed through interpersonal problem solving.
4. To state the steps in a systematic interpersonal problem solving sequence.
5. To identify at least two strategies for facilitating each problem solving step.

Nearly all of the professional tasks and activities for which you are responsible can be conceptualized as some type of challenge or problem to be solved. In one type of problem solving, you act essentially alone to make a decision. You may do this when you decide which intervention, therapeutic technique, or equipment would be best used with particular students. You also independently problem solve when you reallocate time in order to accommodate a disruption in your day's plan, when you design (and redesign) your schedule, and when you set priorities for supplies you need for the next school year.

A second type of problem solving in which you engage is similar to the first in that decisions are made, but it is different in that you share this decision-making with others. This is referred to as *interpersonal problem solving*. Examples of interpersonal problem solving in special services are many: The team meetings you attend to determine the appropriate placement for students represent interpersonal problem solving activities as do conferences you have with colleagues to ascertain how to adapt instruction to meet students' needs. These examples represent two very different interpersonal contexts for problem solving, one fairly broad and involving many people, the other quite specific and involving only two people. Even the other processes in which you are likely to engage with other staff members or parents (e.g., interviewing, planning) are simply specialized applications of interpersonal problem solving. A single set of principles for interpersonal problem solving applies to the entire range of problem solving activities you undertake with others.

Interpersonal problem solving is so fundamental to successful interactions that it is the starting point for our discussion of skills for collaboration. In fact, you will find that it is virtually impossible to collaborate with colleagues and parents without systematically employing an interpersonal problem solving process.

A CONTEXT FOR INTERPERSONAL PROBLEM SOLVING

Before turning to the steps in the interpersonal problem solving process, examining concepts related to understanding problem characteristics will set the problem solving context. Analyze these three interactions:

DIRECTOR: With Jason enrolling at Lincoln School, we're going to have some modifications to make so that the building's accessible. Let's see, what do we need to do?

TEACHER: A ramp needs to be installed at the entrance to the building. There are three steps—impossible for Jason's wheelchair.

THERAPIST: Someone also needs to check the bathroom to be sure the handrails are installed.

PRINCIPAL: What about the chalkboard in the classroom?

DIRECTOR: Let's make a list of the changes to check on and then decide who can deal with them. The carpenters can be here by the end of the week.

TEACHER 1: I don't know how I'm going to get a schedule made up. Too many people want me to be too many places at the same time.

TEACHER 2: I know what you mean. The flexible services for the kids are great, but I'm not sure I can handle what it does to *my* life!

TEACHER 1: Let's start with the "givens." We've got to have one of us available to cover the English classes during first and second hour since we have so many students in those classes.

TEACHER 2: And we promised that at least one of us would be free to meet with teachers during fourth hour lunch.

TEACHER 1: Let's block these things out on a master schedule...

PSYCHOLOGIST: We've agreed that we want to integrate more students next year and that more students should be spending more of the day in general education classes. What would it take to do this?

TEACHER 1: From my point of view, there has to be support for the classroom teachers. We have questions about the kids and may need someone to assist us with them.

TEACHER 2: I'm wondering how the psychologists and social workers could help out. Maybe some of the support could be related to peer groups in classes.

SOCIAL WORKER: We need to think about the parents, too. And the kids. Everyone needs to be prepared for the changes we're proposing.

The situation addressed in the first interaction illustrates a straightforward, *well-defined* problem that can be clearly identified—noting and reducing barriers for a student who will attend Lincoln School. The primary task is to specify the actions to implement and ensure that they are initiated. Well-defined problems are usually fairly easily understood. Difficulties in solving them are often the result of overlooking necessary solutions or encountering obstacles in implementing the solutions (e.g., the carpenters fail to appear).

In the second interaction, the problem is somewhat more complex. The teachers have identified the problem as arranging their schedules, but there is no clear cut single solution. Instead, they are working within a set of factors that have to be accommodated (e.g., the need to "cover" English classes and to have someone available during lunch). This is a *partially-defined* problem in which the goal is clear and some guidelines exist for addressing the goal, but the specific means for reaching it are varied. The problem could have multiple solutions, but the range is constrained by a set of external factors.

The third interaction is the most complex. The problem is identified as wanting to increase integration of students in the school. However, this is an unclear goal: What is increased integration? How much integration should occur? For which students is it most important? How can integration occur? What resources will facilitate integration? The options for specifying and accomplishing the broad goal of increased integration are nearly infinite. This is an illustration of an *ill-defined* problem. It does not have clear parameters, nor is it easily resolved.

While you undoubtedly address all three types of problems in your role as a special service professional, ill-defined problems probably occupy a significant portion of your time. The steps for problem solving outlined in the next section are valid for the first two types of problems, but they are especially critical for addressing ill-defined ones.

Reactive and Proactive Problem Solving

Another dimension on which problem solving may vary is the urgency of the problem solving activity. In *reactive* problem solving, you are faced with responding to a crisis or dilemma. Some event occurs that focuses your attention on a matter to be resolved. Examples of this might include the interactions you have with a parent concerning a sudden change in student behavior, the meeting between you and a teacher to adapt classroom materials to be more appropriate for a given student, and the conference among all the members of a prereferral team to generate interventions that may enable a student to succeed in class. Much of the interpersonal problem solving in schools is reactive.

Conversely, problem solving can be *proactive* when an anticipated situation focuses attention and triggers the problem solving process before a crisis occurs. For example, in the first interaction described above, proactive problem solving is illustrated: Members of a team are anticipating problem areas for integrating a student *before* dilemmas occur. Other illustrations of proactive problem solving include planning a student's program, arranging support services before they are needed, and deciding how to best use staff time given anticipated student enrollment for the next school year.

Using a systematic approach for problem solving is beneficial in addressing both proactive and reactive problems. In fact, one benefit of following specific steps in problem solving is that less time may eventually be required for resolving reactive problems so that more proactive problem solving is possible.

Deciding Whether to Problem Solve

In addition to understanding the type of problem to be solved collaboratively and knowing whether the process will be reactive or proactive, you are faced with a crucial decision prior to beginning problem solving: Is this a problem we should solve?

Your immediate answer to this question might be, "Of course—it's my job!" But that thinking is why special service personnel sometimes repeatedly discuss the same problem without progress. It is also one of the reasons why time is at such a premium for special service providers. The belief that any ill-defined problem, proactive or reactive, *must* be solved if it pertains to a student with special needs undoubtedly arises out of the professional socialization factors discussed in Chapter 1. And while laudable, it should be balanced by an analysis of the realities of the problem situation.

These are questions to ask yourself as you encounter a problem that you and others are being asked to resolve:

1. Are the persons who have responsibility and resources for addressing the problem committed to resolving it?
2. What might happen if nothing is done to resolve the problem?
3. Does the problem warrant the effort and resources that will be required to effect significant change?
4. Are adequate time and resources available to resolve the problem?

Combined, the answers to these questions can assist you to make a decision about whether undertaking collaborative problem solving is warranted. In some cases, the information will lead you to an affirmative decision: Perhaps you are not familiar enough with the situation to make judgments about the impact of not addressing the problem. Or perhaps the individuals involved have expressed a strong commitment to tackle the problem. On the other hand, sometimes the answers to these questions lead you to a negative decision: Perhaps the people who would be key in addressing the problem do not have adequate time to devote to it. Or perhaps the problem—although affecting a student, a program, or some other aspect of the school setting—is beyond the control of the people interested in addressing it.

In addition to enabling you to assess the feasibility of solving the problem, these preliminary questions also assist you to begin assessing the possibility of establishing a collaborative problem solving relationship with the others involved. The questions can alert you to participants' beliefs that there may be many "right" solutions for this or any problem and that group decisions are the preferred approach for this situation. These are applications of the emergent characteristics of collaboration described in Chapter 1.

Because your judgment about whether to problem solve is based on preliminary information, throughout the problem solving process you should continually re-assess the appropriateness of the decision to engage in it. At any point in the process you may find that someone has lost commitment to resolving the problem, or that the problem is no longer within the control of the persons addressing it. If this happens, you may want to reconsider your initial positive decision.

STEPS IN INTERPERSONAL PROBLEM SOLVING

Once you and your colleagues have determined that you can and should resolve a given problem situation and that necessary conditions are in place for successful collaborative problem solving, you are ready to begin the problem solving process. The steps in interpersonal problem solving have been described by many authors (e.g., Bergan, 1977; Conoley & Conoley, 1982; Schein, 1969), and while they seem straightforward, their complexity lies in skillful implementation (Cummings, Murray, & Martin, 1989). The interpersonal problem solving steps and the critical questions associated with each are outlined in Figure 4.1. We explain them in greater detail throughout the remainder of this chapter.

Identifying the Problem

When we ask special service providers to list the steps in an interpersonal problem solving process, they nearly always correctly specify at least the first one: identifying the problem. However, in working with school professionals, we have learned that this step is far more easily recognized than implemented. Problem identification is difficult to accomplish and is often made even more so as the number of participants in interpersonal problem solving increases.

Not surprisingly, research supports the fact that problem identification is the most critical step in problem solving (Nezu & D'Zurilla, 1981) and that the rest of the process can only be successful if the problem statement is accurately delineated (Bergan & Tombari, 1975). We also find that phrasing problems as questions is a successful means of encouraging constructive problem identification; this approach to stating problems is followed throughout this chapter.

Characteristics of Well-identified Problems
When you identify problems, you may be addressing an issue as specific as a student behavior problem (e.g., What strategies could be implemented to increase Jeff's appropriate play with other students on the playground?), or as broad as designing ap-

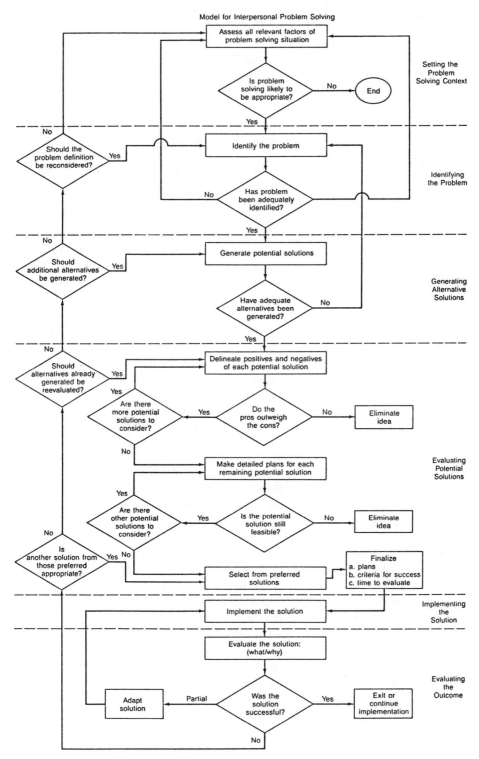

Figure 4.1. Model for Interpersonal Problem Solving

55

proaches for integrating students with disabilities (e.g., In what ways might we increase the extent to which students with disabilities are socially included throughout the school day?). Regardless of the scope of the problem, it should have the following set of characteristics.

An Identifiable Discrepancy Exists between Current and Desired Situations or Conditions. In interpersonal problem solving, you should state the problem clearly enough so that the discrepancy between the current situation and the desired situation is apparent. For example, in a problem situation concerning a student's inappropriate classroom behavior, a description of the current situation might focus on the quantifying detail of how often, for how long, and at what intensity the behavior is occurring. The desired situation might be the specification of appropriate behavior expectations for the classroom, using the same quantifying details. In a problem situation concerning a team's intent to plan a staff development program, the current situation might be information about the staff's knowledge level about a topic of concern; the desired situation might be a description of the knowledge required for proficiency to be demonstrated.

Participants Share the Perception that the Problem Exists. For interpersonal problem solving to occur, shared recognition of a specific problem is required of all participants. This is directly related to the concept of a mutual goal that was presented as a defining characteristic of collaboration in Chapter 1. If a special education teacher is dissatisfied with the progress a student is making in a mainstream class but the classroom teacher believes that the progress is adequate, the shared recognition of a discrepancy between the actual and ideal is missing. Likewise, if a school social worker expresses concern about a student's self-concept, but the student's parents do not perceive a problem, the parents and social worker are unlikely to engage in interpersonal problem solving. Note that in both examples, a different problem might be mutually identified if the participants discuss further their initial perceptions. But unless this occurs, the problem solving process should be interrupted and either terminated or the problem redefined to everyone's satisfaction.

Participants Agree on the Factors that Indicate the Discrepancy. Efforts to clarify what factors define the gap between what is and what should be facilitates clear communication in problem solving. For example, analyze the problem of successfully including a student with a physical disability in a general education class. What is success? Without specifying how to define the current status of the student and the status after some intervention, there is no way to determine whether successful integration has been accomplished. In this example, success could be indicated by the student's improved attitude toward school, parents' and teachers' perceptions of the same, the extent to which other students interact with the disabled student, or any number of additional measures. (Note that you will read about the importance of specifically measuring the factors defining the gap in the later section on finalizing plans.)

Problem Statements Are Free of Strategies that Might Comprise Solutions. The objective of problem identification is to describe in the clearest terms possible the discrepancy between the current and the ideal situations so participants can look for alternative strategies to move from the former to the latter. Therefore you should avoid unnecessarily narrowing the problem statement by inadvertently identifying it as some preferred strategy that is actually a solution (D'Zurilla & Nezu, 1987). To clarify this point, analyze this initial problem statement: "How can we assist this student with learning disabilities to succeed in his math class?" Although the problem is as yet incomplete since the gap has not been specified and the factors defining the gap have not been outlined, it is appropriate because it does not attempt to suggest a single strategy that is needed to ensure success. But what if the problem had been stated in this way: "How can we assist this student to learn his basic multiplication facts so he can succeed in math class?" The latter problem statement includes the assumption that success is dependent on learning math facts. If this problem statement is used, the problem solving process will probably focus on academic strategies and reward systems related to learning basic facts. In other words, the *solution* of learning math facts has been inadvertently inserted into the *problem* statement. In the former statement, however, no such error occurred. In that statement, the problem solving process might include discussion of strategies that include the student, his peers, his teacher, other professionals, his family, and so on. The range of potential solutions is broadened because the problem statement is free of preferred strategies.

The notion of keeping strategies for solving the problem separate from the problem statement is particularly important because of its relationship to the frame of reference concepts presented in Chapter 3. By keeping solutions out of problem statements, you make it more likely that all participants' frames of reference will be accommodated during the problem solving process.

Suggestions for Identifying the Problem
Any of several strategies may facilitate problem identification including the following most common ones.

Think of Problem Identification as Having Both Divergent and Convergent Elements. Too often in schools, problem identification is thought of as primarily a convergent process, that is, one that focuses on rapidly narrowing the problem description. While this may appear expedient, it is usually neither efficient nor constructive. Instead, we encourage you to think of the early phase of problem identification as divergent, that is, as a phase in which the goal is to explore all possible problem definitions so that none is overlooked.

One means of keeping early problem identification divergent is to challenge the assumptions that underlie initial problem statements. For example, this is a problem statement that you might encounter:

- How can we get Josh's parents, Mr. and Mrs. Keller, to participate in the behavior management program that Josh needs?

It has a number of assumptions, including the fact that Josh's parents should be involved in a behavior management program, that Josh truly needs the program, and that "we" should take responsibility for involving Mr. and Mrs. Keller. What would happen if you negated one or several of these assumptions? Perhaps the problem would be reconceptualized as one of these:

1. How can we get Josh's behavior management program to work at school?
2. How can we improve Josh's behavior at school?
3. How could Josh be helped to be more involved in controlling his behavior?

Once underlying assumptions have been challenged and alternative conceptualizations of the problem have been explored, the people participating in the problem solving process are more likely to be able to identify the salient characteristics of the problem and use them to formulate an accurate and precise problem statement. This latter part of problem identification is the convergent part. Challenging assumptions may or may not lead to a redefinition of a problem; the point is that it is a strategy for making the problem identification procedure explicit.

Describe the Problem Precisely. The need for using concrete and specific language in verbal communication was stressed in Chapter 3 and will be clarified in Chapter 5. Its importance cannot be overstated. In problem situations involving students, you encourage others to describe the observable behaviors or performance indicators that characterize the student's academic or social performance. For example, some teachers might call a student unmotivated. Your task during problem identification is to clarify what is meant by "unmotivated." Does this mean that the student is absent? Does it mean that assigned work is not returned to school? Does it imply that the student sleeps during lectures? Only by specifying the exact behaviors or performance indicators that comprise "unmotivated" can the problem be identified appropriately.

In addition to using concrete and specific language, when identifying a problem you will want to confirm that all participants share the same understanding of the particular words used. In the discussion in Chapter 3, we examined ways in which different frames of reference influence how people perceive messages. An example of a word that is often perceived differently by professionals is *integration.* For some special service providers, integration refers to including students with disabilities in general education classes primarily for social purposes; for others, it means inclusion during academic periods. For yet others it means fulltime inclusion. Imagine the difficulties that might result if a group of individuals were problem solving on this topic without establishing a shared meaning for the word!

Confirm Problems with Multiple Sources of Information. One of the dangers in interpersonal problem solving is that the participants will rely on a single source of information to identify a problem. An important strategy for ensuring successful problem identification is the use of multiple sources. In problems related to students, this might entail completing an observation of the target student in several different school settings, reviewing student records, and interviewing parents and teachers. In problems related to programs, teams, or services, this might include confirming district policies, reviewing available data (e.g., needs assessment or a staff development activity evaluation), and interviewing key people to ascertain their perceptions.

Problems can be confirmed in many ways. Sometimes data already exist in the form of student records, district surveys, or state guidelines. In other cases, some type of data collection may be needed, whether formal or informal, quantitative or qualitative. The important point is to be certain that the problem identified is an accurate description of what is actually occurring.

Allow Adequate Time for Problem Identification. All of the strategies for accurately identifying problems require time. Successful problem identification relies on high quality interactions among the interpersonal problem solving participants and opportunities for reflection and analysis. Unfortunately, in many school settings the problem solving context conveys the message that the problem identification step should be completed as quickly as possible so that the more important task of resolving the problem can begin. Such thinking overlooks one key point: Without adequate time, accurate problem identification is unlikely and problem resolution is improbable.

Our recommendation is to begin systematically to increase the amount of time spent identifying problems. In most situations, multiple sessions are preferred for this, especially when additional data need to be gathered. Although this approach may seem awkward and time consuming at first, the long-term benefit is far more efficient problem solving.

Monitor the Problem solving Context. At the beginning of this chapter, we noted the importance of monitoring the problem solving context. This is particularly critical during problem identification. You may not have had enough information initially to determine whether interpersonal problem solving was appropriate; such information may emerge during this problem solving step and cause you to reassess the appropriateness of problem solving. Likewise, you should monitor to ensure that other participants remain committed to solving the problem once its parameters are set.

Generating Potential Solutions

Once you have clearly identified the problem, you are faced with the sometimes daunting task of proposing alternative means for resolving it. The purpose of the second major step of problem solving is to stimulate the creation of the maximum number of potential solutions by the widest range of participants.

Suggestions for Generating Potential Solutions
Studies of both creative processes and critical problem solving have contributed greatly to our knowledge about how to generate potential solutions in interpersonal problem solving. These are some solution-generating techniques designed to encourage divergent thinking:

Brainstorming. The most familiar strategy for generating potential solutions is *brainstorming*. In brainstorming, the participants in the problem solving process call out solutions as they think of them, facilitating their own thinking by listening to the ideas generated by others. The rules typically given for brainstorming during interpersonal problem solving process include these:

  1. Accept all ideas that are offered without evaluating them.

2. Propose ideas freely even if they seem infeasible.
3. Have someone write down the ideas being generated.
4. "Play" with the ideas to generate even more ideas.

In addition, you may find it helpful to set a time limit for generating solutions; this focuses attention on the process, but also acknowledges the time constraints of school-based problem solving.

The following example is an illustration of brainstorming in order to resolve a student problem:

> A special education teacher described a difficult situation she was experiencing at school to colleagues at a district special education meeting. She was responsible for a disruptive student whose behaviors included urinating in hallways, ignoring reasonable teacher requests, and leaving classes and the school grounds without permission. She and her colleagues generated these potential solutions:
>
> 1. Suspend the student.
> 2. Make the student earn his way back into class.
> 3. Refer the family for counseling.
> 4. Never leave the student unattended.
> 5. Hire a paraprofessional for the student.
> 6. Refer the student for psychiatric evaluation.
> 7. Use a group contingency behavior management plan with his classmates.
> 8. Have the student design a reinforcement system.
> 9. Have the student write a contract for appropriate behavior.
> 10. Have the teacher write a contract for appropriate behavior.
> 11. Have the parents write a contract for appropriate behavior at school.
> 12. Have the teacher, parents, and student work together on a contract.
> 13. The teacher should transfer to another school.
> 14. Call the school the student attended last year and discuss how his behaviors were addressed there.
> 15. Have the principal meet with the parents.
> 16. Have the special education director meet with the parents.
> 17. Hire a behavior consultant to work with the teacher, student, and parents.
> 18. Build and use a timeout room with the student.
> 19. Let the teacher hide in the timeout room when the student is being especially disruptive.
> 20. Videotape the student being disruptive and discuss the tape with the student.
> 21. Videotape the student and show the tape to the student's parents.
> 22. Send the videotape to a behavior consultant and ask for recommendations.

This example demonstrates why brainstorming can be such a powerful technique in problem solving. First, notice that playfulness was an integral part of the brainstorming. For example, no one seriously expected this student's teacher to request a transfer to another school, yet surfacing that idea led to the more likely strategy of contacting the previous school staff about the student.

Another brainstorming concept illustrated in this example is *chaining*, that is, linking a series of ideas through a concept or other stimulus. Items 9, 10, 11, and 12 form a chain about using contracts for appropriate behavior. Items 20, 21, and 22 comprise a chain about using videotape to document the student's behavior. In fact, the value of chaining in generating potential solutions is a primary reason why all ideas are accepted without evaluation: Each time you stop brainstorming to evaluate an idea, you decrease the likelihood that any participant will chain with the idea just presented.

Brainstorming is the preferred strategy for generating potential solutions in many problem solving situations. You will probably find it helpful when you and the other participants know each other reasonably well and have comparable knowledge about the problem context. It is especially productive when the size of the problem solving group is relatively small, and it is often used when the problem is not particularly emotion-laden.

Brainwriting. Another strategy for generating potential solutions is *brainwriting*. In brainwriting, participants individually write three or four potential solutions. They then place their list in a pile on the table from which they select someone else's list. The ideas on that list are the stimuli for them to generate additional solutions. This exchanging of ideas continues until no new ideas are occurring. The complete set of ideas is then presented to the group. Figure 4.2 is an example of how brainwriting sheets might look.

Brainwriting is a productive option when discussion of ideas may not be. For example, if you are problem solving about an emotionally charged issue, more ideas may be generated through this written process than through one involving verbal exchange. The same principle holds for topics that might be considered sensitive. Another reason for choosing brainwriting is simply to change the procedure for generating alternative solutions to encourage a fresh perspective.

Nominal Group Technique. A third strategy you may use to generate potential solutions combines aspects of brainstorming and brainwriting. In nominal group technique (NGT) (Delbecq, Van de Ven, & Gustafson, 1975) participants generate and individually record as many potential solutions as they can. These are written down. Then the ideas are shared by having one person state one idea; this is written so that all can see it. Then the next individual shares one idea. This process of persons sharing single ideas from their lists continues until all alternatives are presented. Individuals may "pass" at any time they are asked to share an idea, and they do not have a new option to offer. The total list of ideas is then discussed by participants to identify the most important potential solutions. Each participant writes each of these on a separate card (as many as 10 ideas), and then rates each on a scale from very important (a ranking of 5) to unimportant (a ranking of 1). The facilitator gathers these cards and records all participants' votes for the ideas. If a clear pattern of preference for particular ideas emerges the procedure is complete; if not, additional discussion is held and a second vote is taken.

NGT is valuable when many people need to participate in generating potential solutions and some means is needed to ensure their equal opportunity for participation. This might occur when participants traditionally have had unequal status or when some individuals tend to dominate the group.

Whether you choose to use brainstorming, brainwriting, nominal group technique, or other approaches for generating potential solutions, you should adhere to the rules outlined as part of brainstorming. Sometimes it is tempting to stop to evaluate each idea as it is expressed. But this derails the entire purpose of generating potential solutions; we have seen many problem solving sessions in which participants never return to this

Problem: What steps could we take to involve parents more in school instructional activities?

1. Set up a school parent volunteer program.

---

1. Ask our parent organization for suggestions.
2. Involve grandparents as well as parents.
3. Contact the senior citzens center to check on their interest and availability.
4. Make a list of all types of ways parents *could* get more involved.

---

1. Have current volunteers recruit others.
2. Pay parents to work in school.
3. Ask for help before and after school.

Problem: What steps could we take to involve parents more in school instructional activities?

1. Ask parents how they'd like to be involved.
2. Have parents help before and after school.
3. Open school on Saturday.

---

1. Ask students how they'd like their parents involved.
2. Ask staff at other schools how they involve parents.
3. Ask a state-level consultant to help us create parent involvement.

---

1. Get the state's materials on parent involvement programs.

Figure 4.2.   Sample Brainwriting Sheets

critical problem solving step once the they began prematurely discussing an idea that had been offered.

Evaluating Potential Solutions

The list of potential solutions you generate serves as the raw material for making the specific decision about which solution to implement. In order to make an informed decision, each of the potential solutions should be evaluated. This involves two problem solving steps: judging the positives and negatives of each potential solution and outlining the tasks required to implement each.

Delineating the Positives and Negatives of Each Potential Solution

In this evaluative step, your task is to examine each potential solution from a balanced perspective. This entails listing the positive and negative aspects of each intervention or strategy. For example, in the brainstormed list of options for the disruptive student, the first idea was to suspend the student. Positive aspects of that solution might include these:

1. Removing the student from school would alleviate stress on the teacher and other students.

2. The student's parents would probably become more actively involved in the problem situation.
3. The student would receive a clear message about the inappropriateness of his behavior.
4. The suspension would enable the entire situation to stabilize, and perhaps it could then be examined with a fresh perspective.

Negative aspects of the intervention might include these:

1. Because the student has a disability, the procedure is complex and of limited duration.
2. Suspension is unlikely to solve the student's problem.
3. The student would be losing instructional time.
4. Because the parents both work, the student might be left at home alone for lengthy periods of time.
5. The student may find suspension reinforcing.

On the basis of these positive and negative aspects of suspension, would you retain it as a potential solution? If your response is "no," then you would eliminate it from the list. If your response is "yes," then you would leave it on your list of options for further discussion later.

This step of weighing the advantages and drawbacks should be completed for all the items on the list of potential solutions, although for some the task will be brief. For example, another idea for addressing the student's behavior was for the teacher to hide in the timeout room. This was a preposterous idea that emerged from the playful part of brainstorming and then led to the generation of other possible solutions. This type of potential solution obviously should be quickly discarded.

Outlining Tasks for the Potential Solutions
By eliminating some of the potential solutions on the basis of their positive and negative aspects, you shorten considerably the list of potential interventions or strategies. But you probably still have several options, all of which seem possible. The second evaluation step, outlining the tasks that would be required to implement each of the remaining potential solutions, is the means through which these possibilities are further analyzed and narrowed.

Consider another idea from the brainstormed list. One of the potential solutions is to have the teacher, parents, and student work together on a contract for behavior. What are the tasks that would have to be completed for this option to be implemented? You and your colleagues would have to gain approval from all the persons to be involved before any action could be taken. Once that was accomplished, you would need to clarify the behavior to be addressed in the contract. You might decide that separate discussions should be held with the parents and student prior to the group meeting. A convenient time would have to be found so that the group session could be scheduled. What other tasks would be required?

After considering the tasks associated with developing a contract with teacher, parent, and student input, you should decide whether the contract still seems like a feasible option. If not, you would discard the idea. If it does, you would retain it as a likely solution, and you might select it for implementation.

Selecting the Solution

Following all of the steps described thus far should have led you to a list of several clearly articulated, carefully outlined potential solutions, all appropriate for resolving the problem. Now the task is to select one of these.

This selection can be based on several factors. One consideration may be intrusiveness. If an intervention or strategy will disrupt classroom routine or require changes in staff assignments, it may become the second choice after one that fits into existing routines and staff responsibilities.

Feasibility is another factor that influences selection of solutions. A simple solution that requires no new resources typically is preferable to one that involves separate budget lines. Similarly, a solution that necessitates coordinating multiple activities and people may be less feasible in a busy school setting than one that minimizes the number of implementors.

A third—and admittedly not very systematic—means for selecting among the potential solutions is individual preference. Although all the solutions may be feasible and none particularly intrusive, the people who have the most responsibility for implementing them may simply be more comfortable with one over the others. This consideration should not be ignored; the likelihood of a successful outcome is dependent to some extent on the commitment and attitude of those directly involved in implementation.

As you and your colleagues select a solution, try to identify the basis on which this decision will be made. There are no "correct" criteria for making this judgment, but the criteria used should be clear to all participants.

Implementing the Solution

Now you have selected the solution to be implemented. Because you have done a great deal of planning throughout the problem solving process, many details of implementation plans have already been identified. However, one more planning phase is required before actual implementation of the intervention or strategy is begun.

Finalizing Implementation Plans
In preparation for implementation, your responsibility is to review with other participants the plans that were made during the evaluation step of problem solving. Finalizing these plans typically includes (1) reviewing and refining detailed plans for implementing the solutions, (2) determining the criteria by which success will be determined, and (3) scheduling a time to evaluate the outcome(s) of the applied solution.

Detailed Arrangements. The selected solution is more likely to be successful if you and your colleagues specify all necessary arrangements and assign all responsibilities. Some special service professionals find listing responsibilities helpful in accomplishing this. In the sample chart in Figure 4.3, the first column includes the task to be done, the second

Problem: _____ Date: _____

Solution to be attempted _____ Evaluation Date: _____

Result(s) _____

Action/Task	Person(s) Responsible	Target Completion Date	Outcomes	Comments

Figure 4.3. Problem-solving Responsibility Chart

has the person responsible, the third includes the target completion date, the fourth addresses the outcomes expected, and the final column contains space for writing comments.

Criteria for success. Yet another issue to clarify in the final planning for implementation is the selection of specific variables and criteria that will be used to determine whether the intervention or strategy has been successful. This is consonant with the definition of the desired situation discussed as part of problem identification. In interventions related to students, this could include specific levels of achievement on designated assessment instruments or a quantifiable improvement in attendance. In strategies that address staff problems, this may require the development of a needs assessment questionnaire or survey and clarification of what outcomes will signal success. The form presented in Figure 4.3 includes space for specifying criteria.

Scheduled time for evaluation of outcomes. A final topic to address prior to implementation is a specific time for assessing the success of the solution (or the outcomes). Inattention to this issue is a mistake we repeatedly observe in interpersonal problem solving in schools. Well-intentioned interventions or strategies are abandoned because of failure to assess systematically whether they are having the desired impact.

Carrying Out the Solution

When you have completed all of these steps, you are ready to implement the intervention or strategy. Quite simply, you *do* whatever it is you have planned—whether it is a student intervention concerning academic or social behavior, a staff development plan, a team teaching unit, or an adaptation to the curriculum. The "what" of implementation is as varied as the problem situations you encounter. During implementation you rely on the commitment and expertise of those in your problem solving setting.

Evaluating the Outcome

The evaluation time scheduled during final planning functions as "no-fault insurance" for interpersonal problem solving. During this step of the process, you should determine whether the established goal has been reached. You also determine whether those involved in the problem solving process are satisfied with the impact of the intervention or strategy.

Depending on what you learn during this problem solving step, you will plan different courses of action. If the intervention or strategy is meeting with success, it becomes an opportunity for congratulating each other on that success. In this case, the decision to be made is whether to continue the intervention or strategy for another defined period of time, or if the problem has been resolved, to terminate it. A piece of adaptive equipment created for a specific situation is an example of a "solution" that might be continued over a long period of time; a student reward system is one that you might choose to phase out.

If the implemented solution is only partially successful, your decisions focus on extending or adapting it. You and the other problem solving participants would analyze if elements of the solution are unsatisfactory and need to be modified or if the current intervention needs to be continued for another period of time. In either of these situations, another date for feedback would be scheduled so that you can continue to monitor progress.

An unsuccessful outcome is a third possibility in interpersonal problem solving. And although this is much less likely if the steps in the process have been systematically followed, we recognize that you may need a set of strategies for addressing this frustrating situation.

The first action you and your colleagues may take when faced with an unsuccessful outcome is to analyze the reasons for the lack of success. You might examine the intervention or strategy itself to ascertain whether it was flawed and consider whether the solution was implemented with integrity. You might also reexamine the problem solving context; perhaps you lacked certain information that was important for the success of the solution, or perhaps new information emerged during the problem solving process that is affecting implementation.

Additional possibilities might also account for the lack of success. In fact, your analysis should include a re-examination of each phase of the problem solving process in a search for information that would explain what prevented the intervention or strategy from being successful. A list of questions to guide your analysis and the sequence you should follow for doing this is included in the diagram of the problem-solving process in Figure 4.1, beginning with a negative response to the question, "Was the solution successful?"

Once you and your colleagues have identified the source of the problem, the next task is to return to the point of the interpersonal problem solving process at which the difficulty occurred and complete the steps again, correcting it. This may be as simple as selecting another solution that was previously proposed and evaluated, or it may be as complex as returning to the very beginning of the problem solving process to reanalyze the problem solving context and the presenting problem.

SUMMARY

Interpersonal problem solving is the central process used in collaborative activities, whether you are addressing well-defined, partially defined, or ill-defined problems. Prior to undertaking interpersonal problem solving, you should assess the problem solving context. If interpersonal problem solving seems to be appropriate, then these steps are followed: Identify the problem; generate potential solutions; evaluate the potential solutions by outlining the pros and cons of each and then specifying the tasks that would have to be completed to accomplish each; select a solution from those preferred; finalize implementation plans; implement the solution; and evaluate the outcome of the intervention or strategy. On the basis of the outcome, you may decide to continue with the implementation, make adaptations, or if the outcome is unsuccessful, assess at which point the process may have broken down and return to that step in the interpersonal problem solving process.

ACTIVITIES AND ASSIGNMENTS

1. How do individual and interpersonal problem solving differ?

2. Identify three professional problems you currently are addressing for which interpersonal problem solving might be appropriate. What types of problems are they? Use the questions for analyzing the problem solving context with these problems. How likely are your problems to be resolved? What should you do if they cannot easily be resolved?

3. Why is it important to examine underlying assumptions during problem identification?

4. Use the professional problems you identified in Activity 2 to practice techniques for generating potential solutions. Write one problem statement so that your group or class can all read it. Then select and use one of the recommended techniques to generate potential solutions. Repeat this procedure using different problem statements and different techniques.

5. Identify a problem you are addressing in your school. After generating a list of potential solutions, complete the evaluation steps. First, make a list of positive and negative aspects of each and eliminate those in which the negatives outweigh the positives. Then list the tasks that would have to be completed to implement each of the remaining options.

6. Audiotape yourself engaged in problem solving with a colleague. As you review your tape, analyze how you ensure that you are proceeding from one step to the next. Have a classmate review your tape for the same purpose. Compare your analyses.

7. Set up a class role play in which problem solving is to occur in a team context. Have observers listen for indications of whether each problem solving step has been completed. In a class discussion, analyze the strengths and weaknesses of the interaction.

8. Compare interpersonal problem solving as described in this chapter to the problem solving in your work setting. What steps of the process do you already use? In what steps of problem solving would you like to refine your skills?

RELATED READINGS

Bergan, J. R. (1977). *Behavioral consultation.* Columbus, OH: Charles E. Merrill.

Bergan, J. R., & Neumann, A. J. (1980). The identification of resources and constraints influencing plan design in consultation. *Journal of School Psychology, 18,* 317–323.

Frederiksen, N. (1984). Implications of cognitive theory for instruction in problem solving. *Review of Educational Research, 54,* 363–407.

Heppner, P. P., & Krauskopf, C. J. (1987). An information-processing approach to personal problem solving. *Counseling Psychologist, 15,* 371–447.

Pugach, M. C., & Johnson, L. J. (1988). Rethinking the relationship between consultation and collaborative problem solving. *Focus on Exceptional Children, 21* (4), 1–8.

Schein, E. E. (1969). *Process consultation: Its role in organization development.* Reading, MA: Addison-Wesley.

VanGundy, A. B. (1988). *Techniques of structured problem solving* (2nd ed.). New York: Van Nostrand Reinhold.

CHAPTER 5

Interpersonal Communication

Keeping Perspective

Chapter 5 provides the framework for the skills presented in Chapters 6 and 7. It overviews how interpersonal communication occurs, describes the impact of nonverbal communication on interactions, and outlines essential features of verbal communication.

Learner Objectives

1. To identify the attributes and concepts of interpersonal communication.
2. To distinguish the characteristics of a transactional model of communication.
3. To identify and give examples of four classes of nonverbal cues and describe how they affect communication.
4. To rephrase vague statements and questions using more concrete language.
5. To identify judgmental and evaluative statements and questions and restate them in a more neutral way.

Effective communication is essential to many aspects of your success as a school professional. The term *communication* is used to refer to many different behaviors and processes, and various dimensions of communication are the focus of current research and policy efforts in many human services disciplines, including education. The increasing attention to communication skills in the research on effective instruction, effective treatment, and productive organizations is evidence of its growing importance. This is further underscored by its inclusion in performance assessments for teachers and other professionals. For instance, many professional preparation programs and annual professional performance reviews include an assessment of communication skills. Increasingly, certification and licensure in education and allied professions require similar evidence of communication skill. Just as communication skills are critical in the performance of your instructional, administrative, assessment, or other intervention responsibilities, so are they essential to your effective collaboration with colleagues and parents.

MODELS OF COMMUNICATION

Human communication has been conceptualized in many diverse ways. However because no single communication model is universally accepted, we will consider some conceptual elements that are common to most and clarify the interactional model that undergirds this text.

Common Attributes of Communication Models

In the most general sense, human communication can be thought of as the means by which information is transmitted from one person to another. This description includes three elements. Communication is a *process* of exchanging information between the *sender* and *receiver*. A fourth element, *communication channel*, may be added to refer to the medium through which information is transmitted. Because most messages in human communication are either seen or heard, the most frequently used channels are visual and auditory. The messages are classified as verbal or nonverbal. Verbal messages are comprised of printed or spoken words; nonverbal messages are conveyed by behaviors other than words (e.g., facial expressions, vocal noise, and gestures). Finally, communication includes a *message*, that is, the information that is being relayed during an interaction.

Two other concepts are frequently identified as key to any model of human communication. The concept of *continuous feedback* (Molyneaux & Lane, 1982) specifies that while sending or emitting a message, the sender is simultaneously receiving information related to that message or the environment. For example, when you speak you can hear yourself and judge if you are saying what you intended. If you judge that you have been inarticulate, you may elaborate or restate your message to clarify it. Simultaneously, you are obtaining information from the receiver of your message that lets you know how your message is being received. A confused look, a frown, or a question may cause you to restate your message, whereas a smile, nod, or interested look may encourage you to continue speaking or to go on to a new topic.

The second concept is that messages are *multichannel*. At any given point during interpersonal communication, several messages probably are being transmitted simultaneously over different channels. Sending a single message over multiple channels can strengthen or emphasize the message. You do this when you smile and nod while giving someone a compliment. Alternatively, simultaneously sending discrepant messages through different channels complicates the communication. You do this when you smile while expressing disagreement with another's opinion.

Communication Types

Many dimensions of communication can be used to distinguish and categorize types of communication and generate communication models. For example, the oral communication skills of listening and speaking are often distinguished from the written communication skills of reading and writing. Other dimensions of communication include verbal or nonverbal as discussed previously, receptive or expressive, and formal or informal. An interesting categorization system presented by Schmuck and Runkel (1985) is especially valuable in understanding the various types of communication that you as a special service provider are most accustomed to using. This system classifies communication as *unilateral, directive,* and *transactional.*

Unilateral is one-way communication in which a speaker provides information to a listener. No face-to-face interaction occurs; the listener has no opportunity to query the speaker nor can the speaker clarify or revise the original message. Examples of unilateral communication in your professional activities may include educational film or television, written memos, and audiotaped lecture or training materials.

The *directive* type of communication characterizes much of what occurs between professionals and students in schools. Directive communication is face to face and occurs when the speaker (in schools, usually the adult) sends a message to a listener (generally the student) who indicates receipt and comprehension of the message. This is a frequent mode of communication as school professionals direct, explain, or lecture, and students listen, understand, and comply. This type of communication is complete when the students let the adult know (or when the adult concludes) that the information has been received and understood. Because most adult–student interactions in schools consist largely of directive communication, instructional and special service personnel are likely to be quite accomplished at this type of communication and provide clear, meaningful lectures, explanations, and directions. Other professional situations in which you may experience directional communication are large staff meetings and professional development activities conducted in lecture format.

Despite the prevalence of directive communication in schools, it is in many ways incompatible with the effective interpersonal communication needed for collaborative interactions among adults. Directive communication does not provide for mutual influence or exchange and is sometimes thought to be coercive. The influence is primarily one way with the sender giving information to the receiver who is expected to comprehend and accept it. The characteristics of collaboration would be difficult to establish if one or more participants relied primarily on directive communication. For example, parity cannot be achieved in one-way communication. Why would each of the other characteristics of collaboration be difficult to establish with directive communication?

Alternatively, *transactional* communication is a two-way, reciprocal interaction in which each participant both sends and receives messages while alternately assuming the role of speaker or listener. In this process, participants exchange information: The receiver tries to discern the sender's view and help the sender know whether the intended meaning was communicated. The receiver does this by informing the sender of the perceived message and of his or her personal reactions to it. The sender may then modify, restate, or reinforce the original message in order to clarify the communication. Participants in this complex, reciprocal process are both senders and receivers who mutually influence each other to create the shared meanings that emerge from transactional communication. Contemporary models of interpersonal communication stress that participants both send and receive information throughout their interactions, and in these models each participant may be labeled a *sender-receiver* to emphasize the duality of roles.

Interpersonal communication, the primary concern in this chapter, is an example of a transactional approach. By adding this concept to those already presented we can now offer a more elaborate definition of communication:

> *Interpersonal communication is a complex, reciprocal process through which participants create shared meanings as messages are transmitted continuously from one sender-receiver to another via multiple communication channels.*

This concept of transactional communication grounds our thinking about effective interpersonal communication. Its attributes include those discussed earlier (e.g., process, channel, and message) as well as extensions of them (e.g., reciprocity, sender-receiver, multichannel, and continuous feedback).

COMMUNICATION SKILLS

Despite our understanding and acknowledgement of the multiple, simultaneous, and complex dimensions of interpersonal communication processes, our experiences in learning, studying, and teaching others to use communication skills has convinced us of the necessity of identifying discrete categories of skills and examining them separately. Precisely because of interpersonal communication's complexity, effective skill acquisition requires the isolation and practice of distinct skills. After you acquire discrete behaviors you can practice using them in ways suggested in this text. As you gain comfort with them you will begin to integrate and use them together with other skills to facilitate interaction process skills.

Communication skills and strategies can be classified in many different ways. Some systems categorize skills according to the stage in a relationship or interaction when they are most useful or common (e.g., Okun, 1982). Others categorize them in terms of their role in the interview context (e.g., expressing, responding, and listening) (McKay, Davis, & Fanning, 1983). We categorize communication strategies differently depending on our purposes. We often distinguish *basic communication skills* (e.g., paraphrasing) from more complex multistep *interaction process skills* (e.g., problem solving), particularly when we structure ongoing communication training programs (Friend & Cook, 1988). Alternatively, we sometimes classify communication skills by their intended use in an interaction. In doing so, we surmise the primary intent of the person using them and try to determine whether a particular strategy was intended to provide, gather, or clarify information (Cook & Friend, 1990b). This approach is particularly useful for short-term, focused training activities.

In this text, we treat verbal and nonverbal communication separately and organize our discussion of selected verbal strategies around the use of statements (Chapter 6) and the use of questions (Chapter 7). We use the remainder of this chapter to provide an overview of nonverbal communication factors and then consider principles common to all verbal communication.

Nonverbal Communication

Much valuable information is communicated without words. Skillful use of nonverbal behaviors is considered an essential element in communicating attitudes necessary for establishing and maintaining positive relationships (e.g., interest, acceptance, warmth) and a powerful tool in clarifying, emphasizing, or obfuscating the meaning of verbal messages.

Everyone is aware that "body language" and voice can influence communication, but the impact of nonverbal behaviors is greater than you may have suspected. In fact, the words used in your communication may convey far less information than the nonverbal components do. Mehrabian and Ferris (1967) found that the full impact of an individual's spoken message may be broken down as follows: 7% verbal components, 38% vocal (volume, pitch, rhythm) components, and 55% facial expression.

The study of nonverbal communication is fascinating and has been the subject of extensive investigations. Here we can only point out the significance of nonverbal communication, examine some of the most salient nonverbal cues, and identify some principles that may guide you in using effective nonverbal communication. Hopefully we will whet your appetite for this interesting topic and stimulate you to examine the related readings at the end of the chapter.

Nonverbal Cues

People communicate nonverbally in several ways. Four primary classes of nonverbal cues are (1) body movements such as facial expression, eye contact, posture, and gestures, (2) vocal cues such as quality of voice and the pacing or flow of speech, and (3) spatial relations that include the physical distance between the participants. Minimal encouragers are a fourth class of nonverbal cues that includes both verbal and nonverbal components. Each of these categories of nonverbal cues affects the nature of the communication among people.

Body Movements. The notion that "one picture is worth a thousand words" is based on a recognition of the full impact of nonverbal communication. Without even using words you can communicate a wide range of attitudes and feelings through gestures and facial expression. Consider how gestures and movements add to or change the meaning of the verbal communication in these examples:

> "I'm really interested in what's going on with Sally and William," the counselor said as she set her papers aside and sat down in the chair facing the teacher. She looked at the

teacher and, leaning forward slightly in her chair, she said, "Do you think you have any insights that would help me understand their situation?" Without pause, she said, "Please let me know what you think about their progress." She then sat quietly looking at the teacher, waiting for a response.

"I'm really interested in what's going on with Sally and William," the counselor said as she entered the doorway of the room. She glanced at the teacher then looked back at the papers she was carrying as she said, "Do you think you have any insights that would help me understand their situation?" Then, without pause, she glanced first at her watch, then at the teacher and as she stepped out the door she said over her shoulder, "Please let me know what you think about their progress." She then walked down the hall.

What was the impact of the counselor's body movements? What did they communicate to you? Her body movements in the first example probably suggested that she was interested in the other person's information and ideas. In the second example, her nonverbal message probably contradicted her verbal message. What was the impact of her discrepant verbal and nonverbal communication?

In these examples, only a few movements and gestures were described. In the actual situation one would observe many more movements and gestures that contribute to the message. Eye contact, facial expression, and gestures such as reaching out or touching someone's shoulder also affect the meaning communicated.

Vocal Cues. Paralanguage, the vocal—rather than verbal—component of language, also communicates a great deal of information separate from the verbal content of the message. Paralanguage includes voice tone, pitch and volume, speech rhythm and pacing or tempo, as well as the use and timing of silence.

Many or all of the elements of paralanguage may reach extremes when the speaker is experiencing intense emotions. For example, pitch results from the tightness of one's vocal cords. When you are calm, depressed, or tired your vocal cords are relaxed and your pitch is lower, whereas excitement or anxiety tends to cause your pitch to be higher. The pace of speech also may indicate emotion; rapid speech can signal excitement and enthusiasm or nervousness and insecurity. Thus, you may observe that someone anxious or uncertain about a situation may speak very rapidly at a high pitch while someone more confident and relaxed is likely to speak slowly at a lower pitch. Two additional vocal behaviors—interruptions and the use of silence—also have significant impact on communication; they are discussed more fully at the end of this section.

Spatial Relations. Spatial relations refers to how space is used; it includes the physical distance you keep between yourself and others in an interaction. When considering this nonverbal cue, you may find it helpful to review Hall's (1959, 1966) description of four spatial zones that people seem to use in their interactions with others: (1) intimate distance, (2) personal distance, (3) social distance, and (4) public distance. These zones can be schematically represented by four concentric circles of personally defined space around each person. The smallest circle represents the intimate distance and the largest, outermost circle represents the public distance. Typically, the greater the distance between people in an interaction the less their intimacy. During interactions among colleagues who do not know each other well, the amount of space between them should be great enough to avoid inappropriate intimacy.

Another way of making judgments about appropriate personal space during interactions is the topic of conversation. Generally, when two colleagues discuss a problem that is very upsetting to one of them, the listener should be near enough to the speaker to indicate concern but not so close as to seem threatening or intrusive.

Minimal Encouragers. A category of communication skill that involves both nonverbal and verbal messages is called *minimal encouragers.* This category includes words, phrases, silence, and other nonverbal cues designed to indicate that you are listening and understand what someone is expressing and to encourage the person to continue communicating. These are common minimal encouragers:

Silence
Head nod
"Uh-huh..."
"Hmmmm..."
Quizzical facial expression
"And..."
"So..."
"Yes..."
"Okay...
Hand gesture indicating to keep talking

You use minimal encouragers to ensure that you invite the person with whom you are interacting to continue to share with you all the information perceived as relevant. For example, as you become comfortable with a few seconds of silence, you may also find that it allows others time to gather their thoughts and then share them with you. Similarly, if you nod or use one of the other encouragers, you are also allowing yourself time to phrase your next question or statement.

Clarifying Concepts of Nonverbal Communication

We hope that the examples we have used to illustrate nonverbal communication demonstrate that its impact is highly subjective. We noted that rapid speech may indicate enthusiasm or anxiety, but these are two distinctly different feelings. The physical distance between two individuals should be "near enough to..." but "not so close as to..."; what is appropriate for any particular interaction may be inappropriate for another. No specific prescriptions exist for "correct" body language to use in your interactions. Instead, two critical concepts, *congruence* and *individualism* may help you understand the meaning of your own nonverbal communication and that of others.

Congruence. Communication is not simply a series of verbal or nonverbal behaviors. It is composed of clusters of both verbal and nonverbal behaviors or cues. While an individual is talking, he or she is simultaneously communicating something with his or her eyes, gestures, movements, facial expression, posture, and paralanguage cues and words. As Carl Rogers (1951) noted, believable behavior generally occurs in congruent clusters, that is, several behaviors occur simultaneously that have the same or highly similar meanings. Rogers attributed the characteristic of genuineness to congruence. Incongruence may unintentionally reveal feelings or attitudes one is hoping to conceal (e.g., the principal who chuckles while telling a staff member, "This is serious!") This is illustrated in the following case description.

> The community liaison talked quietly with several parents while others freshened their coffee. When everyone returned to the seating area, he smiled and said, "If we're ready to continue I'd like to describe the role of the community liaison office." He paused and, smiling slightly, looked around the room as people took their seats in the semicircle of chairs. "We are here to talk things over with you. Whenever you have questions or want more information about your child's program we will be here to discuss your concerns and try to answer your questions." He paused, smiled slightly, and looked slowly around the room again. When he made eye contact with a group member, he maintained it long enough to give the member the opportunity to raise a question or offer a comment. "As parents we all have concerns," he continued, as he moved a nearby chair into the semicircle between Diane Long and Bob Clark and sat down. Putting his hand on the arm of Diane's chair and looking at her, he interrupted himself, "Diane, do you remember when my son started talking about getting a job and going to work and I ran checks on the business through the employee relations department at your office?" Smiling warmly and laughing, Diane said, "I surely do! That was one long week in our neighborhood." The community liaison laughed while still looking at Diane, then he leaned forward in his chair, put his elbows on his knees and let his clasped hands fall between them. He glanced down for a silent second. Then, looking up, he said slowly, "Yes, as parents we all have concerns about the decisions our children make and the challenges they must face. We know that we have to let go if we want our kids to have opportunities for independent and productive adult living. But it's hard—especially because we know their special needs." Quickening his pace slightly, he looked directly at each group member and said decidedly, "That's where the community liaison office comes in! We have information about community opportunities, hazards, and supports; and we know your sons and daughters. Maybe most importantly," he continued while sitting up and smiling broadly, "We want to understand what you're experiencing. We've been there!"

The speaker in this example used nonverbal cues to strengthen his verbal message. His body movements or gestures (e.g., eye contact, touching Diane's chair, and smiling) and his vocal cues (e.g., speaking softly or decidedly, laughing, and changing verbal pace) were congruent with his verbal message. Together, his verbal and nonverbal strategies communicated sincere understanding and genuine interest in discussing parents' concerns.

The speaker's use of space was also congruent with his verbal message. By physically joining the group and sitting among group members, he strengthened his verbal message that he was one of them. By leaning into the group while sharing his own feelings, he suggested that the group is a safe place to express intimate and personal feelings. This excerpt does not illustrate the use of minimal encouragers as it focused only on one speaker. Minimal encouragers are used most frequently to encourage someone to *continue* speaking.

Individualism. The concept of individualism emphasizes the subjectivity involved in interpreting nonverbal communication. The meaning of a single nonverbal cue depends not only on the context in which it occurs but also on its specific meaning to the individual demonstrating the behavior and to the person observing it. For example, you may strive to maintain constant eye contact with a colleague to demonstrate your interest and attention. Your colleague, on the other hand, may feel uncomfortable and find your "interested" eye contact to be a penetrating stare that creates a feeling of being exposed or scrutinized too intensely. Similarly, you may observe a colleague sitting with his arms crossed and worry that he is not "open" to your ideas. In fact, he may be cold or alternatively searching for a comfortable position while seated in an armless chair!

In order to develop effective nonverbal communication skills you should examine your own nonverbal behaviors to identify your typical patterns or styles that affect communication positively or negatively and learn to anticipate and identify individual differences in how others react to your nonverbal behaviors. Activities at the end of the chapter should assist in developing this understanding.

Principles of Verbal Communication

In discussing the mutual influence that characterizes interpersonal communication, we stressed that the verbal and nonverbal messages you send greatly affect the types of responses you receive. In Chapters 6 and 7, we consider two primary verbal strategies—statements and questions—and examine how their use affects interpersonal communication. For the remainder of this chapter we focus on two aspects of verbal communication, whether in statement or question form, that have significant impact on interaction—concreteness and neutrality. We then conclude with suggestions for enhancing the effectiveness of verbal communication.

Concreteness
You are more likely to understand verbal interactions if they involve the exchange of concrete, specific information. Such verbal expressions communicate more clearly than the vague or general phrases and expressions commonly heard in personal as well as professional conversations. Imprecise language is difficult to understand and is the cause of much miscommunication. Vague language may so obscure the message that it may not be possible to determine the dimension of information being addressed (refer to Chapter 3 to review dimensions of information needs). For example, words like "handled," "dealt with," "responded," and "concern" could refer to any number of different dimensions.

Level of concreteness is a characteristic of verbal communication that applies across both statements and questions and across all dimensions of information contained in message content. This is illustrated in the following examples and alternatives:

Statement: I was concerned about her reaction.

Response A: I felt somewhat angry and very rejected when she asked to have her son transferred to another class.

Response B: I thought that she might turn her anger on her son when she got home.

The initial statement is very vague. Although its locus addresses both self (I) and other (her), the detail is unclear and it is not evident if the domain (concerned about her reaction) is covert or overt. In Response A, the addition of more specific words makes the message more concrete and clarifies the dimension being addressed. "I felt somewhat angry and very rejected" clearly addresses the covert domain (affect: angry, rejected) and provides more detail (quantifying the intensity of feeling: somewhat, very). This statement also provides detail about the situation (she asked to have her son transferred).

Response B is also offered as an illustration of using more specific words to make the same initially vague statement more concrete. In this example, the information falls again into the covert domain (opinion: "I thought" and affect: "her anger"). The detail provided is situational (what might happen to whom), and temporal (when she got home). In this example, no quantifying detail is given. Although Response B is more concrete than the initial statement, one obvious example of vague language remains. What is meant by "turn her anger"? Did the speaker think the mother would be physically violent, verbally abusive, or silent and rejecting? Any of these labels would offer more concrete information than the phrase used, but none would be as concrete as a description of specific behaviors, such as, "I thought she might spank him and make him quit the team when she got home."

You have probably recognized that concreteness exists on a continuum. As you practice and develop proficiency in clear communication you will learn to judge situationally the amount of concreteness needed for successful interactions. The same principles and information dimensions affect the concreteness of questions as well as statements:

Question A: What approaches might help his adjustment?

Question B: What strategies have been shown to be effective in increasing social interaction in recreational programs?

What information dimensions were made more specific in the alternative question? Perhaps you can generate another question that would improve further the initially vague question. Practice in using words with greater specificity will assist you to communicate clearly and effectively. Additional activities at the end of the chapter provide more rehearsal of this skill.

Neutrality

Neutrality promotes the development of interpersonal trust because it conveys a nonjudgmental and accepting attitude. Although you will often be required to judge situations and evaluate ideas as you work collaboratively, you will want to avoid judging the people with whom you work. Successful collaborators are people who communicate that they are nonjudgmental and nonevaluative about others.

Consider the following alternatives:

Example: I've noticed that you walk around the room while giving directions.

Rather than: You pace around the room too much.

Or: You shouldn't walk around the room so much.

Example: I'm not sure I understand the selection of that activity. What was your rationale behind that choice?

Rather than: Why would you have selected that activity? I know you didn't think it would be effective with these students, did you?

Each example demonstrates how information can be communicated with or without neutrality. Notice too, that positive evaluations and judgments can have undesirable effects on relationships similar to those with negative evaluations. If a colleague generally praises you and expresses positive evaluations of you as a person when discussing a shared project, you may come to expect it and feel criticized when these evaluations are not offered. Evaluations of people can be avoided by focusing your comments on the activity rather than the person. Using concrete, specific language also helps to clarify the focus.

Example: Your calm, quiet speech helped me to slow down and think about what I was saying.

Rather than: You're wonderful! Your voice is enough to help me think things through.

SUGGESTIONS FOR EFFECTIVE COMMUNICATION

In addition to the communication principles given throughout this chapter, we offer several suggestions you may find helpful as you attempt to refine your own verbal and nonverbal communication skills.

Become a Student of Communication

Because communication is the smallest unit of concern in interactions and the most basic set of skills needed in collaborative activities, you will want to learn more and become more skillful with communication skills as you initiate collaborative interactions.

A note of caution is warranted, however. Like most people, you may conclude that you have a high degree of communication skill since you use it regularly in your professional and personal life. As you read about the skills in this chapter and in Chapters 6 and 7, you may believe you have "had that course" or acquired the skills elsewhere. Keep these two points in mind: First, understanding or being aware of communication skills alone will not improve your communication. Only through continuing practice will you improve your skills. Our students repeatedly share with us that focusing on and rehearsing skills is somewhat humbling: Implementing the skills is much more difficult than recognizing them! We concur. Second, regardless of your knowledge or proficiency level after much practice, you will never fully master communication since each new person, interaction, and situation will require you to practice and refine your skills further. We are reminded of this lesson repeatedly as we teach and learn from others.

Nurture and Communicate Openness

Perhaps the most pronounced theme that runs through our work on collaboration, and specifically this text, is the absolutely essential requirement for openness. By *openness*, we refer to your ability to suspend or eliminate judgment and evaluation of information and situations until you have explored adequately the various potential meanings and explanations. For example, when we discussed emergent characteristics of collaboration in Chapter 1, we noted that in order to collaborate, individuals should value joint decision making or at least be willing to experiment with it. This importance of an attitude of openness became even more explicit in Chapter 3, where we discussed the need to be aware of your frame of reference and those of others to minimize misunderstandings in communication and remove blocks to listening. In Chapter 4, we illustrated the importance of fully exploring problems before formulating hasty and inaccurate problem statements. Openness, in the context of verbal communication, refers to suspending or delaying judgment until you have adequate information. It is similar to acceptance mentioned above, but the focus in that discussion was on eliminating judgments about people rather than deferring judgments about situations. In this context we are encouraging you to set aside your biases and explore various aspects of a situation before deciphering the message.

Keep Communication Meaningful

Although it may be entertaining to watch contestants on the T.V. game show *Jeopardy* struggle to create questions for answers they are given, this is not at all the case in interpersonal communication. In fact, nothing may be less meaningful than receiving information you have not sought or answers for which you do not have questions. Specifically, unrequested suggestions and advice, although frequently shared, often have little meaning and may have unintended negative impact. How meaningful and effective would it be if, with no request from you, a colleague said to you over lunch, "I've watched you with Jose, and I think you might have more success if you used a concrete model of the task performance"? The notion of providing a concrete model for this student may have great value, but such unsolicited advice is likely to be unwanted and seem intrusive. It may well make you feel defensive and unwilling to discuss the matter.

A second aspect that influences the meaningfulness of communication is the *amount* of information being communicated. Too much or too little information is not meaningful. Have you had the experience of asking a colleague or co-worker a simple question like, "How is the new student adjusting?" and you get a diatribe with more information than you ever wanted to know about the situation? You may have asked the question in passing or out of general interest and started a verbal landslide. You probably know certain people who tend to give such lengthy responses regularly. Do you try to avoid giving them an opening to speak? This is a common response to such people. Conversely, have you ever found yourself providing too much information to others? As you begin observing your own communication, you may find that you sometimes obscure the meaning of what you are trying to communicate by doing this.

Sometimes this excessive information giving is not a stable characteristic of an individual but rather an aspect of a particular interaction. It may be that the situation is emotionally loaded or particularly complex or the individual is especially distressed by it. Regardless, even highly competent communicators have experiences when they are bombarding others or being bombarded themselves, with too much information.

Alternatively, everyone experiences exchanges in which too little information is shared. You may have had experiences trying to communicate with someone who seems to expect you to be a mind reader. If so, you know how difficult it can be to ensure clear understanding when others withhold needed information.

As you work toward effective interpersonal communication, you should ensure that communication is meaningful by judging the amounts of information wanted by the people with whom you are interacting. When you are relying on information from others, you may find that when they give you too much or too little, your task is either to work to obtain more information, or to focus and narrow the information they are supplying.

Use Silence Effectively

We noted earlier that silence and pauses are important nonverbal behaviors that are related to speech flow and pace or may be used as minimal encouragers. However, beyond these uses, silence is an extremely powerful communication tool. You are undoubtedly familiar with the "deadly silence" parents and teachers use to communicate disapproval or anger to children. You may have even used it or experienced it yourself in adult relationships. Silence can be awkward in conversations, but conversely, very few people seem to understand how powerful it is in communicating interest, concern and empathy, and respect to others. It can also be a very helpful strategy because it allows others to pause and think through what they are trying to communicate; this very often enhances the quality and meaning of their communication.

The definition of silence for our purposes is the absence of verbal noise or talk. But how long must there be no talk before a space in the talk can be considered silence? Goodman (1978) has offered several concepts that help to clarify this. He suggests that the length of time between two speakers' verbal expressions varies within each conversation, and the amount of silent time that qualifies as a "silence response" is relative to each conversation's tempo and patterns of speech, two topics addressed earlier. For example, if two people exchange several comments and pause for about one and a half seconds after each speaker completes a thought and before another starts, then a pause of two or three seconds may be required for a silence response. On the other hand, if two people are talking but only allowing about a quarter of a second of verbal space between taking talking turns, one second may constitute a silence response.

Silence and its impact are more easily understood when you consider the alternatives: interruptions, overtalk, and reduced verbal spacing. *Interruptions* occur when one speaker disrupts another's message in order to deliver his or her own. Interruptions may occur while the speaker is still talking or during a brief pause in speech. When someone is speaking and another interrupts there is a period of *overtalk* where both speakers are talking simultaneously until one relinquishes the conversation to the other. The final alternative, *reduced verbal spacing*, is related to silence and pauses but also distinct from them. It refers to the pace of the turn taking in verbal interaction. It occurs when a new speaker begins talking during what is meant to be a brief pause in someone else's speech. In its most exaggerated form, one speaker appears to clip off the last word or two of the previous speaker's talk.

All of these alternatives to silence (interruptions, overtalk, and reduced verbal spacing) have similarities. They may occur because the person using them has a need to control the situation, demonstrate knowledge, try to reduce the speaker's rambling talk, or simply to be center stage. Whatever the reason, these responses are likely to have negative impact on the conversation and relationship. They say, "Listen to *me*...", "It's *my* turn...", "What *I* have to say has more value than what you're saying." These responses certainly suggest to the other person that he or she is less competent, important, or interesting than the person taking control of the conversation. They are likely to produce frustration and sometimes anger as the person who is verbally "crowded" feels less and less understood and valued.

In your conversations, interviews, and professional discussions, try to develop a habit of protecting verbal space. It will give the other person the opportunity to finish talking and give you the opportunity to consider what the other has said and how you want to respond. In addition to avoiding verbal crowding, this silence response or verbal space conveys that you are interested in the other's comments and are taking the time to comprehend them before responding.

A final point to consider about silence is that the amount of silent space that creates the positive impact you desire varies with each conversational pair. Analogous to inadequate silence, unnaturally long periods of silence can have undesirable effects by conveying disinterest or other negative messages. There are no inviolable rules about verbal spacing: Sometimes, in a fast paced discussion, three seconds is a significant silence. At other times, particularly if the topic is emotional and one or more speakers is describing personal feelings, silences of several seconds or more than a minute may be appropriate. Through experimentation you can learn to determine the desirable amounts of silence in each relationship and conversation within that relationship.

Adapt Your Communication to Match the Task and Relationship

Professionals who are effective communicators tend to adapt their communication according to the task, the relationship, and the characteristics of the individuals involved. This includes choosing language that is clear and efficient, identifying the information content that is needed, and using verbal communication strategies that will best elicit the preferred responses. If you think about the individuals with whom you interact, you will probably include colleagues, administrators, parents, paraprofessionals, and professionals from other agencies. Furthermore, you may differentiate ongoing and regular collegial relationships from more temporary and infrequent interactions, such as annual review meetings. The nature of the relationship and its level of development should influence your choice of the appropriate communication style. As you collaborate in established or developing relationships, one of your responsibilities is to use communication strategies that will best facilitate the collaborative activity. Because there are no simple rules or strategies for adapting your verbal communication, your ability to understand the principles and learn to use many of the skills included in this text may help you to do this.

SUMMARY

Effective communication is critical in all areas of life and it is particularly essential to your success as a school professional. Three primary types of communication include *unilateral, directive,* and *transactional.* Unlike the first two, transactional communication emphasizes that participants in the communication process engage in continuous and simultaneous communication across multiple channels. This model is characterized by mutual influence as participants strive to develop shared meanings. Attributes common to this model include reciprocal process, channel, messages, and sender-receivers. It is also characterized by the concepts of multichannel communication and continuous feedback.

Nonverbal cues are very powerful communication mechanisms. Three classes of nonverbal cues with special significance are body movements, vocal cues, and spatial relations. Another nonverbal behavior, minimal encouragers, consists of nonverbal cues and words or phrases used to indicate listening, understanding, and/or interest encourage the speaker to continue talking. Two significant concepts for understanding nonverbal communication are individualism in responding to and interpreting communication, and congruence in which verbal and nonverbal communication are consistent and void of contradictory messages.

Verbal communication can be classified by grammatical structure—that is, statements and questions that are the topics of the next two chapters. Additionally, principles of verbal communication emphasize the importance of communication of specific, concrete information and the avoidance of judgmental or evaluative comments. Effective communication is characterized by openness, relevance, effective use of silence, and an ability to adapt communication to meet the needs of the task and relationship.

ACTIVITIES AND ASSIGNMENTS

1. Unobtrusively observe others communicating in various situations. Watching and listening to conversations in the staff lounge, at team or committee meetings, or at social events will provide you with opportunities to examine communication and see ways in which participants mutually influence each other. Discuss your observations with your classmates or colleagues.

2. Use the four classes of nonverbal cues as if they were a checklist and observe interpersonal interactions to see if you can identify examples of each class. See if you can describe the ways in which nonverbal cues influence (strengthen or detract) from the messages being conveyed. Does the degree of congruence between the verbal and nonverbal messages affect the communication?

3. Read the following vague statements or questions and imagine a situation in your professional setting where each could apply. Then write four alternative, more specific and concrete statements or questions for each:

   a. How is he doing at school?

    b. She's lazy and insubordinate.

    c. That parent is always involved.

4. Tape-record (with permission) your own interactions with a client or colleague. This may be at a meeting or in casual conversation. Listen to the tape later and identify any verbalizations that communicated bias or evaluation. Try to construct alternative responses that are neutral.

5. Challenge yourself to allow increasingly greater verbal space in some conversations. Lengthen, ever so slightly, the verbal space that follows someone else's talking turn and precedes yours. As you do this in different interactions, observe how it affects the pace and comfort of the conversation.

RELATED READINGS

Danish, S. J., & D'Augelli, A. R. (1980). *Helping skills: A basic training program* (2nd ed.). New York: Human Sciences Press.

DeVito, J. A. (1986). *The interpersonal communication book* (3rd ed.). New York: Harper & Row.

McKay, M., Davis, M., & Fanning, P. (1983). *Messages: The communication skills book.* Oakland, CA: New Harbinger.

Tannen, D. (1990). *You just don't understand: Women and men in conversation.* New York: William Morrow.

Wilson, G. L., & Hanna, M. S. (1990). *Groups in context: Leadership and participation in small groups* (2nd ed.). New York: McGraw-Hill.

CHAPTER 6

Using Statements

Keeping Perspective

Using the discussion of collaboration prerequisites in Chapter 3 and the
basic structure for communication detailed in Chapter 5, Chapter 6
outlines principles for making appropriate statements during interactions
and applies these using situations for providing feedback as a specific
application.

Learner Objectives

1. To identify the types of statements used to provide, seek, and clarify
   information.
2. To give examples of the types of statements used for each of these
   purposes.
3. To describe the affect that different types of statements may have on
   interpersonal relationships.
4. To define interpersonal feedback and list characteristics of effective
   feedback.
5. To describe guidelines for effective interpersonal feedback.
6. To evaluate feedback statements to determine if they contain the
   characteristics of effective feedback.

Statements are an integral part of communication. Consider the message that each of these statements conveys:

- Lee scored at the 4.6 grade level on reading comprehension.
- You should consider asking Kevin's parents to have his medication level checked.
- You said that you're experiencing difficulty in accomplishing the therapy goals in the classroom.
- Barbara seems overwhelmed by her caseload.
- When Jacob began to slip sideways after he was sitting on the floor with the other students, you reached down to reposition him. When one of the other kindergartners pushed him back into the proper position, you sat back.
- I wonder what you're thinking.

You use statements for many purposes: to provide information, to clarify information, and occasionally, to seek information. In this chapter, you will learn that the way you structure, word, and deliver statements has a significant impact on the verbal response you receive and on your relationship with the person with whom you are interacting.

Statements, like all verbal communication, may contain information in any of the dimensions described and illustrated in Chapter 3. Statements address the locus of self or the locus of other, detail (situational, temporal, and/or quantifying), and material that falls into the overt (behavior, event, knowledge) or covert (opinion or affect) domain. Statements with these information dimensions are used to illustrate principles presented throughout this chapter. If you are still uncertain about these concepts as they relate to statements, you may wish to review Chapter 3.

PURPOSES OF STATEMENTS

Statements that Provide Information

The most common function of statements is to provide information to others. You use statements when your primary purpose is to tell others what you think they want or need to know or that you want them to know. You may tell someone that a newly adopted regulation will change services, you may explain how the changing composition of an interagency council will influence your program, or you may describe direct observations you made of a classroom or of a particular student's performance. You may also tell others about a situation or experience you have had or give them suggestions or advice about their own situations. We identify two primary types of statements whose overall purpose is to provide information—statements that describe events or experiences or guide action through explaining or advising.

Descriptive Statements
Often, you use statements to describe events or experiences by providing a verbal account of a situation, behavior, opinion, or feeling. When such a verbal account is offered without evaluation or advice, it is *descriptive.*

Descriptive statements can be used to relate both overt and covert content. The most straightforward means of describing is by providing a verbal account of an overt event, situation, or behavior. This requires identifying observable behaviors or permanent products and describing them without making judgments about them. You probably already have skill in this area because providing precise descriptions of behavior is a basic skill in the preprofessional training of most special service providers.

Because the definition we have given for descriptive statements specifies the exclusion of evaluating or advising, use of evaluative and advising statements as nonexamples is an important strategy for illustrating descriptive statements. The following examples are provided only to help you discriminate among descriptive, evaluative, and advising statements. They are not meant to model effective means of delivering advice or evaluation, two topics addressed later in this chapter. Contrast the ways in which the same event can be described in the following statements:

> DESCRIPTIVE: When Maryanne left the room during the discussion, several team members looked at each other. Tom stopped relating his idea and said, "Should we wait for Maryanne to return?"
>
> EVALUATIVE: You shouldn't have let Maryanne leave like that. It upset the team, and Tom didn't know whether he should continue.
>
> ADVISING: You need to get everyone to agree on ground rules for participation before you have that team try group problem solving again.

The foregoing examples stress overt events—the behaviors of Maryanne, Tom, and the other group members. Those behaviors are described without evaluation or advice in the first statement. The next statements do not meet our criteria for descriptive statements. The second is evaluative ("You shouldn't have" conveys judgment about another). Notice, too, that in addition to being evaluative, this statement contains several inferences (upset the team; Tom didn't know) based on behaviors that were specifically described in the first statement. The third statement is advising ("You need to" suggests action).

Another frequent use of descriptive statements is for describing covert events, attitudes, perceptions, and feelings. Because covert material is not directly observable, descriptions of such events will involve some inference, but the inferences should not be so great as to constitute an interpretation. For example, "I thought the team meeting was efficient, and it seemed like everyone was satisfied with the decision" reflects inferences that, if examined, could probably be traced back to specific behavioral indicators. On the other hand, a statement such as, "I thought the team meeting was efficient, and it was clearly effective in making the right decision" describes the speaker's opinion of the team meeting but makes a large inferential leap and *interprets* the information. It suggests that the speaker is equating effectiveness and efficiency with his sense that a correct decision was made.

Distinctions among descriptive, evaluative, and advising statements of covert material can also be illustrated as in the following examples.

> DESCRIPTIVE: I became so anxious when it was my turn to speak at the inservice that my hands and the papers I held shook. I perspired, my mouth was terribly dry, and I felt all tongue tied. I felt like the floor would fall out from under me.

EVALUATIVE: I'm such a joke as a speaker. I'm really a rotten spokesperson. I *look* nervous and nobody can follow what I'm saying.

ADVISING: I must avoid getting into situations where I'll have to talk in front of other people because they are so upsetting to me. I should have Carlos represent us at meetings.

The topic in these examples is the speaker's feelings (covert) about public speaking. The descriptive statement includes neither evaluation nor advice as it describes feelings (e.g., anxious, tongue tied). This statement goes further in providing a concrete description of the feelings through describing observable behaviors (e.g., shaking hands, perspiration, dry mouth). The second statement is not descriptive because it contains evaluation (e.g., "I'm a joke"; "I'm rotten"). Similarly, the third statement offers advice (e.g., "I must avoid"; "I should have") rather than description.

Although these illustrative statements were designed to provide clear examples of the descriptive, evaluative, and advising concepts, in your day-do-day interactions you are not likely to find such clear-cut examples. Instead, you will generally encounter statements like these:

I observed Timothy in his occupational therapy group and was amazed. He has such a low self-concept that when he made a mistake he marked all over his project in black marker and tore it up. He threw it at the wastebasket and put his head on the table. His behavior was pathetic.

I observed your group, and you shouldn't feel so bad about your lesson. You're a really good therapist and you do a great job with some real "buzzards"! Your presentation took only one minute and you demonstrated all of the three movements we talked about.

The first example contains some descriptive phrases (observed, marked all over, tore it, threw it, and put his head on table). It also contains an evaluative phrase (pathetic behavior) and another high inference reference (self-concept). Similarly, the second example also includes descriptive and nondescriptive elements. Can you identify them?

As you begin to attend more closely to the statements you and others make as you interact, you will undoubtedly find that purely descriptive statements are rare. And, although it is often difficult to describe something without any advising or evaluating, monitoring your own statements can improve your skill. As you will see later in this chapter and in the next, skill in using descriptive statements contributes greatly to effective interaction. By conveying information without judging, purely descriptive statements minimize the likelihood of offending the receiver. These statements promote clear and honest communication without causing listeners to become defensive.

Guiding Statements

Some statements provide information in order to guide action—to urge others to act, feel, or think in a certain way. Two groups of guiding statements are those that explain and those that advise.

Statements that provide information in an instructive way and rely on reasoning, understanding cause and effect relationships, or logic are *explanations*. They translate ideas and interpret information. Use of these statements nearly always means that the person offering the explanation has greater expertise or knowledge than the one receiving it. Explanations can be appreciated, particularly when they are requested such as when you ask a colleague to explain a new regional policy to you or when you ask another specialist to help you interpret assessment results. You will find that this type of statement is particularly valuable when you are asked to share your knowledge to clarify a point, elaborate an idea, or answer a question. The use of explanations is also an effective strategy for developing the shared meanings that are so important in effective communication.

Although the ability to give clear explanations is considered an essential competency for teachers, it is generally classified as an instructional rather than interpersonal skill (McCaleb, 1987). As an instructional skill, explaining typically includes emphasis on clearly presenting material and using examples. Some frameworks also include as components of effective explaining using advance organizers, demonstrations, paraphrasing, or review of salient points. The skills of defining concepts, answering questions, and giving corrective feedback are also considered part of explaining in the instructional literature (Feezel, 1987).

As school personnel, you are undoubtedly familiar with the various aspects of explanations and you are probably aware of their value in your professional interactions. Our caution here, however, is that because you are likely to be proficient in giving explanations, you may tend to overuse them. We suggest that you strive to employ them infrequently because they typify directive communication, not two-way transactional communication. Explanations are most appropriate when they provide others with information they have requested (recall the *Jeopardy* contestants mentioned in Chapter 5 who have answers but no questions). When they are uninvited, explanations may have all of the undesirable effects of unsolicited advice, our next topic.

Closely related to explanations is *advice*, a category of information-providing statements intended to guide action by suggesting, hinting, or even commanding that someone take specific actions or accept certain beliefs. Suggestions are statements of "gentle advice" offered as possibilities for consideration; they communicate clearly that they are tentative and subject to the evaluation of their recipient. For example, when a colleague suggests to you, "You may want to consider some of the new materials we just received," he is giving you a hint or a tip. He is simply offering information for your evaluation and acknowledging that in your role as decision maker you may accept or reject the suggestion.

Advice also may be offered as a direct command that insists on compliance or cooperation. In many interactions, commands may seem overly directive such as when someone says, "You will certainly have to change that" or "You must get some hands-on training." Commands may remind their recipients of someone's inappropriate exercise of authority over them or of years of parental commands. They often suggest the sender's superiority over the receiver. When this happens commands are likely to cause resistance and become less effective than other efforts to guide behavior.

However, commands are not always negative, and they do not always imply that the recipient is inferior to the speaker. Sometimes they are timesavers because they give advisement efficiently when the participants agree that one party has greater expertise in a given area. When such agreement is present it can eliminate the air of arrogance that some people perceive is associated with commands. This situation is illustrated in the following statements made by an adaptive physical education teacher telling a special education teacher how to adapt a classroom game so a particular student can participate. In this example, a series of commands may well be the most efficient approach to guiding the action of a colleague.

- First, point to the target and say, "Throw it there." Then wait 10 seconds to see if Victor responds. If not, physically prompt him to throw the bean bag.

Like explanations, whether offered as a suggestion or command, advice is unlikely to be helpful and may well be detrimental to relationships if given to someone who has not requested it. Unfortunately, advice is a frequently overused response when people are trying to assist others in problem solving. This should not be difficult to understand in the context of the professional socialization factors we discussed in Chapter 3. School professionals are likely to be competent, independent problem solvers, and they may quickly jump to designing solutions and presenting solutions as advice when they begin working with others. However, unsolicited advice is likely to be perceived as intrusive and even arrogant. Recipients of this unrequested information are likely to feel defensive and misunderstood.

Statements That Seek Information

A second function of the statements you use is to seek or solicit information from others. This function may be accomplished through the use of inflection, commands, and indirect questions. To illustrate the use of inflection, imagine this statement spoken with a querying inflection, "The books are no longer available?" Various levels of commands may also be used to request information in conversation. Statements like those below request information without using direct questions. You may notice that the tone changes across these examples, with the first (a command) sounding demanding and the second and third being more invitational.

- Tell me more about the parents.
- I wonder what was going on in the group when he began singing.
- I'd really like to know more about that.

Using statements to seek information is an appealing alternative to excessive question asking as is discussed in the next chapter and may be integrated with questions to avoid creating an atmosphere of interrogation. Using general statements like those above are particularly valuable when initially exploring an issue. You should exercise caution when employing statements to seek information during interactions. As discussions progress and require greater focus, you may find yourself using commands when questions are far more appropriate.

Statements That Confirm or Clarify Information

Statements are often used to confirm or clarify information that has already been shared. When used in this way, they may be addressing simultaneously the combined purposes of providing information and seeking information. Frequently, statements designed to confirm or clarify are restatements of already available information offered to ensure that participants are developing common meanings and understanding each other. Common forms of clarifying statements are *paraphrasing, reflecting, summarizing*, and *checking*.

Paraphrasing

In paraphrasing, you restate in your own words what you think another person has just said. Paraphrasing focuses on relatively small units of information that were discussed by just one other individual, and it involves little or no inference.

> A teacher and principal are discussing how to handle a problematic situation that includes parents of a student with disabilities.
>
> TEACHER: I'm not sure I should meet alone with his parents. We had a falling out last month.
> PRINCIPAL: You had conflict with his parents recently.
> TEACHER: Well, they were furious at me when I told them his grades at our conference. The father got red in the face, hit the table a couple of times, and left really angry. He won't return any of my phone calls.
> PRINCIPAL: So it's still unresolved and you think they—especially the father—are still angry with you.
> TEACHER: Yes, but I did get to talk to the mother on the phone. She apologized and explained that her husband's been working two shifts, is really tired, and has been getting angry easily. He also feels guilty because he can't help with homework while he works so much. The mother says he wants to meet with me to see how we all can help their son...I'm not sure.
> PRINCIPAL: Even though the parents seem to have gotten over their anger and want to respond constructively, you're still not certain you should meet with them.
> TEACHER: Yes...It may be calm now, but I've given two tests since our last meeting. He failed both of them. His father's having problems with his temper.
> PRINCIPAL: His father may get angry again if you tell him about the test grades.

This excerpt illustrates the definition of paraphrasing and provides an opportunity to examine how paraphrasing functions to influence the relationship. By accurately restating the main points in the teacher's statements, the principal demonstrated that she had been attending to and accurately understanding what the teacher was relating. She thus conveyed interest in the problem as well as in the teacher as a person.

The principal's paraphrase also helped to clarify the information provided. If any of the principal's restatements had been incorrect, the teacher would have been able to rephrase or modify them so they would be more easily understood. Because the principal's paraphrases were succinct and captured the essence of the teacher's comments, they also helped to focus the discussion and encourage the teacher to examine the situation more closely. This strategy maintained the teacher as the central figure and helped the principal and the teacher establish a shared understanding of the situation. These relationship effects may become more clear if you contrast that example with this alternative:

> TEACHER: I'm not sure I should meet alone with his parents. We had a falling out last month.
> PRINCIPAL: I agree. We don't need conflict between parents and staff. Let's have the counselor meet with them instead.

The principal may appear to be supporting the teacher, but such a quick response reveals the principal's tendency to solve problems independently and suggests both lack of concern for the teacher and her perception of the problem as well as lack of respect for the teacher's own resources.

Reflecting

Reflection, a clarifying statement more complex than paraphrasing, was popularized by the psychologist Carl Rogers nearly 40 years ago. It focuses on circumscribed information provided by a single individual, but it also includes inferences on the part of the speaker. In reflection, you describe what another person has said and try to capture the affective meaning of the message. Because you cannot observe another's feelings, you examine the verbal and nonverbal information provided in both the overt and covert domains and infer what this information communicates about the emotional meaning. Reflection is a way of making explicit information that is being conveyed implicitly during interaction. It demonstrates that you understand another's feelings as the following vignette illustrates.

Imagine the previous example of the teacher and principal discussing an angry father if it ended like this:

> TEACHER: Yes....It may be calm now, but I've given two tests since our last meeting (heavy sigh). He's failed both them (laughing and looking away). His father's having problems with his temper.
>
> PRINCIPAL: His father may get angry again if you tell him about the test grades. Your laugh and clenched fists make me think you're frightened about this.
>
> TEACHER: Yes, I met another angry father alone last year, and he was really a bully and pushed me. I know he was *trying* to scare me, and he was successful. I'm afraid to meet alone with people like that. Can you meet with us?
>
> PRINCIPAL: His father may get angry again and possibly even pose a physical threat. You'll feel safer if someone could meet with you and the parents. I'm quite sure I'm available, but if not, can we reschedule the meeting?

In this excerpt, the principal restated the teacher's messages in her own words and reflected the teacher's feelings. In doing so, she conveyed her understanding of the situation from the teacher's point of view. This response is often integral in building relationships and in promoting a sense of trust since it conveys that the speaker's ideas and feelings are valued.

These illustrations of reflection are presented out of context and can only suggest how it functions. In fact, our examples may unintentionally suggest that reflection is a simple type of verbal statement. Although the wording may be simple, the accurate perception and reflection of someone's verbal and nonverbal messages is a complex endeavor.

When you reflect, you convey understanding of the other's frame of reference. Understanding accompanied by congruent nonverbal behaviors is referred to as *empathy*, and its importance in promoting trust in relationships is widely recognized. Additionally, hearing your own messages reflected will give you the opportunity to consider complex thoughts a little longer and may allow you to have a better understanding of your own experiences.

It is important to recognize that reflection does not go very far beyond the speaker's overt messages. Its intention is not to explain anything new to the speaker. Reflection is thus distinguished from *interpretation,* which does go beyond the information the speaker has presented. Interpretation attempts to explain the speaker's experience in terms of a theory or a level of understanding beyond what the speaker knows. As Goodman (1978) points out, interpretation is usually an attempt to show an understanding of the speaker that is better than the speaker's self-understanding.

Consider this alternative response to the teacher's concern about meeting with an angry parent:

> PRINCIPAL: You're afraid the father will be angry and violent. This is a lot like your conflict with many of the male teachers. Once again, you're having conflict with a man and feeling threatened by him. Perhaps I should meet with you when you see the parents.

This example is exaggerated to emphasize the potentially intrusive nature of this type of response and to support our contention that interpretations should be used very little, if at all, among school professionals in work settings. They may be very appropriate in more help-oriented or therapist–client-centered relationships, but interpretation is likely to go beyond the scope of what is appropriate among colleagues.

Summarizing

Summarizing consists of one or more statements that restate, in concise form, several preceding statements made by the individuals involved in the interaction. It is a means of ensuring that all individuals involved understand what has been said, and it functions in much the same way as a summary section in the middle or end of a lengthy piece of expository text. Summarizing differs from paraphrasing in at least two significant ways. When you paraphrase, you are simply restating what one other person has just said. Paraphrasing is relatively immediate and it is a response to a discrete, self-contained piece of information. On the other hand, summarizing is not as immediate and it is a response to several pieces of information often presented by more than one participant. The following examples heard at team meetings illustrate this point.

> Let's see if we can agree on the major points. Mrs. Evans, you've said you're concerned about Tom's disruptive and off task behavior in your math class; Mr. O'Rielly said Tom's behavior is appropriate but wants him to have an extra period of art since he does so well in that class. And, Tom, you want to drop the math class until next semester because you feel like you're too far behind to ever catch up. Does anyone want to correct anything or add comments?

> It seems like we've considered all the main issues. Cathy, you've described your efforts to implement peer tutoring, self-instructional materials, and language master activities in the classroom. Despite all the planning you and the grade level team have done, Hope still requires too much assistance to work independently in your classroom. And Naomi, you've

seen Hope work semi-independently with the language master when you sit near her and you'd like to try to provide some in-class assistance. Have I missed anything?

Checking

Sometimes the clarifying or confirming function of communication is referred to as *checking, perception checking*, or *checking for accuracy*. All of these referents have the same purpose that we have described as clarifying. We mention this here and again in Chapter 7 because this function is so frequently addressed through combining a statement and question. In fact, if paraphrasing, reflecting, and summarizing are to be maximally effective they themselves will be checked, or followed up with a question to ensure agreement and accuracy. The final questions in the preceding illustrations of summarizing are examples of checking.

GIVING VERBAL FEEDBACK

Although you will use statements throughout your interactions, one specific situation in which they will be relied on extensively is when you provide verbal feedback to others. And since effectively providing feedback is an essential but often poorly applied communication skill, the ideas in this section should provide opportunities to practice both your general skill for making statements and the specific application of them to giving feedback. In the strictest sense, all transactional communication, whether verbal statements, questions, or nonverbal messages, is feedback. As noted in Chapter 5, you simultaneously send and receive messages when you interact with others, and so it is not possible to communicate without feedback. Most simply, feedback is providing others with information about their behaviors or performance. It can be given for many different purposes including:

1. providing objective information about observed behaviors of others or observed conditions;
2. providing information about the impressions or feelings that these behaviors or conditions cause; and/or
3. clarifying what the observed behaviors or conditions may mean or signify to the individual involved.

Characteristics of Effective Interpersonal Feedback

If you wish to collaborate successfully with others, you will need to be adept at giving effective feedback. You will also want to learn to solicit and accept feedback from others as a means of securing valuable information about your own communication behaviors and about your collaborative relationships. This is true whether your collaboration is aimed at helping each other develop and refine the skills presented in this text or targeted at work-related activities.

Any effective feedback statement will include most of the following five characteristics:

Feedback Is Descriptive Rather than Evaluative or Advising

An individual is more likely to listen when someone simply describes what has been observed. As noted earlier, descriptive information is not threatening and not judgmental. The implication of this for feedback is depicted in the following examples.

> Example: I noticed that you raised your voice.
>
> Rather than: You talk too loud all the time; You shouldn't yell; or Have you tried keeping a calm voice?

When you describe a personal observation, the other individual is free to use it or not as he or she sees fit. On the other hand, evaluative or advising feedback conveys that the other person should take action or change. This is likely to cause the person to feel defensive and criticized.

As you may have surmised, avoiding judgmental comments requires the elimination of both negative and positive comments. The following statements easily might be seen as evaluative and are likely to be threatening to the person hearing them:

- You didn't do that very well.
- Your system doesn't make any sense.

Equally important, however, is the fact that positive comments also convey a judgment. Some examples are these:

- You did good work...
- You had a nice style when you...

Individuals who make positive judgments also are likely to make negative ones. The person receiving the feedback is justified in assuming that those who give praise or compliments also make critical evaluations—whether they are stated openly or not.

Feedback Is Specific Rather than General

Descriptions of specific behaviors are more easily understood than are general comments. "You sounded angry" communicates much less than, "I noticed that every time you spoke you frowned, raised your voice, and put your hands on your hips." As emphasized in Chapter 5, specific and concrete language helps to ensure clear communication.

Feedback Is Directed toward Behavior or a Situation
that the Individual Can Change

In order for feedback to be useful, it needs to be directed at something the receiver can control or do something about. Feedback directed toward an attribute or situation the receiver cannot control is generally pointless and likely to interfere with effective communication. Physical traits such as height, age, or sex and situational aspects such as the size of the room or the administrator's leadership style are not behaviors that an individual can change. Telling someone that his age and physical appearance make it hard to talk to him could be more detrimental than helpful. On the other hand, information such as "You were busy filing papers when I was talking to you," or "I notice that you usually look at the desk when I'm talking" is information that may be acted upon. You only increase others' frustration when you remind them of some attribute that cannot be changed.

Feedback Is Concise

Concise feedback is easier to understand than feedback that contains extraneous detail or information. When first learning to give feedback you may feel obligated to give very detailed information or to make many statements. When giving feedback *more* is not necessarily *better*, too much information or too much verbiage, irrelevant information, and redundant statements distract from the main message. For example, compare the two following feedback statements. Which is more likely to help a teacher understand the confusion?

> In terms of your language, I mean the words you used, you used complex and technical words that I didn't understand. The vocabulary you used was too specialized for me to understand. I didn't know what all your vocabulary meant so I didn't understand your main points. Everything has to be explained well or I get really disturbed and close out everything you say.

> When you used technical terms I got lost. It would help me if you would define your terms and make your point again.

Feedback Is Checked to Ensure Clear Communication

Perceptions of any event usually differ among individuals. Several people may participate in the same situation and yet experience it differently. Similarly, when you give feedback, the receiver may not receive the information the way it was intended. Although most of our examples of characteristics of effective feedback have focused on statements, questions are often needed for checking. An effective method for checking others' understanding of the feedback you have given is to ask them to rephrase your feedback to see if it corresponds to what you intended. For example, you might say,

> I'm really concerned about whether I'm communicating clearly. Would you mind summarizing my comments?

Frequently when receiving feedback, the person will spontaneously confirm or appear to understand the feedback with a general comment such as, "Yes, I did do that" or "That's right." In this situation it may still be advisable to check for understanding. This checking might be done by rephrasing or questioning as shown here:

> Rephrasing: So it is correct to say that you...
> Questioning: You said, "That's right." What particular observations were correct?

You may also want to check the accuracy of your observations that are the subject of your feedback, particularly if you are uncertain about what you observed. In checking for accuracy you might ask if the receiver agrees with the your description of the observation. Two examples follow:

- It seemed to me that you were asking questions of James more frequently than you did the others. Would you agree with that?
- Does it seem accurate to you that you asked James more questions than you did the others?

Suggestions for Giving Effective Feedback

Although our suggestions for giving effective feedback are not as easy to illustrate as were characteristics of feedback statements, three are extremely important. Feedback should be solicited, direct to a person, and well timed.

Feedback Is Solicited Rather than Imposed

Feedback, like advice and explanations, is most effective when someone has requested it. An individual who requests feedback is more likely to use it than one on whom feedback is imposed. Unsolicited feedback may make the receiver feel defensive and assume a "Who asked you?" attitude. When you first attempt to work collaboratively with a colleague, you should not assume that your colleague actually wants feedback. One way to avoid ineffective interaction is to wait for your colleague to provide an opportunity for you to give feedback. Then you need merely to confirm the request. The most direct way of ensuring that your colleague wants the feedback you believe he has requested is to respond to his apparent request with a question such as, "Are you asking for my feedback?" or "Do you want to know about that?" The following excerpt illustrates this:

> STATEMENT: I don't know why Jimmy doesn't follow directions. Do you think I'm not giving them clearly? How can I be more successful with him?
> RESPONSE: It sounds like you'd like to examine how you give directions. Would it be helpful if I shared my observations on that?

Most frequently your colleague will not ask for feedback and you will face the prerequisite task of finding a way to be invited to provide it. Depending on the openness and attitude of your colleague, you may emphasize different aspects of the situation and use different communication skills to set the stage for giving feedback.

Feedback Is Direct to the Person Rather than Indirect

Feedback is most effective when it is given directly to the person who can use it by the person who has made some observation. For example, instead of asking the principal to tell your coteacher about ineffective teaching behavior, generally you should tell him or her personally. Similarly, although many school professionals write notes to communicate with other adults, notes may also decrease the effectiveness of feedback. Indirect feedback is more easily misinterpreted than is feedback given directly to the person involved. This is due in part to the lack of transactional communication.

The giver cannot check the feedback for accuracy, and the receiver cannot adequately clarify it.

Feedback Is Well Timed

The immediacy of feedback is a subject of considerable attention in the research on learning, particularly in reference to learning new skills. Corrective feedback is most beneficial to learners when it is given immediately following the relevant event or behavior. This is not always possible or appropriate for interpersonal feedback, partly because it is not necessarily meant to be corrective or instructional in nature. But several guidelines can help you to determine the appropriate timing for feedback.

You should always ask yourself, "Is now the best time to give feedback?" If your colleague is extremely busy or rushed, the feedback may seem like an irritating intrusion. Or if some event has left your colleague upset and confused, immediate feedback may be seen as unduly demanding or even critical. Our recommendation here is to provide feedback as soon as appropriate so that it is recent, but also so that it demonstrates your sensitivity to your colleague's receptiveness.

When you find you must delay giving feedback you should use recent examples in your feedback statement. Your colleague who receives feedback is more likely to understand and benefit from recent examples than from those that are more distant and possibly forgotten. The more time that passes between the event and the feedback, the less vivid the event will be in her memory.

In general, when giving feedback to others, ask yourself these questions:

- Will this person understand me?
- Will this person be able to accept my feedback?
- Will this person be able to use the information?

The most significant consideration is that the feedback be constructive to the recipient. What you are about to say should be helpful and appreciated by this person. These considerations, along with use of the other characteristics and strategies we have presented, should maximize the effectiveness of the feedback you give to others.

SUMMARY

Statements are the primary verbal means of providing information to others. Statements that describe events or experiences and those that attempt to guide action are the most frequent forms of statements that provide information. A second purpose of statements is to seek information (e.g., commands or indirect questions). Confirming or clarifying information is the final purpose of statements and frequently achieved through paraphrasing, reflecting, or summarizing.

A communication skill that relies largely on the use of statements, giving interpersonal feedback, illustrates several principles of communication. Characteristics of effective feedback include these: It is descriptive, specific, directed toward behavior, concise, and checked. Additionally, for feedback to be maximally effective, it should be solicited, direct to a person, and well timed.

ACTIVITIES AND ASSIGNMENTS

1. Think of a problem one of your colleagues has mentioned having with a student. Imagine an interaction in which you try to assist your colleague to solve the problem. Write down eight to ten statements you would probably make. Then classify the purpose and format of each. Do you use certain types of statements more than others? What is the primary purpose of most of the statements you wrote? Is this what you believe is the best approach to helping someone solve a problem? Review your responses to the above questions and construct different types of statements if you find you are not using an appropriate range.

2. Explain to a colleague or a parent that you are trying to improve your verbal communication skills and ask permission to audio tape an interaction with them. Review your tape and classify each statement according to its purpose and format. Consider which statements could be improved and write improved versions. Discuss your tape and written responses with a classmate or colleague.

3. Study and critique the text material on interpersonal feedback. Write an original example for each of the five characteristics described in the text. Write a separate statement to illustrate each characteristic even though a good example may simultaneously include several of them. Review your work with a classmate or colleague.

4. Critique each of the examples below to determine if they include the characteristics for effective feedback. Revise statements as necessary to include all characteristics.

   a. After you smiled and said, "OK," Jimmy looked very relieved. Then when you nodded for him to join the group, a big smile covered his face. Is that what you observed, too?

   b. The way you handled Jimmy seemed better today. He has made a lot of progress in his spelling and your patience with his bad behavior has improved tremendously.

   c. You've really managed to get Sandy to behave in class. You should be very proud of yourself for doing such a great job!

5. Observe someone interacting with one or more individuals (e.g., a parent and child in the community, colleagues in a meeting, a friend at a party). Then write feedback statements describing what you observed. Evaluate your feedback statements against each of the five characteristics of effective feedback.

RELATED READINGS

Brammer, L. M. (1985). *The helping relationship: Process and skills* (3rd ed.). Englewood Cliffs, NJ: Prentice-Hall.

Corey, G. (1981). *Manual for theory and practice of group counseling.* Belmont, CA: Brooks/Cole.

Egan, G. (1982). *The skilled helper: Model, skills and methods for effective helping* (2nd ed.). Monterey, CA: Brooks/Cole.

Hargie, O., Saunders, C., & Dickson, D. (1987). *Social skills in interpersonal communication* (2nd ed.). Cambridge, MA: Brookline Books.

Okun, B. (1982). *Effective helping: Interviewing and counseling techniques* (2nd ed.). Monterey, CA: Brooks/Cole.

Verderber, R. F., & Verderber, S. K. (1983). *Inter-act: Using interpersonal communication skills* (3rd ed.). Belmont, CA: Wadsworth.

CHAPTER 7

Asking Questions

Keeping Perspective

Chapter 7 is in many ways analogous to Chapter 6. It focuses on a specific type of verbal communication skill—asking questions—and draws on communication information presented in earlier chapters. Strategies for enhancing your skill in asking questions are presented, and interviewing is outlined as a common situation in which question asking skills are employed.

Learner Objectives

1. To explain the importance of question asking in collaborative interactions.
2. To describe the major purposes of questions.
3. To analyze questions to determine their format and degree of concreteness.
4. To describe strategies that may facilitate effective question asking.
5. To state the purpose of interviews.
6. To outline activities that should occur prior to an interview, during it, and after it.

Questions are a primary verbal means of soliciting information during interactions, including collaborative activities. They are crucial at the outset of interpersonal problem solving to elicit pertinent information, and they continue to be essential throughout the process for clarifying interactions and sharing ideas and information. Skillful use of questions can mean the difference between an interaction that is successful and one fraught with misperceptions and parallel communication.

Because questions are used in casual conversation, informal collaborative interactions, as well as in more formal situations such as interviews, mastering the skill of asking well-phrased, appropriate questions should be a priority. This is especially true for teachers who may have to learn to modify existing behaviors because many of the question-asking techniques they learned in teacher preparation are focused on querying students, a communication situation tremendously different from interacting collaboratively with other professionals and parents.

As with any verbal communication, the way you phrase a question will greatly affect the quality of response you receive. And so, prior to asking a question, you should decide what type of response you desire and what type of questions would best elicit that information; then you can phrase your question accordingly. At the same time, you should strive to clarify your questions and also embed them within interviews, one common question-asking context.

In Chapter 6 we reminded you about the importance of dimensions of information in statements. The same can be said for questions: They, too, address information dimensions of locus (self or others), domain (covert or overt), and detail (situational, temporal, and quantifying). We again refer you to Chapter 3 if you find you are encountering difficulty in recognizing the application of these concepts to either questions or statements.

PURPOSES OF QUESTIONS

As you learned in Chapter 5, virtually all of your communication with others both provides information to them and enables you to gather information from them. When you look more closely at how questions are used in interactions, you will find that they can be categorized as having one of three primary intentions or purposes. The intentions parallel those for statements addressed in Chapter 6; because the topic has been previously addressed, it is treated here only briefly. Refer again to Chapter 6 to review these concepts.

Questions That Seek Information

The most straightforward function of questions is to query others for information. You often ask querying questions when your primary purpose is to seek information about a topic on which you do not have information. You might ask whether a student's program is effective, what steps need to be taken to arrange a new service for a student, or when the next team meeting will be. All of these questions have information-seeking as their foundation, as do these examples:

- What are your professional development goals for this school year?
- How many different reading series have you used with her?
- What led the parents to involve an independent evaluator?
- What kinds of feelings underlie her response?

Questions That Provide Information

Another function of some of the questions you ask may be to provide information to the persons with whom you are interacting, either by evaluating or attempting to guide action by giving suggestions or advising. Evaluative questions, although seemingly constructed to query and spoken with a questioning inflection, typically convey far more information than they elicit. For example, think about the impact of these questions:

- What about all the problems that intervention is likely to cause for the parents?
- How could you go about contacting the rehabilitative services so that they're aware of the problem?
- What do you think would happen if you asked Marie's parents to take her for an ophthalmological exam?
- You haven't talked to the physical therapist, have you?
- Why would you want even to attempt that type of intervention?

Questions that evaluate have limited value in interactions. Did you find yourself feeling defensive in response to the illustrative questions? If so, your reaction is a common one.

Some of the questions you ask could have an even stronger message than those just described. Such questions are actually direct commands or advice with a querying format attached as an afterthought. Like statements that are meant to guide others, these questions are used to direct or advise a person to take an action or to respond to a situation in a prescribed manner. For example, consider these questions:

- You'll call Tom's parents, won't you?
- Why don't you try giving him only one task at a time?

Like questions that evaluate, you should seldom use questions that advise. They, too, may be perceived as negative by respondents. Furthermore, they tend to make others feel like they are being "put on the spot" because the advising question usually implies that there is only one right answer to give—and that right answer has been predetermined by the person asking the question. Generally, if your purpose is to convey information you should do so with statements, not with questions.

Questions That Clarify or Confirm Information

Sometimes you ask clarifying questions to confirm information that you already have obtained but may not fully understand:

- Did you say that Michael has gotten only 3 out of 10 spelling words correct this week?
- Did you mean that you favor the tutoring option over the after-school program?
- What did you mean when you said his parents are aware of the problem?

As you strive to develop the shared meaning that is so critical in interpersonal communication, questions that clarify information constitute an extremely important strategy. They allow you to check your perception of the information being shared with your colleague's perception. Clarifying questions may serve the same purpose as paraphrasing or reflecting. In fact, they are often used in conjunction with these types of statements. After paraphrasing information provided by a colleague you may check your mutual understanding with brief confirming questions (e.g., "Did I describe your situation correctly?" or "Have I understood what you were saying?").

CHARACTERISTICS OF QUESTIONS

In addition to understanding the purposes of questions, your skill in using questions relies on your ability to recognize and manipulate various characteristics of them. By considering format and degree of concreteness you can phrase your questions effectively and efficiently.

Question Format

An essential characteristic of questions is their format, the way in which words are put together to create the question. Although format is not usually a critical dimension of the statements we make during interactions, it is especially important for the information-seeking purpose of questions. You may receive widely varying responses to questions simply on the basis of their wording (Baldwin, 1987).

Open/Closed

An *open question* is defined as one for which an infinite range of responses is possible (Benjamin, 1987). For example, if you ask a colleague, "What did John do in your class today?" you cannot predict the nature of the response you will receive. Other examples of open questions include:

- What would you like to see the team accomplish this year?
- How could I help you adapt materials for Jason?

Sometimes you want to encourage others to continue speaking or to obtain their perception of an event or situation without imposing any limits to their responses. In such instances the appropriate type of question to use is open.

In contrast, a *closed question* is one in which the range of responses is limited either explicitly or implicitly (Benjamin, 1987). First, you may explicitly limit the range by specifying the response options in the questions, as in the following two examples:

- Would you prefer that we meet before school, during lunch, or after school?
- Does Jennifer have no friends, just one friend, or several friends?

A second way in which you may limit response options is implicit, that is, by inferring them in the wording of the question. Analyze these examples:

- Can you meet during lunch today?
- How old is Carey?
- How many friends does Jennifer have on the team?

In the first example, the inferred limit on the response is *yes/no*. In the second, the limit is set because there is only one correct answer. In the third, the limit is established by the inference that there is a finite number of students on the team with whom Jennifer may have friendships.

One basis for deciding whether to use open or closed questions should be whether you are seeking an elaborated, divergent response or a simple, convergent one. Closed questions may be used to limit the scope of the conversation or confirm information. However, sometimes you will find that even though you ask a closed question, you receive an elaborated response, for example, when a question, "Has Laura's time management improved?" launches a five-minute description of her latest rash of missed classes and incomplete work. Conversely, even an open question such as, "What does Kevin say about school when he's at home?" may only elicit the very narrow answer, "Nothing." Your choice of open or closed question format nevertheless establishes general parameters for the type of response you intend to receive.

Another consideration in selecting between open and closed formats is the nature of your relationship with the person from whom you are seeking information. Sometimes your concern about building a relationship will be as great or greater than your need for specific information. In these cases, you may decide to ask open questions that allow your colleague to offer freely any information. There is less of a sense of precise or correct answers when questions are open. With closed questions, the person being queried may become defensive or feel as if she is being tested since the range of appropriate responses is limited.

Direct/Indirect

Most of the questions you ask have a direct format. That is, the question is phrased as an interrogative and if written, would end in a question mark. All of the examples in the previous section were direct questions.

An alternative question asking format is *indirect*. In this format, it is not clear that anyone is being queried as the question is phrased as a statement, not a question at all (Snow, Zurcher, & Sjoberg, 1982). This topic was mentioned in Chapter 6. Perhaps you have used indirect questions similar to these:

INDIRECT: It would be interesting to know what would happen if we included Chris in the community-based training program.
DIRECT: What would happen if we included Chris in the community-based training program?

INDIRECT: I was thinking about the possibility of asking Jason's parents to talk to the other
parents about accessing support groups.

DIRECT: What do you think about the possibility of asking Jason's parents to talk to the other
parents about accessing support groups?

Asking indirect questions may be appropriate when you are unsure whether a direct question would offend another person. Notice that by using the first person, the implied responsibility for the idea contained in the question stays with the question asker; the person answering the question need not assume ownership for the idea expressed. In contrast, when you ask direct questions, you turn responsibility for the response to the other person. Thus, in awkward or uncomfortable situations, or in other cases in which you want to be certain you are not imposing a potentially unwanted idea, the indirect format may be preferable.

An indirect question format also carries a risk, however. Your question could be perceived by the other person as rhetorical; if this occurs you may not receive a response. You then would rephrase the question to be direct if you judged that a response was required.

Single/Multiple

Another element of how you format your questions concerns the number of questions you ask at one time (Hargie, Saunders, & Dickson, 1987; Morrissey, 1986). In general, *single* questions are preferable to *multiple* questions. Which of these question-asking examples is likely to result in the most constructive interchange?

When you think about the changes we've been making for Liz over the past couple of weeks, which ones seem most responsible for the improvement in her behavior?

What do you think of the changes we've made for Liz over the past couple of weeks? Do you agree that they're really helping her behavior? Which one do you think has been most effective?

In the first example, one well-phrased question is asked, and the other person has the option of sharing ideas and perceptions. In the second example, a nonexample really, three questions are asked, and the respondent would be left wondering which one to answer.

Multiple questions occur for several reasons. First, you may have the habit of beginning to talk even while you are phrasing your question. This may cause you to need several tries to arrive finally at the question you intended. Another reason for multiple questions relates to specificity. You may first ask a vague question, then realize that it will not convey the message intended, and so then try again and perhaps again. A third type of multiple question occurs when you are conversationally rushing past the person with whom you are speaking. That is, you may ask at one time an entire series of questions you wish to have answered. Examples of these types of multiple questions are listed below:

Thinking and Talking at the Same Time

"Is Joyce mastering her math facts? How about her problem solving? Is she turning in her math homework? Overall, how successful is Joyce in her mainstreamed math class?"

Moving from Vague to Focused Questions

"How is Reginald doing? How has he adjusted to his vocational program? What issues are still coming up in having Reginald work with his job coach?"

Asking a Question Series at One Time

"What are the highest needs the teacher listed on the professional development questionnaire? What resources do we have available for meeting their needs? When can we meet to begin planning the professional development program for next year?"

Regardless of the reason for multiple questions, when you use them you leave your interaction partner wondering how to respond. That person may wonder which question you really meant to have addressed. He or she may also answer on the basis of the question remembered, often the first or last question. Alternatively, you may put that person in the position of being suspicious or defensive; multiple questions sometimes convey the impression that you are "fishing" for information.

Our simple recommendation is to avoid multiple questions. If you have several questions to ask, phrase each one well, in a logical sequence, and permit the other person time to respond. If you tend to ask multiple questions out of carelessness, monitor this behavior and learn to use a pause of a few seconds before asking a question in order to phrase it.

Degree of Concreteness

Just as statements can be phrased with varying levels of specificity or concreteness, so too, can questions. At times you will pose very general questions such as when you are initiating relationships or just beginning to explore a situation. Most often, however, you should ask questions that elicit more specific and concrete information; we refer to these as *focused* questions.

A *focused* question specifies the topic sufficiently so that the respondent can clearly discern the specific type of information requested. With few exceptions, you should use focused questions in your interpersonal interactions (Brown, Kratochwill, & Bergan, 1982). Perhaps the most convincing evidence of this comes from an experience most special service providers have had: Do you remember a time when you asked a question such as, "How is Katie doing?" because you specifically wanted to know about Katie's reaction to the intervention you had spent hours designing? If so, you may have found that your vague or unfocused question resulted in an accounting of Katie's overall progress, her upcoming surgery, the progress she was making in other areas, and so on. A more focused question such as, "How is Katie succeeding in the language program we designed?" would have probably elicited the information you preferred.

Focused questions play an important role in clear communication. When questions are too vague you may have to interpret someone's response or at the very least, ask additional questions in order to secure the information intended. And occasionally a vague question may lead the respondent in a direction that pulls the entire interaction off a constructive course.

Making questions more focused in order to obtain specific and concrete information can be achieved in several ways. First, by considering carefully the purpose of your question, determining the information dimensions you wish to tap, and then selecting the most appropriate format, you will greatly improve your ability to gather specific, concrete information. Second, particular wording or phrasing considerations can also help you to increase question focus. The latter focusing techniques, including pre-suppositive and prefacing statements, can be used to affect any response whether the question is open, closed, single, direct, or indirect.

Presupposition

Presupposition refers to the question's content that conveys to respondents an expecta-tion of what they should know. Presupposition exists in questions along a continuum from little to great. The following questions contain a high level of presupposition:

- What is the greatest concern you have about having Erin in your classroom?
- What behavior management system are you using with Evan?

In the first question, the presupposition is that the respondent has concerns and that these are prioritized. In the second, it is that the respondent is using a behavior manage-ment system with the student.

The following questions have little presupposition:

- Do you know whether Pat is returning?
- How did you do that?

Presupposition is a potent tool for focusing interactions. Especially when used in an open question, it is a means of embedding a particular topic to which you want a response targeted. It thus enables you to query in a way that maximizes the likelihood you will receive elaborated, accurate information that is concrete and specific. To illustrate, consider the following versions of the same basic question that you might ask parents about their satisfaction with their child's current educational program:

- Are you satisfied with your child's program this year?
- Are you satisfied with the progress your child has made in her program this year?
- What aspects of your child's program have you been most satisfied with this year? What aspects have caused you the most concern?

In the first version of the question, little presupposition is contained in the question. If you use this question form, there is a significant chance that the parents will give a yes or no answer and that they will not explain what their specific reactions to the program have been. In the second version, a greater degree of presupposition is included by making the assumption that the student has made progress, but since the question is closed, the response may be similar to that for the first. The third question contains a high level of presupposition; it is assumed that the parents have identified strengths and weaknesses of the program and that some of these are more important to them than others. Further, since their format is open, these questions are likely to enable the parents to discuss in more detail their response to the program.

Prefatory Statements

Well-phrased questions are the heart of effective question asking, but sometimes phrasing questions well includes structuring the statements that preface them to specifically establish the context for them (Wolf, 1979). Several types of statements you might use during an interaction to respond to others (e.g., those that describe, advise) were presented in Chapter 6. Here we are concerned with statements you may use when you want to ask a question and must first literally set it up. You are establishing parameters for the question and the response, sometimes by raising possible answers, sometimes by reminding the other person of previously discussed issues, sometimes by cuing the other that you are going to change the subject. The statements you use to accomplish this are called *prefatory statements.*

Each of the following questions is preceded by a prefatory statement. What purpose does each accomplish?

- We've considered an immediate program change for Tim as well as several interventions that might eliminate the need for the change. At this point, what strategy do you think would be best for Tim?
- Yesterday you mentioned that the adaptation to Maria's communication board was not working. I wanted to get back to you about that. What seems to be the problem?
- We've been talking about finding ways for teachers to be released to attend team meetings. I am also concerned about the scheduling difficulties of arranging for the occupational therapist to be here. What are our options for adjusting the OT's schedule to match the team's?

In the first two examples the prefatory statement focuses the respondent's attention on specific aspects of the topic the person asking the question wants addressed. In the final example, it also signals the person about a change in topic. The result is that the respondent may be more prepared to participate in the interaction.

In addition to the general prefacing statements just illustrated, two specific types may sometimes be appropriate during your interactions—*exemplar* and *continuum.* In an exemplar, you phrase a prefatory statement that provides examples of the types of answers that you might be seeking. For example, in the following segment of the interaction, an administrator set up options in her prefatory statement:

- We've agreed that we'd like to have a series of meetings with teachers to clarify how we could be more supportive of mainstreamed students. There are quite a few options for doing this. We could use the upcoming institute day, or ask the superintendent for an extra day at the beginning of the next school year. Another option would be to discuss this at the staff meeting. I'm sure there are others. What ways do you think would be best for holding these meetings?

The examples of alternatives for conducting the meetings help the others to think about options. And yet the phrasing of the question clearly conveys that the administrator has not already selected any of the options named.

The other type of prefatory statement, *continuum,* is similar to an exemplar but is used when feasible responses tend to fall along a range. For example, you might use a continuum prefatory statement to raise options for reward or punishment systems to employ with a student, to describe potential levels of staff involvement in decision making on a special services team, or to raise programming options that are progressively more restrictive. The following interaction segment illustrates a continuum prefatory statement:

- Through the years, Marvin's teachers have used a wide variety of behavior management techniques with him. Some have preferred to rely almost totally on a system of rewards, others have used a combination of rewards and punishers, and still others have found that punishers are most effective. What type of behavior management system have you found most appropriate for Marvin?

In general, the statements that preface your questions become integral to them. You can use prefatory statements to raise issues you believe should be noted, but that are not being discussed. You may also implicitly give the person you are interacting with permission to address a sensitive or awkward topic by mentioning it.

SUGGESTIONS FOR EFFECTIVELY ASKING QUESTIONS

In addition to the principles for constructing effective questions given throughout this chapter, several techniques may help you to refine your own question asking skills:

Use Pauses Effectively

A key to effective question asking is pausing (Hargie, Saunders, & Dickson, 1987). Two types of pauses can facilitate question asking: The first comprises the pauses you make for a moment before you ask a question. You use these to ensure that your question is phrased and worded in order to convey exactly the message you intend. Second, you may pause after asking a question to allow the person you are questioning time to think about, phrase, and deliver a reply.

In our work in schools we find that many special service providers find this technique initially frustrating, but once they master it they find it very powerful. Perhaps you know that you have a tendency to keep talking if someone does not respond immediately to a question you have asked. Do you follow it with another question? Do you propose a response for the person? Both these habits seriously interfere with one of the primary purposes of question asking, to obtain information.

Monitor Question-asking Interactions

Another strategy for becoming a successful question asker is to monitor your understanding of the relationship between how a question is asked and the type of response obtained. If you begin consciously to observe others ask questions, you will increase your own skill in discriminating appropriate from inappropriate questions. Another variation of this strategy, of course, is monitoring your own question asking skill. How often do you use a closed question when your intent is to obtain an open response? In what situations do you tend to resort to vague instead of focused questions?

Ultimately, you may sometimes successfully interact in a collaborative activity even though the quality of your questions is mediocre. However, this may create other problems. For example, some people want to interact and tend to respond in great detail to even closed questions. They may do so by taking their cue about the type of response desired from the way a question is asked. Thus, in some situations you may need to be especially careful that your questions are accurate and well phrased. Otherwise, the information you receive may be simply a reflection of what you unintentionally conveyed that you wished to hear!

Make Questions Meaningful

Too many or too few questions during an interaction can seriously limit communication clarity (Benjamin, 1987). Have you ever participated in a question asking situation that sounded like this?:

> COUNSELOR: Did you try that strategy we discussed?
> TEACHER: Yes.
> COUNSELOR: Did it work?
> TEACHER: Yes.
> COUNSELOR: Are you satisfied with how things are going now?
> TEACHER: Not really.
> COUNSELOR: Why? Is it still her behavior?
> TEACHER: Yes.

You get the sense that a verbal ping pong match is occurring! How could you combine prefatory statements and different question formats to improve this interaction?

At the other end of the continuum, asking too few questions is just as inappropriate. Consider this exchange:

> PSYCHOLOGIST: Tell me what you're concerned about with Miguel.
> TEACHER: He has a poor attitude toward school.
> PSYCHOLOGIST: Clarify that, please.
> TEACHER: He is often late, he seldom completes assignments, and he doesn't respond to rewards.
> PSYCHOLOGIST: And you've tried the contract system we discussed.
> TEACHER: Yes. It was effective for awhile, but then Miguel lost interest.
> PSYCHOLOGIST: Explain what you think happened.

With no questions but many commands and other statements the interaction becomes directive, and the sense of parity and mutual participation are seriously undermined. Furthermore, you become aware that emergent characteristics in a collaborative relationship (e.g., trust, respect) are not nurtured using this approach to interactions.

CONDUCTING INTERVIEWS

When we discuss the topic of question asking with students and field-based profession-als, they frequently assume that questions are used primarily as an interviewing tech-nique. Although we hope that this chapter has illustrated for you the tremendous range of uses for questions, it is true that interviewing provides an opportunity for you to focus your attention on your question asking skills. We stress interviewing, therefore, as an application for illustrating the use of question asking.

An interview is an interaction process with multiple purposes. In school-based professional interactions, a primary purpose is for one party to obtain information from the other. Interviews can be thought of as occurring in steps or stages (Westhead, 1978): First, you prepare for an interview by generating appropriate questions and arranging the setting so that it is as comfortable as possible. Second, you introduce the interview by stating its purpose and ensuring that the persons being interviewed are comfortable. Next, you ask the substantive questions of concern, and then you close the interview by reviewing the information collected, checking its accuracy, and stating the actions, if any, to be taken later. Finally, after the interview, you carry out responsibilities you agreed to during the interview. The success of an interview requires knowledge about the context and process of interviews and skillful use of various verbal statements, as well as skillful question asking. And so to assist you to use interviews effectively as a specialized process in your collaborative activities, you should consider these suggestions.

Prior to the Interview

Have you ever attempted to interview a teacher about a student's progress while standing in the classroom doorway so that the teacher can "keep an eye on" the students? Perhaps the teacher was repeatedly distracted by student misbehavior. You were probably inter-rupted several times as students sought the teacher's assistance. And both you and the teacher may have been uncomfortable because you did not have a place to put your notes and materials. Neither of you may have been particularly satisfied with the outcomes of such an interview.

The goal of your activities prior to an interview should be to create an interaction situation that is conducive to effective communication. To accomplish this, you should arrange an appropriate setting for the interview, prepare yourself for the interview, and assist the person with whom you will interact to prepare.

Arranging the Setting
The physical characteristics of the interview setting will have a significant impact on the psychological comfort of the person being interviewed and thus on the quality of the information shared. Figure 7.1 summarizes a wide range of factors to consider if the setting is to be optimum. The items collectively address privacy, comfort, and equality of status. Although you may not be able to produce all of the checklist conditions in your school setting, you should strive to maximize privacy, comfort, and equality of status.

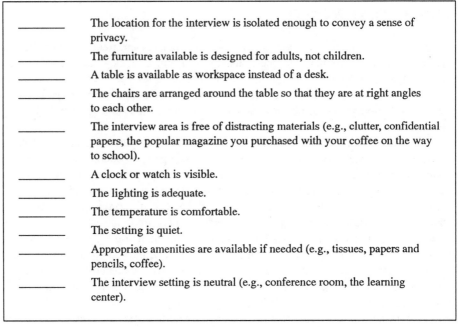

_____	The location for the interview is isolated enough to convey a sense of privacy.
_____	The furniture available is designed for adults, not children.
_____	A table is available as workspace instead of a desk.
_____	The chairs are arranged around the table so that they are at right angles to each other.
_____	The interview area is free of distracting materials (e.g., clutter, confidential papers, the popular magazine you purchased with your coffee on the way to school).
_____	A clock or watch is visible.
_____	The lighting is adequate.
_____	The temperature is comfortable.
_____	The setting is quiet.
_____	Appropriate amenities are available if needed (e.g., tissues, papers and pencils, coffee).
_____	The interview setting is neutral (e.g., conference room, the learning center).

Figure 7.1.   Checklist for Interview Settings

Preparing Yourself

You will obtain more information in a more efficient manner if you prepare yourself carefully for the interview (Horowitz & Kimpel, 1988). This requires two distinct tasks: First, prepare the questions you plan to ask. For an informal interview, this may be a matter of jotting a few notes or simply gathering your thoughts prior to the interview. For more formal interviews, you may choose to write out the questions to be used and the order in which they will be asked. Second, anticipate how your interviewee will react to the questions. Consider the topic from that person's perspective. Is it sensitive or emotion laden? Might the person be confused by your questions? What areas might need clarification? How will you respond to the interviewee's reactions?

Assisting the Other Person(s) to Prepare

Too often, interviews are unsuccessful because the person being interviewed was surprised by certain questions and became suspicious of the interviewer's motives, or was simply unprepared to address the topic the interviewer had planned. When you function in the interviewing role, you can avoid these problems by sharing information in advance with the person you will interview. Specifically, you should let the person know in advance that you need to conduct an interview. This seems like an obvious and necessary courtesy when considering parents or perhaps administrators but is frequently overlooked when the person is a colleague with an office or classroom down the hall. In addition, you should clarify with the other person the topic for the interview. With a colleague, a general comment about the topic may be sufficient. With parents, others outside the immediate school setting, or sometimes with colleagues, it may be beneficial to provide a specific set of questions you plan to ask as well as a list of the topics or a summary of the information that may be discussed.

During the Interview

Once you are seated face-to-face with the person you are interviewing, what should you do to ensure that the interview accomplishes your goals? Answering that question involves examining each phase of an interview separately.

The Introduction

The purpose of the introduction to any interview is to establish the ground rules for the interview and put both the person being interviewed and yourself at ease. The introduction includes completing these tasks:

1. Spend a short period of time chatting to establish a relaxed atmosphere.
2. State the purpose of the interview.
3. Indicate how much time should be needed for the interview. This assists you and the other person to keep to a schedule as needed.
4. Thank the other person for their time and effort.
5. If you plan to take notes or record the interview, explain what you plan to do and, particularly with recording, obtain permission. You may find that in most cases, notes are a more expedient recording option since tapes have to be reviewed, a time-consuming task. However, you may also have to learn to be comfortable with the additional time it takes to jot notes while interacting with another.

The Body

The substantive part of the interview commences once the introduction has been completed. During this stage, you will rely heavily on the skills discussed in this chapter and the last for seeking and gathering information. In addition, these interviewing suggestions (Brinkley, 1989) may be helpful:

1. Carefully order your questions and statements. Usually, ordering means focusing on low-inference information in the overt domain early in the interview and minimizing or leaving until later the high-inference observations and discussion of content in the covert domain. For example, you probably should ask a colleague about events that have happened in the classroom setting early during the interview, delaying discussion about the affective components until later.
2. Cluster your questions and statements by topic. Clustering assists the logical flow of information during the interview. For example, you may find it best to group all discussion pertaining to a student's academic functioning together and likewise to cluster discussion about social skills.
3. Use silence and minimal encouragers. The more you talk during an interview, the less likely it is that you will achieve the purpose of it.
4. Monitor time. Once time limits have been established, try to adhere to them, even if it means needing to schedule an additional interview session. This is a matter

of courtesy; colleagues, parents, and others have other obligations, and you will want to be sensitive to their needs to meet those obligations.

The Close

The closing of an interview should provide an opportunity to summarize what has occurred during the rest of the interview and to conclude the interview in a manner that leaves a sense of closure for all participants. These are suggestions for closing your interviews:

1. Review the major topics. Highlight all perspectives discussed. Your summary should be an accurate description of the interview.
2. Outline any plans that were made during the interview. This is an opportunity to clarify who has agreed to do what after the interview has concluded. You may find that it is preferable to specifically write this information so that no confusion occurs at a later point in time.
3. Set a time to follow up on any actions taken. Follow-up may occur in subsequent face-to-face interactions, by telephone, or through correspondence.
4. Ask whether any additional topics should be addressed. If the other person introduces a new topic and time is becoming an issue, you may decide to schedule an additional interview. You should clearly convey to the other person that the only reason for delaying discussion is the time factor. If you are perceived as avoiding the topic, you will sabotage the quality of the interview atmosphere.
5. Indicate what you will do with the information obtained. If you have taken notes, you might offer to duplicate them for the other person. Clarify whether the information should be shared with others.
6. Express appreciation for the person's time and effort.

After the Interview

How much follow-up occurs after an interview depends on the purpose for the interview. Of course, if you agreed to provide materials, complete a task, or contact another resource person during the interview, you will fulfill these responsibilities. If you suggested sharing the notes or tape of the interview with the other person, you should do so as soon as possible.

The single most critical element for you to consider after an interview is confidentiality. Unless you have clarified with the interviewee that the information conveyed during the interview will be shared with others, you should make every effort to protect the confidentiality of the information, even if it seems innocuous to you. For example, sometimes special service providers share with other teachers the success that a particular teacher is having with an instructional technique. Although that seems harmless and perhaps flattering, it could cause problems: The teacher who has been used as an example may wonder why the other techniques she is using are not being praised, she may be annoyed at being used as an example, and other teachers may feel some resentment because of the attention to the teacher. The point to be made is this: Assume that information shared during an interview is confidential. If you are not sure about the information, check with the other person before repeating it so that you do not violate a confidence and thus damage the quality of your working relationship.

Final Thoughts on Interviewing

Our description of techniques for interviewing describes the process as it should occur in ideal conditions. Admittedly, you may find that you have to interview parents or colleagues when insufficient time is allocated, no private space is available, or your respondent is uncooperative or uncommunicative. In such situations, our advice is to assess the situation and adjust two factors: (1) your expectations for what you will be able to accomplish during the interaction and (2) the extent to which you attempt to follow all the recommendations we have offered. For example, if you are interviewing a parent who becomes angry, it may be nonproductive to summarize points and propose follow-up strategies. An alternative would be to telephone the parent at a later time and using the interaction skills you have been learning, propose the follow-up you prefer. Similarly, if only 10 minutes is available for an interview, you probably should make the judgment to dispense with introductory comments (except purpose). Being able to assess interaction situations and adapt the skills and techniques you possess is an indicator of a high degree of interaction competence.

SUMMARY

Question asking is the primary means through which you seek information during collaborative activities. Three key characteristics of questions are purpose (seek, clarify, or provide information), format (open/closed, single/multiple, direct/indirect), and concreteness. Questions are often surrounded by statements or words that are not directly part of the question, but serve to clarify or facilitate questions. One type of such supportive words or statements is prefatory statements, including exemplars and continua. Questions are sometimes used within the process of interviewing. Care should be taken prior to, during, and after interviews to ensure that appropriate information is sought, clarified, and acted upon.

ACTIVITIES AND ASSIGNMENTS

1. To practice recognizing the characteristics of questions, set up a game of question tag. One person begins by asking a question and then calls the name of a classmate. That person must make the question more specific by varying one (and only one) characteristic. If correct, that person stays in the game and calls on another to respond to the question, again changing it by one dimension. If incorrect, he or she is "out." To make the game more difficult, expand the number of question dimensions each person must change or specify the dimension in which the changing characteristic must lie.

2. Listen to a professional interviewer on radio or television. Analyze the questions the person asks according to the information outlined in this chapter. How would you rate the quality of the interviewer's question asking skill? How is the situation in which an interviewer asks

questions different from the situations in which you ask questions? What impact might this have on the answers respondents give? The value of this exercise derives from studying the interviewer, not the interviewee, because of the differences in responses likely to occur between interviews in media and day-to-day situations.

3. Question asking is a sophisticated skill that requires attention and considerable practice, but attending to all its dimensions simultaneously can lead to frustration and a sense of being tongue tied. An alternative is this: Select one or two of the question characteristics based on a self-assessment of your skill needs. Then practice asking questions that focus on those dimensions. Once those are mastered, select another, and then another until attending to the way in which you phrase questions becomes an automatic part of your communication. Ask a classmate to assist you in assessing your question asking skill.

4. Set up an informal role play with your classmates. Work in triads with one person facilitating the interaction by asking questions, one person responding to the questions, and one person functioning as the observer. Choose a topic of conversation that is of concern or interest to your group. Role play for five minutes. Then stop for feedback from the observer regarding the different question dimensions used by the speaker as well as the level of specificity in the questions. As time allows, rotate roles. Simplify the exercise at first by agreeing to focus on one or two question dimensions and adding more later.

5. Audiotape yourself during a collaborative activity in your school setting. Write down each question that was asked, highlighting those that you asked. Classify each of your questions for purpose and characteristics as well as those of the others. A variation of this activity is to ask the other persons to listen to the tape with you and discuss your questions and why they elicited particular responses. Then exchange tapes with a classmate and repeat the analysis. Compare your results and resolve any discrepancies.

6. What could you do to remind yourself during an interaction to use appropriate question asking skills? Develop a plan for improving your skills. If possible, involve a colleague who might be able to provide feedback.

7. Recall an interview in which you were present, but not the facilitator. To what extent were the tasks and activities for interviewing carried out? What recommendations would you now make to the person who facilitated that interview.

RELATED READINGS

Benjamin, A. (1987). *The helping interview with case illustrations.* Boston, MA: Houghton-Mifflin.

Bogdan, R. C., & Bicklen, S. K. (1982). *Qualitative research for education: An introduction to theory and methods.* Boston: Allyn & Bacon.

Bradburn, N. M., & Sudman, S. (1979). *Improving interview method and questionnaire design: Response effective to threatening questions in survey research.* San Francisco: Jossey-Bass.

Macan, T. H., & Dipboye, R. L. (1988). The effects of interviewers' initial impressions on information gathering. *Organizational Behavior and Human Decision Making, 42,* 364–387.

Merriam, S. B. (1988). *Case study research in education: A qualitative approach.* San Francisco: Jossey-Bass.

Molyneaux, D., & Lane, V. W. (1982). *Effective interviewing: Techniques and analysis.* Boston: Allyn & Bacon.

CHAPTER 8

Resolving Conflict

Keeping Perspective

Chapter 8 considers the interaction process of resolving conflict. As you read this chapter, you might consider it a very highly specialized version of problem solving that may be needed during an interaction. The statement and question skills you learned in Chapters 6 and 7 are the means through which you carry out conflict resolution strategies.

Learner Objectives

1. To define the term *conflict*.
2. To explain why you should expect to encounter conflict in your professional role.
3. To describe three major causes of conflict.
4. To explain factors in the school setting that may influence the amount and degree of conflict that occurs.
5. To explain the five styles that special service providers typically use during interactions in which conflict occurs.
6. To describe your conflict management style.
7. To outline and use three types of strategies for resolving conflict in collaborative interactions.

Have you ever experienced a situation similar to any of these?

> You have just completed an inventory of your curricular materials and supplies when you receive a memo that details an entirely different accounting procedure you are to use. You telephone your supervisor and comment that you have finished the task and do not want to do it again. Your supervisor is sympathetic but says you must.

> A "perfect" office has just become vacant. You want it. You hear that a colleague has also requested it.

> The parents of a student refuse to give permission for an assessment, despite the student's failing grades. You are a member of the special service team that agrees the student should be considered for possible eligibility for special education services.

Each of these incidents and many others like them occur in schools each day. Some are relatively trivial and mostly annoying to those involved. Others concern the fundamental decisions made about students' educational needs. All are examples of conflict.

UNDERSTANDING CONFLICT

Conflict has been defined by numerous authors (e.g., Wall & Nolan, 1987). Definitions generally note that conflict is any situation in which one person (or group) perceives that another person (or group) is interfering with his or her goal attainment. If you review the foregoing examples, you can easily identify the needs of the participants and the interference each may have been perceiving.

Traditionally, school professionals have disliked and avoided conflict. They were reasonably successful at doing so when school culture emphasized isolation. Now, however, it is unlikely that conflict can be avoided. The same approach that Tjosvold (1987) uses to analyze why conflict is inevitable in business settings can be applied to traditional schools to explain why this is so.

First, in the traditional school design, each individual had clearly delineated tasks to accomplish and did these without relying to any great extent on others. As we discussed in Chapter 1, this picture accurately describes special service providers, too. However, in today's schools, this isolation and delineation of individuals' tasks are outmoded. Increasingly, staff members are expected to work together in groups to accomplish unit planning, staff development, and many other tasks. As professionals spend more time working jointly, they are more likely to experience conflict. A clear example of this for special service professionals is the use of teams: When professionals from several disciplines with different frames of reference are making decisions about student needs, they are likely to differ occasionally about desired outcomes.

Second, the traditional value system of schools tended to stress downplaying emotions and keeping the school somewhat impersonal. Emerging trends, however, support schools being explicitly nurturing environments for students and staff alike, and meeting wide ranging needs of the school community is a priority. As more needs are expressed conflict is likely to emerge since meeting some individuals' needs will interfere with those of others. For example, in special service areas this may occur as professionals request smaller caseloads in order to implement innovative programs.

Finally, a third reason that conflict is increasingly a normal state of affairs in schools is because of changes occurring in leadership roles. In traditional schools, principals were considered effective when they were strongly directive in making decisions for the school. They were expected to solve any problems that arose. Now, however, participatory management approaches are preferred, and principals are viewed as facilitators who rely on staff contributions to make consensus decisions. This increased involvement in decision making by school professionals also increases the opportunities for conflicts. For example, when special services staff gather to write mission statements or outline long-term plans for program development, they often find conflict an integral part of the activity.

Because it is highly likely that you will experience conflict in your professional role, you should understand how it can be beneficial. Conflict, by itself, is neither good nor bad. It is the judgment you make about conflict that determines whether you perceive it as having positive or negative outcomes. Consider these potentially positive results from conflict:

1. Decisions made after addressing a conflict are often high in quality because of the intense effort invested in discussing perspectives and generating acceptable alternatives.
2. The professionals who implement decisions emerging from conflict are likely to have a sense of ownership of the decisions and to be committed to carrying them out.
3. Conflict typically causes professionals to sharpen their thinking about their points of view so that they can clearly communicate them to colleagues. The result is a more carefully reasoned discussion that may include a wider range of ideas and options.
4. Professionals who successfully manage conflict often develop more open, trusting relationships with one another. This facilitates their subsequent interactions.
5. The practice in effectively communicating during the stress of a conflict can make it easier to address other conflict situations.

Notice that we are not saying that conflict interactions are simple or enjoyable. But conflict does not have to be viewed as exclusively negative. If you look upon it as an opportunity, it will be one. And expanding your understanding of why conflict occurs and how it can be managed will help you to do so.

CAUSES OF CONFLICT

When you examine conflict you experience in your professional role, you may find that you can identify different reasons why conflict occurs. These can be categorized by the goals that are involved:

Conflict between Individuals with Different Goals

One major cause of conflict is any situation in which two individuals want different outcomes, but they must settle for the same outcome. For example, in a suburban school district team members and parents are disagreeing about the mission of a proposed program to integrate students with moderate disabilities into general education classes. Some school professionals believe that few students will be able to be integrated because they cannot succeed in academic settings without significant modifications. Others believe that the program should have as a goal making needed modifications, and they want all students integrated for at least half of each school day. The parents also have different opinions. Some are not in favor of integration; they prefer the current service delivery system with limited mainstreaming. Others want their children fully integrated into general education.

Each of the groups in this example wants a different outcome concerning the integration program; they have differing goals. However, when a decision is made about the program, all the groups must settle for those guidelines. Only one group's outcome goal can be attained. Other common examples of conflicts caused when individuals with different goals have to settle for the same goal are disagreements between parents and school professionals about the amount of service a student will receive and disagreements among professionals about how special education services should be arranged in their school. What additional examples of conflicts occurring for this reason have you observed in your professional role?

Conflict between Individuals with the Same Goals

The second major cause of conflict occurs when professionals each have the same goal, but they cannot all access it. School scheduling is an example of this cause of conflict: In the local high school, scheduling students with special needs is a major challenge. In the past, the master schedule has been created by first blocking in the academic courses, then the vocational and special subjects, and finally the special education classes. However, with increased integration of students, the special education teachers are finding that appropriate general education classes are not offered when their students are free to schedule options. These teachers are requesting that the scheduling of special education classes occur immediately after the academic classes and before the others. The special subject teachers argue that far more students are affected by art, music, and physical education classes, and that those classes should thus have a higher priority. The teachers of the honors classes are asking that other classes be arranged so that students who attend classes at the local university in the afternoons are not penalized.

In this example, the various parties have the same goal: receiving priority treatment in the scheduling process. Unfortunately, when one group is given priority, the others cannot have it. Some group is likely to be dissatisfied with the result of this conflict. You have probably witnessed or participated in many conflicts with this cause: When you wanted classroom space that was promised to another staff member, when only two individuals could go to a professional conference and seven requested to attend, and when a position in a preferred school opened and several individuals requested a transfer. Scarce resources often result in conflicts caused by similar, competing goals.

Conflict within Individuals

One additional cause of conflict is an internal discrepancy that you perceive among your own goals. We mention this cause of conflict for the sake of completeness, but this is an *intra*personal dilemma that does not necessarily affect others. A brief example illustrates this source of conflict: Suppose a student is to receive 60 minutes per week of direct services complemented by systematic consultation to his teacher. You know that you should not schedule the student for three such 60-minutes periods each week, but you also believe strongly that you can deliver higher-quality services that will better meet the needs of the student by doing so. You delay for several days finalizing your schedule for the year while you worry about the appropriate ethical decision to make. Internal causes of conflicts such as these are extremely common in schools where professionals are changing their roles and expectations for their services are evolving rapidly.

Internal conflict may cause unclear communication which then affects professional interactions. As you discuss the above student with the teacher, for example, you may inadvertently convey the message that you believe the student should receive direct services. If you do this while communicating that indirect services are the most appropriate, the teacher may wonder which message is the accurate one. If this same student is the topic of discussion at a special service team meeting, the internal conflict could even lead to interpersonal conflict: Although you agreed in a previous meeting that the service for the student was inappropriate, you may now vacillate about the service's appropriateness.

Factors Influencing Causes of Conflict

Understanding the causes of conflict provides a framework for identifying and managing conflict situations; however, other factors interact with these causes to affect the frequency and intensity of conflicts in your school setting. Two factors are especially important to consider: organizational variables and individual personal characteristics.

Organizational Variables

The conflict you may experience in your role is influenced significantly by the organization and administration of your school. For example, your principal's leadership style affects conflict. If the principal tends to use a laissez-faire style, you may notice that you and your colleagues often find yourselves in conflict with one another while you compete for the available resources. Without leadership to set guidelines on the distribution of resources, you monitor how others obtain resources, disagree with their allocation, and compete with one another for them.

Another critical organizational variable that affects conflict is the pattern of communication among the various components of the organization. You can observe many different types of dysfunctional communication that create conflict situations. One type occurs when similar information is not available to all affected members. For example, the school psychologists and social workers receive information that the procedures for conducting placement team meetings are changing. The special education teachers do not receive this information. At a subsequent team meeting, the special education teachers challenge the change in procedures initiated by the social worker and question whether the change is mandatory or optional. Because the communication was dysfunctional, a conflict was caused.

Another dysfunctional communication pattern that affects the likelihood of conflict occurs when information is conveyed differently by the individuals who communicate with the same staff members. You experience this when you attend a meeting with all the other members of your discipline and learn a new piece of information about how to write information on Individualized Education Plans (IEPs). A week later, you attend a meeting for all special service providers and a different set of instructions is given on the same topic. Finally, you are present at the building faculty meeting when the principal explains the change, and you hear a third version of the change. Shortly after this series of meetings, several staff members experience conflict about the correct IEP procedure. Their differences are attributable to the adequacy of information they each received about the change.

As you examine the causes of conflict you encounter in your professional role, it is important to attend to these and the many other organizational variables. Doing so enables you to look beyond the simple cause of the conflict and to comprehend and make decisions on the basis of a more sophisticated understanding of the situation.

Personal Variables

The other group of factors that may affect the causes of conflict in your school are the personal characteristics of your colleagues. Everyone uses selective perception to some degree when they listen; depending on the strength of this selectivity they may inaccurately perceive information shared. The result may be a cause of conflict that is based in either differing goals or competing goals. Both occur in the following interaction:

> A special education teacher who is meeting with the coordinator of special services has the opinion that the coordinator tends to make decisions without adequately conferring with those affected by them.
>
> TEACHER: I heard that you were planning to move my class to another location next year. What's happening?
>
> COORDINATOR: That's right. I just put a memo in the mail to you about it. Because of space limitations and the projected growth for the building, for the next year you'll be sharing space with the speech/language specialist. We'll try to arrange schedules so that you are in the room together as little as possible, and we are ordering a sound-absorbing room divider to help out. If possible we'll only have to do this for the first semester; once the addition is ready, you'll have a new classroom.
>
> TEACHER: I object to this. You're not even considering the needs of my students. They are distractible and sharing a room is going to interfere with their learning. It seems as though the least you could have done is discuss this with me before making the decision. We're going to lose at least half a year of instruction.
>
> COORDINATOR: It's the best we can do for now.
>
> TEACHER: I'm sure the parents will object to this. (Teacher thinks: I could call a parent or two and let them put pressure on the coordinator to prevent this.)

In this example, the teacher was only perceiving certain aspects of the message. Notice how the teacher's frame of reference influenced her interaction with the coordinator.

As discussed in Chapter 3, each professional's unique combination of training and experience affects their functioning in their roles. So, too, does that combination affect how they will perceive information in interactions and affect causes of conflict.

CONFLICT MANAGEMENT STYLES

The next component in learning to understand and manage conflict concerns the style you are likely to use when participating in a conflict interaction. Before you read any further, complete and score the questionnaire in the appendix at the end of this chapter. This will enable you to assess how you manage conflict and to consider your preferred style as you examine the descriptions that follow.

Figure 8.1 visually represents the common conflict management styles. Notice that the styles vary along two dimensions: cooperativeness and assertiveness. Avoidance styles have the least amount of both these characteristics; collaboration has the greatest amount of each.

Most people have a preferred conflict management style. As each style is explained, keep in mind that no style is entirely positive or negative; depending on the situations in which it is used, each has both merits and drawbacks.

Competitive Style

One style often used for addressing conflict is competitive. People who use this style tend to try to overpower the others with whom they have a conflict. Their goal tends to be "winning" the disagreement, regardless of the potential negative repercussions of their strategy. This style is often associated with the use of power.

A competitive conflict management style might be appropriate when ethical issues are at stake, or when you are certain that you are right. Occasionally you may use this style when a decision must be made, and you perceive that you have more responsibility for it than others. The disadvantages of this style relate to its inappropriate use: If you frequently compete during conflict interactions, you may find that others stop interacting with you in a meaningful way. Too much use of a competitive style can seriously damage the collaborative relationships you wish to develop.

Avoidance Style

People who prefer avoidance as a conflict management style usually try to ignore the discrepancy between their own goals and those of others. They often face a conflict by turning away. If you have ever participated in a meeting in which an issue needed to be surfaced, but everyone appeared to have tacitly agreed not to discuss it, you were experiencing an avoidance style. Notice that in this situation the conflict is not being resolved and may continue to plague the group.

In some instances, avoidance is appropriate. If a conflict is extremely serious and emotionally laden, temporary avoidance may enable the individuals involved to regain control of their emotions. Similarly, if there is not adequate time to constructively address a conflict, avoidance may be the preferred strategy. It may likewise be useful to avoid

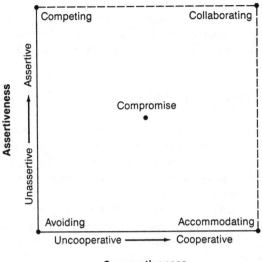

Cooperativeness

Figure 8.1. Five Conflict-handling Modes (Source: Thomas/Kilmann, *Thomas-Kilmann Conflict Mode Instrument*, Copyright 1974, Xicom, Inc., Tuxedo, New York. Reproduced with permission.)

the conflict if the issue is relatively inconsequential. However, using avoidance may create difficulties in your collaborative relationships. For example, if you and a colleague disagree on the technique that should be used to teach a student, avoiding discussing the topic can exacerbate the conflict. Avoidance is a seductive strategy because it gives the appearance that all is well; its hidden danger is that a situation may become more conflicted by inaction.

Accommodating Style

If you scored high in accommodating, your typical style is to set aside your own needs in order to ensure that others' needs are met. Your characteristic response to conflict is to "give in." Occasionally, special service providers use this style because they believe it may help to preserve positive relationships with colleagues.

An accommodating style can be beneficial when the conflict issue is relatively unimportant, or when your analysis of the causes of conflict suggests that you cannot alter the situation. Accommodating has a distinct advantage in that it brings conflict to a quick close. By accommodating you are resolving the conflict and turning your attention to other issues. The drawbacks of accommodating include the risk of feeling as though others are taking advantage of you in your professional role, the potential that the issue about which conflict is occurring is one for which you do have the correct answer, and the possible devaluing of your ideas when you quickly accommodate on an issue. Essentially, accommodation can be especially appropriate for professionals whose self-assessment demonstrates to them that they should overcome the tendency to try to "win every battle"; it is inappropriate for those who feel powerless in their professional relationships.

Compromising Style

Many school professionals use a compromising style in conflict management. They give up some of their ideas related to an issue while demanding that others do the same. The result typically is an outcome that may not exactly meet the needs of any participant but is acceptable to all. Compromise is more assertive and cooperative than avoiding but less so than collaborating.

Because compromising is a style whose strength is expedience, it is often appropriate when limited time is available to manage a conflict. It is also useful when the issue at hand is not especially problematic and when two individuals who tend to be competitive are locked in a conflict situation. And although compromise seems like an ideal style since it infers that part of each individual's goal is achieved, it, too, has drawbacks. For example, sometimes when typically competitive professionals decide to compromise, they may feel dissatisfied; later additional conflict may occur. Their resolution of an issue may be a bit like the compromise seaside vacation planned by two friends, one of whom wanted to go to the East Coast while the other wanted to go to the West Coast: They ended up in Kansas.

Collaborative Style

If you most frequently use a collaborative style to address conflict, you use high degrees of both assertiveness and cooperativeness. Collaboration in the context of conflict management is consistent with the conceptual foundation laid earlier in this text. Use of a collaborative style requires commitment to the defining elements we described, as well as to the emergent characteristics. It often includes developing a completely new alternative to the conflict situation: A collaborative response to the vacation example might be to plan a series of minivacations that take the friends on a tour of the entire perimeter of this country. Another alternative might be for the friends to decide that the vacation was not the issue at all: Both were looking for a renewing experience by the water, and so they decide to spend a week in a lakeside retreat setting only 50 miles from where they live.

Of course, we believe that collaboration is an extraordinarily critical style for special service providers. This entire book serves as an illustration of our sense of its importance. However, in conflict situations as in others, collaboration is not always the preferred approach. It is time consuming, requires that certain defining elements be in place, and can only be undertaken as professionals learn about and come to trust one another. Thus, collaboration is sometimes not even an option for resolving conflict.

By learning to monitor your conflict management style in your professional interactions you will grow in your knowledge about how you handle such situations. By knowing your preferred style, you can also learn to observe other, different styles and practice adding them to your interaction skills. Finally, by combining knowledge about what causes conflict, understanding of your response to conflict, and information about the specific strategies described below, you will have the tools needed to more successfully manage conflict interactions.

SUGGESTIONS FOR RESOLVING CONFLICT

What should you do when you are experiencing conflict in your role? Unfortunately, there is no simple formula we can give you that will lead to satisfactory solutions for all conflicts. In fact, some conflicts cannot be resolved. Instead, we can remind you of several points made in earlier chapters on interpersonal problem solving and interpersonal communication and outline additional techniques. Your skill in applying them will in large part determine your satisfaction with the outcomes and the satisfaction of the others with whom you have conflict.

Problem Solve

A constructive way to think about conflict management is to envision it as a special example of a problem-solving process. Use the specific steps outlined in Chapter 4, defining the problem as the topic of the conflict. If a conflict occurs while you are problem solving, you will, in essence, be embedding a conflict management problem-solving process within the larger problem-solving process.

Use Clear Communication

Although all the communication skills addressed in Chapters 5, 6, and 7 are useful in the context of conflict management, especially important are the skills of paraphrasing and questioning. Combined, your use of these skills will allow you to gather and clarify information needed to understand the point of view of the others with whom you have a conflict; this will assist you in constructively resolving it.

Clear communication may be the heart of effective conflict management. First, if communication among professionals is concrete and specific, some conflict may be avoided. Second, if conflict does occur, it is through clear communication that each professional's perspective can be understood and considered. Think about conflict situations in which you have participated. Have you noticed that when other participants are able to clarify their viewpoints the conflict situation is constructive, even if stressful? When the viewpoints are not clarified, the stress remains and is possibly magnified by the sense that individuals are not communicating.

Negotiate

A common conflict management technique that we have not previously addressed is negotiation. Negotiation is a process that begins with each party involved in the conflict asking for more than is reasonable to expect and then, using a series of offers and counteroffers, reaching an agreeable resolution (Rubin, 1989). An example of a principal and a special education teacher deciding on materials needed in a new classroom illustrate this strategy:

ADMINISTRATOR: What are your needs for materials for your room?
TEACHER: I've reviewed the records of my students and looked through the catalogues. I have a list here of the materials I need. Also I would like to be able to request an additional

$500 for instructional supplies once I have the opportunity to work with the students. One other item concerns equipment. I would like to have a computer in the classroom.

PRINCIPAL: (looking at the list and her notes) I'd like to be able to provide all these items, but it's just not possible within the budget. How about if I managed to obtain the top 20 prioritized items on this list and agreed that we would discuss additional resources next year?

TEACHER: That's a problem. I'm concerned that in a new classroom I'll need more than the items with the highest priority. And the computer issue is important to me.

PRINCIPAL: Perhaps we can resolve that one. There are three loaner computers in the learning center. We could locate one in your classroom; the only time you would have to share it would be when the others were in use. That shouldn't happen too often.

TEACHER: That's fine. But what about the other items?

PRINCIPAL: I simply can't promise you the amount of budget you are requesting for materials and supplies. What would be a reasonable solution?

TEACHER: What if you furnished the initial materials and I prepared a request for the Parent-Teacher Organization to assist in supplying additional materials I might need later in the year, especially computer software.

PRINCIPAL: I can do that. I would want to work with you on the proposal, though.

TEACHER: Great! Then we've agreed you'll fund the initial list of needed supplies, I'll borrow the computer, and we'll approach the PTO about additional needs.

Although you might not think of negotiation as a strategy you typically use in your professional interactions, you probably informally negotiate every day, whether it concerns the amount of time you need on the agenda at an upcoming meeting, or the role that you will play in carrying out an instructional intervention. In conflict situations, the strategies you use in such informal negotiations should be more deliberate.

Successful negotiators keep these considerations in mind:

1. Understand the your own motivation as well as that of the others involved in the conflict. Is the basis of the conflict a value difference? Is it an issue of limited resources and the stress caused by the situation? Is it a matter of differing opinions about interventions? Exploring your own underlying motives as well as determining those of others enables you to make judgments about reasonable expectations and areas for likely productive discussion.

2. Clarify the issues. This step requires the clear communication mentioned earlier. If you and the other person(s) in a conflict do not have a mutual understanding of the issues, it is unlikely that you will resolve them.

3. Set your expectations. This requires examining your ideal solution to the conflict and then tempering it with your understanding of motivations as well as other factors influencing the situation. This step is goal setting; it sets a direction for your perception of how the interaction should proceed.

4. Discuss each issue involved in the conflict. Sometimes, it is tempting to have a general discussion of all the issues related to the conflict. The result is typically unclear communication, and sometimes it is additional conflict. It is preferable to explore each part of the conflict separately, much as you were advised to do with problems in Chapter 4.

5. Make and respond to offers. This is the part of negotiation that includes give and take among participants. Perhaps you have resources that could be part of the

discussion; you offer those while others decide their value and the role they could play in a negotiated agreement. Perhaps you could agree to take over a responsibility similar to your own that is part of the conflict issues. Perhaps you could suggest a means of enlisting the support of others to create conditions that would alleviate the conflict (e.g., in a conflict about time, deciding to request from the school board an additional half-time staff member).

6. Monitor for ethics and integrity. Negotiation in conflict situations can only be successful if you work in good faith. If you withhold information or manipulate others' words, you may worsen the situation instead of improving it. At the same time, you should continue to be aware of the ethical issues involved in serving the needs of students with disabilities. Of course, violations of students' rights is never acceptable. Finally, the concept of ethics and integrity extends into the relationship you have with the others in the conflict situation. Your goal for concluding a negotiation should be to enable everyone to "save face," while at the same time resolving the dilemma.

Additional Suggestions

In addition to the strategies already suggested, keeping these points in mind may also assist you to manage conflict effectively:

1. Focus on issues, not people, whenever you experience conflict. Instead of saying, "You don't understand the impact of changing the intervention on the entire class," you might say, "The strategy we're discussing now is problematic because of its potentially negative impact on other aspects of the classroom routine." The former makes the disagreement an adversarial situation based on people; the latter acknowledges disagreement but anchors it on the proposed intervention instead of the person who proposed it.

2. To the greatest extent possible, keep the conflict focused on issues that have the potential to be agreed upon. This reminds you as well as the others that you have a common ground from which to work to manage the conflict. For example, it is often more constructive to address specific interventions or approaches than individuals' underlying beliefs about how students should receive education services. The former can be addressed; in most cases, the latter cannot.

3. Reduce the emotional component of the conflict. If the issue in conflict has raised strong emotional responses, you may find that it is not possible to proceed, and temporary avoidance is needed. However, you can also sometimes diffuse emotions by responding positively to others' negative comments, not responding to comments that might cause you to become angry, and by acknowledging the feelings that others are expressing.

4. For particularly serious conflicts in which there are far-reaching implications, you may find it is helpful to ask a third party to assist in resolving the conflict. In most places, for example, mediation is used prior to due process hearings. In mediation a neutral third party listens independently to the views of each party, tries to explain those views to the other party, and facilitates the parties' problem-solving process to manage the conflict. A less commonly used strategy is

arbitration, in which a third party listens to all perspectives and then independently reaches a decision to resolve the conflict.

5. And we would be remiss if we did not include a final strategy: the option for you to adapt to the issue or exit the situation. That is, at some point it becomes self-defeating to continue to try to address a conflict if the other person does not view the matter as an issue, or if you cannot influence the conflict situation. Resolving the matter within yourself so that you no longer fret about it may be the most viable option. If that is not possible and the issue is critical, you may choose to leave the school setting.

SUMMARY

Conflict is any situation in which people perceive that others are interfering with their ability to meet their goals. Although school professionals, including special service providers, traditionally have tended to avoid conflict, current trends are increasing adult–adult interactions and making conflict much more likely. Such conflict can be constructive and helpful. Conflict is generally caused either when two individuals want different outcomes but must settle for the same one, or when they want the same outcome, but it cannot be available to both. These causes are influenced by a wide variety of organizational and personal variables.

Most individuals have a preferred conflict management style that is competitive, avoiding, accommodating, compromising, or collaborative. Each of these has advantages and drawbacks. You should learn to use each style as appropriate in combination with specific strategies that may assist you to create constructive outcomes in conflict situations.

ACTIVITIES AND ASSIGNMENTS

1. Think about conflicts that you have experienced in your professional role. To what extent were these conflicts the result of the three causes of conflict described in the chapter? With a classmate, generate additional examples that illustrate each of the causes of conflict.

2. What factors in your professional setting influence the number and intensity of the conflicts occurring there? Is their influence positive or negative? Which of the negative factors might be amenable to change?

3. Ask a colleague to rate you on the Thomas–Kilmann Conflict Scale. Compare this rating to your self-assessment. How similar are they? What accounts for the discrepancies? Using information already presented in this text, analyze and discuss why a colleague would view you differently from how you view yourself.

4. Select a conflict situation that is common among your colleagues or class members. First, role play different styles for managing the conflict. Then discuss additional strategies for constructively addressing the conflict that are consistent with each style.

5. Special service professionals may not think of themselves as negotiators, despite the importance of negotiation in many of their activities. Describe instances in which you found yourself negotiating. Based on the information presented in this chapter, what did you do appropriately? What did you do that you would now do differently?

6. Think about what you have learned about conflict. If you could write a list of rules for making constructive use of conflicts in your professional setting, what would you include?

7. Observe two or more people who seem to be having a conflict. If asked, what advice would you give them for resolving their difference?

RELATED READINGS

Blake, R. A., & Mouton, J. S. (1984). *Solving costly organizational problems.* San Francisco: Jossey-Bass.

Cameron, K. S. (1986). Effectiveness as paradox: Consensus and conflict in conceptions of organizational effectiveness. *Management Science, 32,* 539-553.

Canary, D. J., & Spitzberg B. H. (1987). Appropriateness and effectiveness perceptions of conflict strategies. *Human Communication Research, 14,* 93-118.

Deutsch, M. (1973). *The resolution of conflict: Constructive and destructive processes.* New Haven: Yale University Press.

Druckman, D., Broome, B. J., & Korper, S. H. (1988). Value differences and conflict resolution. *Journal of Conflict Resolution, 32,* 489-510.

Fisher, R., & Ury, W. (1982). *Getting to yes: Negotiating agreement without giving in.* New York: Penguin.

Sillars, A. L., Coletti, S. B. F., Rogers, M. A., & Parry, D. (1982). Coding verbal tactics: Nonverbal and perceptual correlates of the "avoidance-distributive-integrative" distinction. *Human Communication Research, 9,* 83-95.

Tjosvold, D. (1984). Putting conflict to work. *Training and Development Journal, 42,* 61-64.

APPENDIX: THOMAS–KILMANN CONFLICT MODE INSTRUMENT[*]

Consider situations in which you find your wishes differing from those of another person. How do you usually respond to such situations? Following are several pairs of statements describing possible behavioral responses. For each pair, please circle the "A" or "B" statement that is most characteristic of your own behavior. In many cases, neither the "A" nor the "B" statement may be very typical of your behavior; but please select the response that you would be more likely to use.

1. A. There are times when I let others take responsibility for solving the problem.
   B. Rather than negotiate the things on which we disagree, I try to stress those things upon which we both agree.
2. A. I try to find a compromise solution.
   B. I attempt to deal with all of his/her and my concerns.
3. A. I am usually firm in pursuing my goals.
   B. I might try to soothe the other's feelings and preserve our relationship.
4. A. I try to find a compromise solution.

---

[*]Thomas/Kilmann, *Thomas-Kilmann Conflict Mode Instrument,* Copyright 1974, Xicom, Inc., Tuxedo, New York. Reproduced with permission.

B. I sometimes sacrifice my own wishes for the wishes of the other person.

5. A. I consistently seek the other's help in working out a solution.
   B. I try to do what is necessary to avoid useless tensions.

6. A. I try to avoid creating unpleasantness for myself.
   B. I try to win my position.

7. A. I try to postpone the issue until I have had some time to think it over.
   B. I give up some points in exchange for others.

8. A. I am usually firm in pursuing my goals.
   B. I attempt to get all concerns and issues immediately out in the open.

9. A. I feel that differences are not always worth worrying about.
   B. I make some effort to get my way.

10. A. I am firm in pursuing my goals.
    B. I try to find a compromise solution.

11. A. I attempt to get all concerns and issues immediately out in the open.
    B. I might try to soothe the other's feelings and preserve our relationship.

12. A. I sometimes avoid taking positions which would create controversy.
    B. I will let the other person have some of his/her positions if he/she lets me have some of mine.

13. A. I propose a middle ground.
    B. I press to get my points made.

14. A. I tell the other person my ideas and ask for his/hers.
    B. I try to show the other person the logic and benefits of my position.

15. A. I might try to soothe the other's feelings and preserve our relationship.
    B. I try to do what is necessary to avoid tensions.

16. A. I try not to hurt the other's feelings.
    B. I try to convince the other person of the merits of my position.

17. A. I am usually firm in pursuing my goals.
    B. I try to do what is necessary to avoid useless tensions.

18. A. If it makes other people happy, I might let them maintain their views.
    B. I will let other people have some of their positions if they let me have some of mine.

19. A. I attempt to get all concerns and issues immediately out in the open.
    B. I try to postpone the issue until I have had some time to think it over.

20. A. I attempt to immediately work through our differences.
    B. I try to find a fair combination of gains and losses for both of us.

21. A. In approaching negotiations, I try to be considerate of the other person's wishes.
    B. I always lean toward a direct discussion of the problem.

22. A. I try to find a position that is intermediate between his/hers and mine.
    B. I assert my wishes.

23. A. I am very often concerned with satisfying all our wishes.
    B. There are times when I let others take responsibility for solving the problem.

24. A. If the other's position seems very important to him/her, I would try to meet his/her wishes.
    B. I try to get the other person to settle for a compromise.

25. A. I try to show the other person the logic and benefits of my position.
    B. In approaching negotiations, I try to be considerate of the other person's wishes.
26. A. I propose a middle ground.
    B. I am nearly always concerned with satisfying all our wishes.
27. A. I sometimes avoid taking positions that would create controversy.
    B. If it makes other people happy, I might let them maintain their views.
28. A. I am usually firm in pursuing my goals.
    B. I usually seek the other's help in working out a solution.
29. A. I propose a middle ground.
    B. I feel that differences are not always worth worrying about.
30. A. I try not to hurt the other's feelings.
    B. I always share the problem with the other person so that we can work it out.

Scoring the Thomas–Kilmann Conflict Mode Instrument

Circle the letters below which you circled on each item of the questionnaire.

	Competing (forcing)	Collaborating (problem solving)	Compromising (sharing)	Avoiding (withdrawal)	Accommodating (smoothing)
1.				A	B
2.		B	A		
3.	A				B
4.			A		B
5.		A		B	
6.	B			A	
7.			B	A	
8.	A	B			
9.	B			A	
10.	A		B		
11.		A			B
12.			B	A	
13.	B		A		
14.	B	A			
15.				B	A
16.	B				A
17.	A			B	
18.			B		A
19.		A		B	
20.		A	B		
21.		B			A

	Competing (forcing)	Collaborating (problem solving)	Compromising (sharing)	Avoiding (withdrawal)	Accommodating (smoothing)
22.	B		A		
23.		A		B	
24.			B		A
25.	A				B
26.		B	A		
27.				A	B
28.	A	B			
29.			A	B	
30.		B			A

Total number of items circled in each column:

Competing   Collaborating   Compromising   Avoiding   Accommodating

In which column did you receive the highest score?
That is your preferred style for managing conflict.

CHAPTER 9

Managing Resistance

Keeping Perspective

Chapter 9 is a companion to both Chapters 8 and 10. It addresses
resistance, a difficulty in interactions that is often more subtle than
conflict and therefore more difficult to manage. Resistance often occurs
when new programs or services are implemented, and so the material
presented in this chapter also has immediate and direct relevance to the
program planning concepts that will be considered in Chapter 10.

Learner Objectives

1. To define the term *resistance*.
2. To give examples of justified resistance based on personal or
   situational variables.
3. To describe fears and concerns that may cause professional resistance.
4. To describe and provide examples of indicators of resistance.
5. To define the term *persuasion* and explain its use in managing
   resistance.
6. For each of the four theoretical approaches to persuasion, to outline
   and use two strategies for addressing resistance in your professional
   interactions.
7. To state general principles for constructively managing resistant
   interactions.

Have you ever had the sense as you were interacting with others that, although they were not obviously disagreeing with you, they certainly were not supporting your position? And perhaps you had the impression that they would undermine your ideas by inaction or subtle negative actions. If so, you may have been sensing others' resistance to your ideas.

Resistance is a complex and elusive condition that occurs in nearly every type of professional interaction, including those that occur in truly collaborative relationships. While in conflict situations the involved parties typically know the disagreement exists and can choose whether or not to resolve it, resistance may be verbalized or demonstrated in ways that could have multiple interpretations. It is thus difficult to recognize and often frustrating to address. And so part of your skill repertoire for effectively interacting with your colleagues should include an understanding of resistance and a set of strategies for addressing it.

UNDERSTANDING RESISTANCE

Resistance has been a topic of concern in many fields. In business, the management of employee resistance to technological advances and procedural modifications has been explored in attempts to improve both productivity and morale. In the helping professions, resistance has been examined in relation to individuals' receptivity to therapeutic change. And in education, resistance has been addressed in the context of teachers' reactions to innovation, including school improvement (e.g., Jwaideh, 1984) and specialized services such as consultation (e.g., Piersal & Gutkin, 1983; Rosenfield, 1985).

What all of these applications have in common is the fact that resistance is associated with change. Specifically, *resistance* most typically occurs as a response to an interpersonal change or an organizational change that has a personal impact. Karp (1984) provided a succinct but accurate characterization of resistance when he defined it as the ability to not get what is not wanted from the environment. The double negative in the definition is critical: Resistance only occurs in response to a perceived impending change. If no change exists, resistance vanishes.

The use of negatives in the resistance definition, however, should not lead to you conclude that resistance itself is undesirable. In fact, the opposite is true. Resistance is a defense mechanism that prevents us from undertaking change that is too risky for our sense of safety. Each of us will become resistant if our personal threshold of safety is reached. Additionally, resistance is sometimes the appropriate response. In some instances, it leads to an appropriate decision not to participate in an activity or change. The concern in professional relationships arises when resistance becomes a inappropriate barrier to effective interactions and needed innovation.

Think about the type of issues that contribute to resistance in these two examples:

> The social committee for a high school faculty is considering options for the annual staff gathering. The committee members have discussed the need to explore innovative options since staff have expressed dissatisfaction with previous banquets. One committee member says, "Let's spice up the entertainment we have. I know a place nearby that will give us a discounted rate on half-day white water rafting trips. We could go rafting and then have a picnic." Another committee member immediately replies, "Right. I can just see myself bouncing down the river in a raft. That can be dangerous. And if anyone got hurt it would be me."

Ms. Hill, the school psychologist, is meeting with Mr. Neal, the fifth-grade teacher. They are discussing whether it would be helpful to write a behavioral contract as an intervention strategy for Reggie, a mainstreamed student with behavior disorders who is inattentive in class and who has been swearing at the teacher and other students. As Ms. Hill explains the contract possibility, Mr. Neal comments, "You know, I don't mind having Reggie in my class. He's certainly not dumb. But I don't know about this contract idea. It's not really fair to the other kids to give Reggie special treatment. I predict I'll get parent phone calls about this." After more discussion about Reggie's needs and the merits of contracts, Mr. Neal reluctantly agrees to try the intervention.

A week later, Ms. Hill stops by Mr. Neal's classroom to check on Reggie.

"How's the contract working for Reggie?"

"Well..."

"What's going on?"

"Actually," says Mr. Neal, "I tried it for two days and it just wasn't fitting into my classroom routine. Besides, Reggie probably didn't like being singled out. We need to change it, but for now, with the holidays coming, I just don't have the time to attend to this. Let's talk after the beginning of the year."

In the first example, the resistance to river rafting is fairly straightforward; the teacher appears to be concerned about the *physical* safety of the proposed adventure. In the second example, the resistance is more difficult to discern clearly, but it still related to safety: Mr. Neal's response might be interpreted as meaning that he is concerned with his *psychological* safety. Perhaps he is unfamiliar with the contracting approach Ms. Hill proposed, and he does not want to let her know this. Perhaps he is overwhelmed by the pressures of his job (a new language arts curriculum, an overcrowded room, several students receiving special education services), and he simply cannot manage one more demand.

Given the amount and pace of change currently taking place in schools, it is not surprising to find that resistance is common. And when you reflect on the changes occurring in the education of students with disabilities and other special needs, you should conclude that resistance is likely among special service providers as well as between special service providers and general education staff. The fact that many of the changes taking place in schools and especially in school-based special services result in increased adult–adult interactions only compounds the issue because such interactions increase the likelihood that each individuals' resistance will be known by and will affect others. For example, a teacher resistant to a new recommended instructional strategy may be able to keep that information from colleagues by using just enough of the visible parts of it to convey acceptance. However, resistance to a strategy being collaboratively implemented with the school psychologist must be known by not only the teacher, but also the psychologist and possibly others.

CAUSES OF RESISTANCE

Although many causes of resistance have been described in the professional literature (e.g., Margolis & McGettigan, 1988; Piersal & Gutkin, 1983; Waugh & Punch, 1987), they can be summarized as addressing just one critical concept: Resistance is an emotional response based on a rational or irrational fear or concern related to whatever change is proposed or occurring.

One way of examining the types of fear that may lead to resistance is to categorize them. For our discussion, they may primarily pertain to (1) the change itself, (2) the impact of the change on the person who is resistant, (3) other persons initiating, participating in, or affected by the change, or (4) homeostasis.

Concerns about the Proposed Change

One common source of resistance is professionals' and parents' objections to a proposed change because of their perceptions of the anticipated outcomes associated with it. For example, parents may be resistant to a proposal to move their children's segregated special education class into the local school; they believe that their children are receiving excellent services and should not be exposed to the problems they perceive that children with disabilities will confront in the local school.

Another example of fear related to the change itself may be the philosophy or value system some individuals associate with the change. If you are a speech and language therapist who believes strongly in the value of therapy offered in separate settings, then the plan to have you work with students primarily in classes may cause you to be resistant. Alternatively, if you believe that integrative therapy should be the standard in your field, you are likely to be resistant to a plan in which you will provide only articulation therapy in a separate clinical setting. For occupational and physical therapists a similar issue may arise concerning developmental versus functional curriculum. For general education teachers, this type of resistance may arise when considering adapting their learning materials and performance standards for students with disabilities. In all these examples, resistance is attached to a belief system that is associated with a specific change.

Concerns about the proposed change and the resultant resistance are often escalated by inadequate explanations of the change. Some individuals become resistant because they are responding to partial information. In general, the more ambiguity there is in explanations of change the more likely it is that serious resistance will result.

Concerns about the Personal Impact of the Change

According to Menlo (1982), fear about the personal impact of change is the category into which most professional resistance falls and includes the following issues:

First, some individuals faced with changing their professional functioning may be afraid of failing. They may anticipate that they do not have the skills to participate in the change, and they may perceive that they cannot acquire them. This sense of potentially diminished competence can create a tremendous fear for professionals who are used to working in isolation and deriving reinforcement from their personal sense of competence.

Another related concern is the fear related to the frustration that may occur while learning new skills and practices. Whenever professionals make meaningful changes in activities, programs, or services, they require time to adjust to the changes, become proficient, and perform differently. Because time is a luxury that simply cannot be afforded in many schools, professionals often are expected to assimilate change rapidly and immediately function effectively. This understandably leads to feelings of frustration because too many expectations are being placed on professionals without the resources to learn about them and carry them all out. This example is an obviously rational objection to change. Without accommodations, this may be a change professionals should refuse to make.

One other example of fear about change that relates to personal outcomes concerns losing autonomy. School professionals are accustomed to completing their job responsibilities with a great deal of autonomy. They generally have to rely on their own judgments to carry out their roles effectively. When a change is proposed, particularly one that appears to threaten this autonomy, fear may result for professionals who are used to working in isolation. Resistance is a logical outcome.

Concerns about Others Involved in the Change

The third category of concerns that may lead to resistance focuses on the other individuals participating in the change. First, concern may be directed at the person initiating the change. Have you ever decided before hearing about a new strategy, service, or program that you probably did not want to participate just because you were dissatisfied with former interactions with the person whose idea it is? Perhaps you did not respect that individual. Perhaps you experienced a great deal of miscommunication. Perhaps you and the other person have discrepant personal styles. Your resistance to the idea may stem directly from your feelings about the person. It should be noted that this is another example of resistance that may have a strongly rational basis. And again, an informed decision may be to refuse to participate.

The second major type of concern subsumed in this category is the threat of change in your relationships with others. If you participate in a change, it may have an affect on how other staff members view you and affect your resulting status with them. For example, a newly hired special education teacher at the secondary level is asked by the special education director to begin developing a plan with the basic skills teachers to spend two class periods per day coteaching in social studies and science. The basic skills teachers are opposed to the coteaching idea, and the committee they were supposed to have formed to work on the project has only met once. If you were the special education teacher, how would you respond? One approach would be to support the concept and develop the program alone, hoping to positively influence colleagues in the process. Another would be to let the basic skills teachers know about the request and then to collaborate with them to avoid meeting it. Even if this were not appropriate, the latter option might appeal to the special education teacher if he or she feels unaccepted by the other teachers and has concerns about how they would respond if the program were developed. This type of situation clearly has many alternative solutions. The point here is that the relationship issue may supersede others and lead to resistance.

Homeostasis

Homeostasis refers to the tendency of some individuals and systems to prefer sameness to change. Individuals often seek to achieve homeostasis by maintaining the status quo; once they become accustomed to a particular way of carrying out responsibilities, working with students, and otherwise fulfilling their professional obligations, they may be unable to consider alternative ways to do those tasks. How much homeostasis plays a part in resistance varies greatly from person to person. For example, some professionals have an idiosyncratic system for logging their work with students. When their school district proposes an alternative format, they resist simply because they do not want to change, even if the new approach seems preferable to their own. Other professionals welcome the system that makes the logging format consistent. Individuals with a high need for homeostasis are likely to fear any type of change and respond with at least some resistance.

Organizations also seek to maintain some level of homeostasis, and in doing so may encourage resistance. In some school settings, it is considered the norm to resist to *any* change, regardless of its source. We have worked in school settings in which staff members quickly stated that the schools were difficult places to initiate new programs because staff simply did not like change. Although this situation relates to individual homeostasis, it is distinguished from it because of its pervasiveness in the school's culture as a norm. In this situation the mores of the organization are stronger than the characteristics of the individuals within it. Several staff in the school may be risk takers or change agents, but their individual characteristics are overshadowed by the pervasive norm.

Any number of organizational elements can lead to such resistance, but one common culprit is leadership. If the leadership of a school has developed a reputation for initiating each new idea that is proposed without giving staff adequate time to develop and assimilate these and without long-range plans for institutionalizing the change, staff may become overwhelmed by change and consequently resistant. When this norm is operating the resistance phenomenon may be schoolwide.

INDICATORS OF RESISTANCE

In the example that began this chapter, you were asked if you had gotten "the impression" that resistance was occurring. Although that is a vague term, it is often an accurate one for assessing the presence of resistance. Every behavior that indicates resistance has alternative interpretations that appear to be rational, legitimate explanations, but that when examined closely, actually function as means of avoiding change. Thus in order to address resistance, you will need a clear picture of how resistance is likely to be manifested. The following behaviors, when they appear repeatedly and in response to requested change, are common indicators. They are the ways professionals and parents are likely to convey their fears and concerns.

Refusing to Participate

Perhaps the clearest indicator of resistance is seen when an individual says "No, thank you" to a potential change. You may have heard comments similar to these as you attempted to discuss an alternative instructional procedure with a colleague:

- I figure this is just a fad so why should I do it. By next year it'll probably be gone and we'll have something else new to replace it.
- I just can't deal with doing that right now. I have too many other responsibilities.

- I don't want to deal with this issue. There are other people to draw on. Count me out this time.

In each example, a person politely declined to participate in the change being discussed. This might be considered the most preferred indicator of resistance since it is not particularly subtle and thus gives you a clear signal that resistance exists. It is also significant because it forms the fulcrum between conflict (as discussed in Chapter 8) and resistance. If your initial response to a refusal is to advise or demand participation (even in a friendly manner), then conflict may emerge since competing goals then exist. If your initial response is to say, "Let's talk about the issues you see," then the interaction continues to be resistant because you have not imposed a competing goal on the interaction. In the subsequent conversation, if the issues are resolved the resistance is eliminated, but if they are not, resistance is confirmed.

Supporting without Substance

Like most professionals, you undoubtedly have participated in interactions in which another person nods repeatedly in response to the idea being discussed. Eventually, you may have been tempted to make an outrageous comment just to assess whether that person was processing *any* of the information. With tongue-in-cheek we refer to this as the "puppies-on-the-dashboard syndrome" as the behavior is so reminiscent of those outdated car ornaments. This may be an indicator of resistance and may even be accompanied by comments such as, "Yeah-that's great," "Okay-I see," "That makes sense," and often "Uh-huh."

When you analyze interactions in which you have sensed resistance, you may find that you have overlooked this indicator. When individuals give verbal and nonverbal cues that a spoken message is being received and agreed to, you may interpret the cues as conveying support and feel reinforced by them. Only by asking for feedback and otherwise attending to a broader range of meanings for the response can you discern the incongruity between the apparent response and the actual one.

As you monitor your interactions for this indicator of possible resistance, you will become more proficient at recognizing it. Remember that sometimes parents and colleagues will resist by using this strategy because they perceive it is easier initially to agree overtly with your ideas and subsequently not act upon them than it is to openly disagree with you and possibly initiate conflict, or at least a lengthy discussion.

Displacing Responsibility

When have you heard responses to one of your most promising ideas that are similar to these?

- The other parents are going to complain.
- I understand that the state has said this is not legal.
- The law doesn't allow it.
- Have you talked to any school board members? I heard the board is going to veto this program.

- I'm sure Mr. Carl (principal) indicated at the first faculty meeting that these adaptations are optional.
- Mrs. Frank (parent) will never permit us to do this. She has been very clear about the services she'll accept for Vivian.
- (mother) His father will object.

In each example, the person speaking refused to take responsibility for accepting or rejecting change and has placed the responsibility elsewhere, whether on policy (e.g., the law), individuals (e.g., his father), or groups (e.g., the school board). By creating a real or imagined external authority, the resistant individual attempts to present legitimate reasons to reject the change. The ultimate use of this strategy may occur when the reason given for not participating in a change is because "they won't like it," even though "they" is never identified.

Deferring until a Future Time

Repeated procrastination in implementing an intervention, scheduling a meeting, or arranging a service may also be an indication of resistance. For example, consider a series of interactions in which the occupational therapist tries to arrange a meeting with a teacher to plan classroom based activities, and the teacher responses follow a chronology like this:

September

It's a good idea, but everything is so hectic with the start of the year. Let's give it a little time and then try it.

October

It's close to the end of the grading period and parent conferences are coming up soon. Once all of that is out of the way, perhaps we can pursue this.

November

The holidays are almost here and you know how disrupted the schedule gets. Starting now would be a waste of time with all the special events coming up. Let's hang on until the beginning of the year when there's more time to make this idea work.

Notice that a resistant individual with a high level of skill in deferring participation may be able to postpone change indefinitely, perhaps even for an entire school year. In school districts with high rates of staff turnover or staff reassignment, resistant individuals may be able to avoid unwanted change completely.

We hasten to clarify that we are not ascribing every schedule delay to resistance. The vagaries of events beyond professionals' control may be the culprit for delays in many instances. However, a pattern of such delays is often an indicator of resistance.

Relying on Past Practice

Just as Tevya reveled in tradition in the musical *Fiddler on the Roof*, others with whom you interact may similarly enlist this reason for not participating in change. Expressions that convey reliance on tradition include these:

- We've always done it this way.
- If it's not broken, don't fix it.
- The way it is has always been good enough for us.
- We can't just rush into this type of intervention. It's too different from what we're used to.

This indicator of resistance is often attributed to midcareer or senior colleagues who are not keeping pace with the evolution of the field. Although some individuals may fit this characterization, it is inappropriate to indiscriminately apply this generalization. Many individuals with considerable experience are very supportive of new ideas and seldom resist in a way that is not constructive. At the same time, some inexperienced professionals rely on variations of tradition in their resistant interactions. For example, sometimes special service providers who have been in the field for many years welcome opportunities to implement innovative programs as a means for updating their skills and revitalizing their perspective. On the other hand, sometimes professionals just entering the field claim that their professional preparation did not train them for an alternative program approaches or strategies.

As you interact with colleagues and parents, look for indicators of resistance. If you carefully assess these, you will be better prepared to understand and respond, either by acknowledging the appropriateness of the resistance, or using strategies such as those outlined later in this chapter.

ASSESSING WHETHER TO ADDRESS RESISTANCE

The next consideration when you perceive resistance is occurring is to decide whether or not it should be addressed. To do that, you should examine the extent to which the resistance is appropriate, whether the effort to address the resistance is warranted, and others' commitment to change.

Determine Whether Resistance Is an Appropriate Response

The concept that resistance is sometimes appropriate has already been mentioned, and overall you may have noticed that this chapter on resistance does not necessarily focus on overcoming it, that is, somehow making it go away. Instead, as you approach resistant interactions, you should first consider the situation from the other individual's point of view. If the change will place too great a burden on the person, the resistance may be a positive reaction and should not be addressed. This notion has particular relevance when the change in programmatic, as will be addressed in Chapter 10. In general, if you remember that addressing resistance should have as a goal respecting it, exploring it, and potentially (but not invariably) reducing it, you will be more effective in your professional relationships. Although our examples tend to make others the resistant people, keep in mind a point made at the beginning of this chapter: We *all* resist, given the right circumstances.

Assess Whether Addressing Resistance Is Warranted

Another consideration when deciding whether to respond to a resistant situation is the appropriateness of attempting to address it. The same questions presented in Chapter 4 for deciding whether to problem solve are applicable for resistance as well. In some instances, the best response to resistance may be no response at all. For example, if a colleague is planning to leave her job at the end of the year, your efforts to address her resistance to a new therapeutic technique may not be worth the effort. The same could be said for others who are transferring to other schools or retiring. Other situations that may not warrant addressing resistance are those in which administrative support is lacking, contextual variables (such as a lack of resources) make the proposed strategy unfeasible, or you cannot make the commitment needed to pursue addressing it.

Consider the Extent of Others' Commitment to Change

Understanding the likelihood that others will change can assist you to gauge your own commitment to change. Individuals are more likely to participate in a change if they feel they have a moderate or low level of positive or negative feeling about the nature of the change. They are less likely to change if they have strong feelings about it. The implication of this is that your proposals for change are less likely to be successful if you offer them when emotions are strong. A more constructive alternative would be to wait until feelings are less intense and then reevaluate later the appropriateness of using the strategies mentioned later in this chapter.

PERSUASION AND RESISTANCE

If you decide that a resistant situation should be addressed, one major strategy that you may use to have a positive influence is *persuasion*. Persuasion is your ability to convince another person to agree to your perception or plan regarding an issue or idea. For example, you may be faced with the task of convincing a resistant colleague that change in the daily schedule is necessary and appropriate. Similarly, you may attempt to convince a parent that the educational services proposed by the team are in the best interests of the child.

Persuasion has been carefully studied in the context of advertising and business communication, and many ideas about how to persuade another professional or parent can be gleaned from this work. In addition, fields such as counseling have contributed information on how professionals influence others. Examples of the areas of inquiry from these disciplines include the effect of gender, message content, and situational variables on the outcome of persuasive efforts. If you are especially interested in this topic, we recommend you explore the wealth of information available that can only be sampled in this chapter.

Personal Qualities

When you think about yourself in relation to your colleagues, how do you think they perceive you? The answer to that question could be critical in understanding the extent to which you are able to persuade others. The personal qualities that you have and that others perceive you have will in part determine whether you can convince others of your point of view. Kenton (1989) refers to these qualities as credibility and includes those presented in Table 9.1.

Notice how the characteristics that contribute to persuasiveness relate to collaboration. Each category noted in Table 9.1 may contribute to or detract from the sense of parity that exists in the professional relationship; each may also affect the emergent characteristics of trust and respect. This concept is easily illustrated with the example of status (prestige category). Having status as a valued colleague is essential for collaboration; it also establishes a base for persuasion. Conversely, being perceived as having too high a status or too low a status may negatively affect both parity in the collaborative relationship and the ability to persuade.

This same example of status can also illustrate another point: Persuasion is a complex process, often affected by subtle individual variables. Specifically, in contrast to the potentially negative impact on persuasiveness attributed to extremely high status above, the opposite may also occur. In some interaction situations, collaboration is not the goal, and individuals perceived as having very high status may easily, sometimes too easily, persuade others. One familiar situation in which this frequently occurs is a doctor–patient relationship. In schools, it may occur when teachers or other professionals give instructions to paraprofessionals.

TABLE 9.1. PERSONAL QUALITIES CONTRIBUTING TO CREDIBILITY

Quality	Examples
Goodwill and fairness	Focus on the other person Concern for the other person Unselfish
Expertise	Professionally prepared Experienced Qualified Competent Intelligent
Prestige	Rank Power Status Position
Self-presentation	Verbal ability Ability to "think on your feet" Similarity Dynamism Energy Confidence

(Adapted from Kenton, S. B. (1989). Speaker credibility in persuasive communication. Journal of Business Communication, 25(2), 143–157 Reprinted with permission.)

Persuasion Approaches for Addressing Resistance

Having positive personal persuasive qualities is only one dimension of persuasiveness. Approaches for managing resistance through persuasion are heavily influenced by many theories that describe how individuals respond when faced with an idea or activity to which they are resistant (Shelby, 1986). In the following sections, we present just a few of the major approaches for conceptualizing persuasion and the strategies that result from them.

Behavioral Approach

One major approach for examining persuasion is based in the behavioral theory that is well known to special service providers. In essence, this approach has as its premise the belief that individuals will be persuaded when they learn to associate positive attributes with the targeted idea or activity (Miller, 1980). As long as negative attributes are pronounced, resistance is likely. The individual who is persuading, then, is looking for strategies that will shape the preferred association.

This case study illustrates a learning approach to resistance management:

Mary Ellen, Judy, and Dan, the speech and language specialist, special education teacher, and special education director, respectively, are discussing the feasibility of a cotaught class for students with communication disorders. The special education teacher, who currently is the only teacher for the class, is supportive of the idea as is the director. The speech and language therapist is resistant to the idea.

DAN: I realize that it will take awhile for everyone to get used to this new coteaching arrangement. I also know that you have been looking for a position in the district, Mary Ellen, that would not require too much traveling. What I am planning to do is consider the coteaching job a full-time assignment and that's why I thought that you would enjoy it.

MARY ELLEN: Let me be sure I understand this. If I take this coteaching position, I wouldn't have any travel to other schools?

DAN: That's right.

JUDY: I'm really looking forward to the possibilities, Mary Ellen. Do you remember when we went to that conference on special education innovations, and we attended that session on coteaching. We had a great time that day brainstorming what the options would be and the speakers were so positive. When we tried the ideas out on that colors unit, it worked better than I thought it would. I enjoyed the experience we had working as a teaching team.

To persuade Mary Ellen about the cotaught class, Dan agreed to consider it a full-time assignment. He was using the straightforward behavioral technique of providing reinforcers in order to get Mary Ellen to agree to the change. Alternatively, he could have attempted to use a punisher. For example, he could have informed Mary Ellen that if she chose not to participate in the new class, she would be assigned to seven schools distributed throughout the school district and carry an extraordinarily heavy caseload. Of course, typically incentives are preferred over punishers as a strategy for persuasion.

Judy was using another behavioral principle in her attempts to persuade Mary Ellen. She was associating a positive event that Mary Ellen recalled with the proposed change, the cotaught class. Using this technique represents an effort to have coteaching become a stimulus for a positive perception. If repeated systematically and reinforced, Mary Ellen may eventually associate coteaching with positive work conditions.

The following resistance management strategies are grounded in behavioral theory:

Seeking Ways to Provide Incentives. Using the most basic notion of a behavioral approach—providing rewards—applies to persuasion, too. For special service providers, incentives could include a trading-off or reduction of workloads, as Dan suggested for Mary Ellen; for general education teachers this might involve assistance with classroom chores or the provision of a paraprofessional to assist. If you think of any situation in which you need to persuade others, you can probably identify incentives that could be offered in order to affect the outcome positively.

Considering Whether Negative Consequences Are Necessary. This sounds harsh, but in actuality is not. The most concrete example of this may be the strategy of simply withdrawing from the resistant situation, as when a special education teacher has repeatedly attempted to persuade a general education teacher to change assignments to meet a mainstreamed student's needs. Instead of providing incentives such as volunteering to work with the student in the classroom, the special education teacher might find that, within the limits of ethics, simply not offering additional help is more effective. In a short period of time the student needs may become so intrusive that the teacher turns to the special educator for assistance and becomes less resistant to accommodations. Dan could have used this type of option if he had assigned Mary Ellen to multiple schools.

Relating the Proposed Change Issue to a Positive Image. To many teachers, the word *change* is a negative stimulus; they immediately associate it with anxiety, stress, more work, and more meetings. One strategy for persuading others is to associate the change with a reduction of anxiety, work, and meetings. Obviously, this strategy is effective only to the extent that the reduction of workload can, in fact, be operationalized.

Providing Opportunities for Others to Become Familiar with the Change through Observation. This strategy is based on the assumption that if a professional observes others successfully carrying out a similar change, he or she will be better able to do it as well. For some educators, and perhaps for Mary Ellen, this may include visiting neighboring school districts with similar activities or services being offered. For others it may be just an observation period in a nearby colleague's classroom or therapeutic setting. Of course, this technique is most effective if important characteristics of the change are highlighted for the person observing and if the similarity to the person's setting is emphasized.

Consistency Approach
A second major approach for exploring persuasion as a response to resistance is derived from consistency theory. It assumes that individuals strive to have consonant cognitive structures; when they sense they are receiving information that is inconsistent with their conceptualization of a topic or issue, they seek to resolve the perceived inconsistency.

Festinger's (1957) work in the area of cognitive dissonance dominates this approach to persuasion. It suggests that when no dissonance exists in a person's cognitive structures that individual is unlikely to change. However, if a new idea is introduced that calls into question, but does not destroy, other already known information, the individual seeks to resolve the dilemma and is more likely to change. Consider the following interaction that illustrates this concept:

> Several teachers are in the lounge discussing the new program that will entail having students with moderate disabilities in the school building. Kelly and Karen are expressing concerns about the proposed program; Gene is a teacher with much experience and high status in the school.
>
> KELLY: I just don't think this is a good idea. It's not fair to those kids. They need someone to look after them. The other kids can be so cruel—I'm sure there will be problems with students picking on them.
>
> KAREN: You're right. We're just not set up to have that kind of student in this school. And I heard that we may have some of them in our classes. It's totally unfair that no one involved us in planning for this. I don't like this kind of surprise.
>
> GENE: Wait a minute. You're acting like this is more serious than it is. Do you remember when Paul attended school here? He was that student who is moderately retarded. I had him in class; he was great. And one of the best things that happened was that the other kids were unbelievably good with him. They probably learned more important lessons that year by having Paul in our class than they did from me.
>
> KAREN: But he was an exception. And why didn't anyone ask us about how this should be done?
>
> GENE: No, he wasn't. You should see what they are doing at Park Junior High where my wife teaches. They have all sorts of kids in their building. Everyone seems to be fine about it. And, by the way, there is a meeting tomorrow about this. Didn't you see the notice? If you'll go, I'll go, too.

In order to begin addressing the resistance being expressed by Kelly and Karen, Gene was challenging their thinking and thus creating dissonance. When he pointed out the inconsistencies in Kelly's statements and when he referred to his own experiences, he conveyed the message that ideas Kelly and Karen had believed to be true might not be. His next strategy would be to open subsequent discussions on the topic to influence their thinking further.

In general, three major persuasion strategies emerge from consistency theory:

Pointing Out Discrepancies in Others' Thinking that May Create Dissonance. This is the strategy that Gene was employing. He mentioned a specific positive situation familiar to Karen that did not have the negative outcomes she was predicting for the present situation. At the same time, he stressed the positive aspects of her past experience. Care must be taken in making such comments, however, so that they are not perceived as too confrontive.

Creating Discrepancies that Can Be Brought to the Attention of Resistant Individuals.
To illustrate creating discrepancies, imagine a history teacher who is resistant to the possibility of mainstreaming a student with a disability into his classroom because he

fears the student will be ostracized and will require too much teacher attention. One strategy would be to arrange an informal meeting between the history teacher and another subject area teacher who has worked with the student and who can share the positive experiences the student had in a mainstream setting.

Linking the Proposed Change with the Resolution of the Discrepancy. Persuasion involves more than simply creating dissonance; it also involves efforts to influence how the dissonance will be resolved. In the example just presented, the dissonance exists because of the history teacher's belief that the mainstreamed student cannot be successful and the other teacher's perspective that the student can be successful. To influence the history teacher to resolve the dissonance by agreeing the student could succeed, you might comment on his ability to work with other difficult students, the fact that he would be on the "cutting edge" for the district integration program and in compliance with emerging policy, and the satisfaction he would experience by working with the student. What other points would you make to establish the link between accepting the mainstreamed student and the resolution of the cognitive dissonance?

Perceptual Approach

Like a consistency approach, a perceptual approach to persuasion is grounded in the assumption that individuals' unique frames of reference affect their receptivity to change. However, in a perceptual approach, it is also stressed that individuals' frames of reference set parameters on their willingness to tolerate change (Sherif & Hovland, 1961). If the change message being conveyed falls within an individual's tolerance level, then change is possible if presented in an effective manner. Conversely, if the change is beyond that person's tolerance level, it is unlikely to be considered, regardless of the strategies used to persuade. The individual who is persuading has to determine the others' tolerance range and propose only ideas that fall within it, being aware of the fact that the information shared is not as important as how the information is perceived (Shelby, 1986).

In the next case study, practices based on this approach are highlighted:

Dr. Ramirez, the school principal, is introducing to her staff the new resource program for students with behavior disorders.

DR. RAMIREZ: You've all been talking about the new resource program for students with behavior problems that we're introducing this year. I'd like to say a few words about it before I turn the meeting over so the planning team can share the details of the program. This program marks a new step in our services for students here at Daniel High School. We're going to be able to better meet the needs of all our students by having additional staff to address discipline issues and by providing support to you as teachers. The program will be similar to the one that we began for students with learning disabilities several years ago. You'll also notice that it dovetails closely with the tutoring program. And as with those programs, we will pilot this year in some classes, work out the bugs, and then expand the program next year and the year after that. Now, let me turn this over to the team—beginning with the chair, someone you know well and have worked with for nine years now—Greg Russell. Greg?

(Greg continues the meeting. He is an integral part of the high school already, a special education teacher who is senior class advisor and the initiator of a successful innovative discipline program.)

Dr. Ramirez was relating the new program for behavior disorders to ones already well established and well received in the school. In doing so, she was hoping to reduce staff anxiety by anchoring the change in familiarity. Some of the strategies for addressing resistance supported by perceptual approaches include the following:

Relating the Change to Others' Knowledge and Experience. Keeping both the nature and the description of the proposed change within others' knowledge and experiential base is a basic strategy of a perceptual approach for persuasion. A simple illustration of this point concerns the use of technical vocabulary. If you have a strong background in behavioral approaches, you may tend to speak to others in the language of reinforcers, extinction, and punishers. If you change your language so that your message sounds more familiar to your colleagues, you may find that less resistance will occur.

Proposing Changes within the Value System of Others. This, perhaps, is one of the most powerful strategies based on a perceptual approach, and it is an extension and elaboration of the above. It is the idea that proponents of change examine the value system of the participants in the change and tailor ideas to stay within that value system. Any other approach is likely to create an unnecessarily negative reaction.

Gaining Public Commitment. One strategy for ensuring that a proposed change falls within individuals' tolerance levels is to obtain their overt commitment to the change. Once they have made such a commitment they are more likely to try to expand their own levels of tolerance for change in order to follow through on it. That is, a perceptual approach suggests that public commitment for an idea raises significantly the probability that individuals' support for it will continue through implementation.

Functional Approach

A functional approach to persuasion considers change as it relates to individuals' needs. It suggests that for individuals to be persuasive, they should identify others' needs and enable those needs to be addressed. For example, professionals in schools may have a need to feel control over their immediate work setting (e.g., classroom, caseload, schedule), a need to have their efforts on behalf of students appreciated and acknowledged, or a need for a high degree of structure in their roles. Changes, then, should be designed and presented as responsive to those needs. This approach is implemented in the following interaction:

Barb, a special education teacher, and Andrea, an occupational therapist, are talking informally in the teachers' lounge. Barb has been considering trying to have some of their shared students spend more time in the classroom.

BARB: One thing that really is starting to bother me is the way my kids stream in and out of the program all the time. I know all of you providing related services need to do your jobs, but it's getting to be impossible to run a coordinated program with kids disappearing every few minutes. With you, speech, physical therapy, social work, and reevaluations, I feel like installing a revolving door in my classroom. I'm not in control of my students anymore even though I was hired to make sure they learn.

ANDREA: I wondered how you felt about that. It can't be easy keeping track of what everyone is doing. But while you were talking I've been thinking about something that came up at our weekly therapists' meeting. It was suggested that we carry out more therapy in classrooms. Now I can see why that was said—it would drop the number of students leaving. I wonder if a different approach to my services, at least, could help you out.

In this example, Barb has clearly communicated a need for a sense of control over what is occurring with her students. Andrea has recognized it and introduced the idea of in-class services by relating it to Barb's needs. If we followed their conversation further, we might find that Andrea's suggestion was sufficiently responsive for Barb to agree to experiment with a coteaching strategy. Or we might discover that although Barb adamantly rejects coteaching, Andrea's responsiveness to her needs was powerful enough to encourage Barb to consider adapting in another way her instructional approach for students.

Generally, strategies based on a functional approach emphasize creating a sense of ownership on the part of the individuals affected by the change. Specific strategies based on a functional approach might include the following:

Involving Others Early in Planning Stages. Whether you are discussing a single intervention, a modification for a classroom, a program change, or the restructuring of an entire service delivery system, the change will be more readily accomplished if you include others in planning. Doing so enables you to be responsive to others' needs since they will provide input. It also provides the others with an opportunity to create an outcome in which they feel vested. Change thus becomes less threatening, and so the potential for resistance is decreased. As you will see in Chapter 10, this is also a critical element in program planning.

Being Sensitive to Adult Learning Preferences. As adults, certain conditions may make change easier for us. In fact, an entire area of study has evolved to address adult learning. Examples of these preferences include (1) incorporating ideas based on the life experiences of participants, (2) using novelty to introduce an idea, and (3) engaging participants in meaningful activities related to accomplishing the change. Although none of these techniques may seem strongly persuasive, each has the potential to add enough appealing character to the proposed change to make it attractive to the individuals affected by it.

Clarifying Ownership of the Task of Activity. Ownership was mentioned in the first suggestion, but the topic requires additional discussion. Whenever people are working together toward a goal, they should specify how ownership will be assigned. If change is the issue, the more that individuals feel like they have contributed to designing and implementing the change, the more likely it is that they will participate in it. Of course, a key to creating this sense of ownership is participation in the development of the change plan.

Obtaining and Using Feedback from Participants. Feedback is one type of information that participants in change can contribute. The obligation of change facilitators is to use such information in a meaningful way. For example, suppose you were working with a general education teacher on accommodations for a student with a mild disability. Before you discussed specific accommodations, you might ask what the classroom goals are, what the teacher's priorities are, and what approaches seem most suited to the class. Based on this input, the discussion of alternatives could proceed. In a second phase, the special educator and general educator should meet to discuss whether the accommodations are being successful. If the general education teacher mentions a problem, the appropriate response from the special education teacher is to explore how that feedback could be used to alter the arrangement. Counterproductive approaches would be for the special education teacher to defend the accommodation or explain how the teacher could make it more effective.

ADDITIONAL SUGGESTIONS FOR MANAGING RESISTANCE

This discussion of persuasion has arrayed a menu of approaches for addressing resistance, and it was intended to provide a framework through which you can generate others. In addition to such specific strategies, however, you may find the following broader principles helpful in responding to resistant interactions.

Look for Resistance

Lange's (1984) advice to consultants is also timely for professionals who work in any collaborative endeavor. Because resistance is common (although not inevitable) when new interventions, services, programs, and other changes are pending, you should not assume that because no obvious resistance is appearing that it is not occurring. Professionals must look for others' coping mechanisms for responding to change. As many, many others have noted, "Change is hard."

Here is another concept that may clarify the importance of seeking resistance: Resistance could be considered a healthy indicator that others are comprehending and becoming involved in whatever you are proposing. On the other hand, the absence of resistance could be an indication that others have either not understood you or not become involved enough to anticipate the impact of the change. With this in mind, you may find seeking resistance a worthwhile pursuit.

Gauge Your Response to Resistance on the Basis of Your Evaluation of a Wide Range of Factors

No single response that a colleague or parent makes should be construed as resistance. Instead, the emergence of patterns of statements and behaviors such as those outlined in this chapter may signal that resistance is occurring. Remember that your conclusion that resistance exists is a perception you have, and as such it should be checked for accuracy. The following are examples of statements that can assist you in determining the meaning of others' responses:

- I'm concerned about your silence as I'm explaining this intervention. What is your impression of the intervention?
- When I mentioned coteaching, you grimaced. What kinds of experiences have you had with coteaching?

For additional suggestions on feedback, refer to the ideas presented in Chapters 6 and 7.

Prevent Resistance If at All Possible

In some ways, you might think of this entire book as being about the prevention of resistance. In strong collaborative relationships, participants are sensitive to each others' individual goals and needs, and resistance is often a response that occurs but that can be managed satisfactorily as participants communicate effectively. The specific application here pertains to collaborative interactions in which change is the topic, as when two special education teachers are considering an alternative way to arrange their schedules, when an occupational therapist and administrator discuss the adoption of a community-based approach to services, or a psychologist and general education teacher discuss a social skills training unit. When such changes are imminent, using effective communication skills to systematically problem solve can facilitate the quick and successful resolution of resistance by clarifying the relevant issues, deciding if they should be addressed, and if so, using one of the strategies outlined in this chapter.

Stress Voluntariness When Resistance Exists in Your Interactions

Think of the last time someone told you that you *had* to complete a professional task, whether an inventory, a curriculum change, or a staff orientation program. It is likely you resisted simply because you were given no choice. Your input was not sought, much less valued. When you interact with others concerning change, you should be certain to convey clearly that choice is an option. Conveying that the proposed change is the only "right" answer devalues the contribution that the other person could make. Instead, a general principle for addressing resistance is to respect the rights of others to object to change and to encourage them to discuss their points of view. By stressing this, the individuals are able to explore whether they share commonalities that might lessen the resistance.

SUMMARY

Resistance is the ability to avoid what is not wanted from the environment. Resistance is an emotional response to change; it is based on a variety of fears professionals may have about any proposed change. Resistance may be demonstrated with any of these indicators: (1) refusing to participate, (2) supporting an idea without intending to act on the idea, (3) transferring responsibility for not participating to others, and (4) deferring participation. Four approaches to conceptualizing persuasion offer many strategies for addressing resistance: a behavioral approach, a consistency approach, a perceptual approach, and a functional approach. In general, careful application of collaboration principles greatly contributes to the constructive management of resistance.

ACTIVITIES AND ASSIGNMENTS

1. Recall a situation in which you perceived that a colleague was resisting a change. What types of fears or concerns may have been causing the resistance?

2. Review the indicators of resistance described in this chapter. Generate an example you have experienced or observed in your work setting that illustrates each one. If you think about the colleagues with whom you most frequently interact, what do you find are their characteristic patterns of resistance?

3. To assist you in recognizing indicators of resistance, create a group exercise for practice: Prepare slips of paper, each containing one of the manifestations of resistance. Distribute these. The group can then take turns so that one person discusses an issue of interest with a classmate; the classmate role plays the manifestation of resistance drawn. Other class members should analyze which indicator of resistance was being illustrated and the verbal and nonverbal ways in which it was conveyed.

4. Create a checklist of the strategies for addressing resistance you find most helpful. Analyze a change currently anticipated or occurring in your work setting. To what extent have the strategies you prioritized been employed? How could the change process be made more constructive?

5. The four approaches to persuasion presented in this chapter form a framework for positively influencing resistant interactions. Use one resistant situation as a basis to describe how a professional might use each approach to persuade the other individual about the change. Do certain approaches tend to be more valuable for specific types of resistance?

6. For each of the approaches for persuasion, generate at least two additional strategies that might assist you to prevent or minimize resistance.

7. If you suddenly found yourself in charge of an innovative program for providing services to special education students in mainstream settings, what steps would you take to minimize resistance?

RELATED READINGS

Friend, M., & Bauwens, J. (1988). Managing resistance: An essential skill for LD teachers. *Journal of Learning Disabilities, 21,* 556–561.

Fullan, M. (1985). Change processes and strategies at the local level. *Elementary School Journal, 85,* 391–420.

Gutkin, T. B., & Ajchenbaum M. (1984). Teachers' perceptions of control and preferences for consultative services. *Professional Psychology, 15,* 565–570.

Hawryluk, M. K., & Smallwood, D. L. (1986). Assessing and addressing consultee variables in school-based behavioral consultation. *School Psychology Review, 15,* 519–528.

Margolis, H., & McGettigan, J. (1988). Managing resistance to instructional modifications in mainstreamed environments. *Remedial and Special Education, 9*(4), 15–21.

Randolph, D. L., & Graun, K. (1988). Resistance to consultation: A synthesis for counselor-consultants. *Journal of Counseling and Development, 67,* 182–184.

Rosenfield, S. (1985). Teacher acceptance of behavioral principles. *Teacher Education and Special Education, 8*, 153–158.

Shelby, A. N. (1986). The theoretical bases of persuasion: A critical introduction. *Journal of Business Communication, 23*, 5–27.

CHAPTER 10

Program Planning and Implementation

Keeping Perspective

Collaboration can occur without developing a new program, but current trends in special services often assume the former will occur by accomplishing the latter. The program development ideas presented in this chapter should assist you to apply the knowledge you have about the characteristics and dilemmas of collaboration and thus to plan programs that facilitate collaboration because they are responsive to those factors. In addition, engaging in program development may, in itself, be an opportunity to establish collaborative relationships by using the interaction processes and interpersonal communication skills that have been stressed throughout this text.

Learner Objectives

1. To describe the steps in program planning and implementation.
2. To identify strategies for enlisting stakeholder support for new programs.
3. To describe a process for assessing individual and group readiness for programs that emphasize collaboration.
4. To design a plan for implementing a schoolwide program that includes professional collaboration.
5. To develop an evaluation plan for a program that emphasizes collaboration.

Many professionals who are refining their own skills for collaborating are also charged with the task of developing new programs that stress collaboration, or revitalizing existing programs to increase opportunities for professional collaboration. For example, you may have the responsibility for initiating a schoolwide peer coaching program, teacher assistance team, or an integrated therapy program. Or you may be working with general education teachers to expand a coteaching project from an informal arrangement between two teachers to a schoolwide option for service delivery to students with disabilities. Whether your focus is a large-scale, formal program that affects an entire school or district or an informal one that seemingly affects only a few colleagues and students, your efforts are most likely to be successful if you systematically address relevant program development issues.

STAGES FOR PROGRAM DEVELOPMENT

Several authors have proposed models to facilitate program development and the successful implementation of various innovations in schools. Loucks-Horsley and Hergert (1985) described a seven-stage model for school improvement, whereas Sparks, Nowakowski, Hall, Alec, and Imrick (1985) proposed a six-step model for effective staff development. Similarly, Reisberg and Wolf (1986) outlined a five-step approach for implementing school consultation programs.

The stages for program development depicted in Table 10.1 comprise the five-stage framework we recommend for school professionals. These stages reflect many of the essential concepts stressed in others' work on program development as well as our own experiences working with many professionals in tremendously diverse school settings as they have implemented collaborative programs. The stages apply both to new projects as well as those being refined and to formal as well as informal collaborative efforts.

Stage One: Establishing the Program and Its Goals

The primary purposes of this initial stage are to clarify your intent, begin to negotiate for resources, build relationships, establish a planning structure, assess the context, and set goals. Much of what you accomplish in this first stage will consist of communicating your intent while getting a "lay of the land" by determining receptivity and commitment for the program and establishing a planning structure.

Clarifying Intent
Once you have decided to undertake program development, fundamental questions are, "What do I want to see happen?" "What outcomes would be acceptable?" Having a picture of what you want the project to accomplish will enable you to identify the key stakeholders—those individuals or groups who will be most affected by your project. Stakeholders will probably include at least one administrator and some of your colleagues, students, and their parents. You may find these questions helpful for determining stakeholders:

- With whom am I going to work directly?
- With what other people or groups does that person work directly?
- Who will be influenced by my program?

TABLE 10.1.   STAGES OF PROGRAM PLANNING AND IMPLEMENTATION

Stage One: Establishing the Program and Its Goals

1.1 Clarify intent
1.2 Secure resources for planning
1.3 Build relationships
1.4 Establish a planning structure
1.5 Assess needs and set goals

Stage Two: Planning for Implementation

2.1 Identify and describe the ideal outcome
2.2 Match the context and resource
2.3 Design implementation strategies
2.4 Specify component parts
2.5 Establish timelines

Stage Three: Preparing for Implementation

3.1 Create awareness
3.2 Select implementors
3.3 Set expectations
3.4 Make logistical arrangements
3.5 Train personnel
3.6 Design an evaluation plan

Stage Four: Implementing the Program

4.1 Expand professional development activities
4.2 Carry out program activities
4.3 Evaluate the program

Stage Five: Maintaining the Program

5.1 Refine the program
5.2 Plan for and provide support

After these individuals are identified, you will want to ensure that you and they reach a shared understanding of the program intent. For example, if you are proposing to team teach with a general education teacher, you, the principal, and the teacher all need the same definition of what team teaching involves. The principal could assume that you and the other teacher are dividing responsibility for the existing curriculum and that the division of labor will provide more planning time for both of you. The teacher with whom you are planning to team teach may think the arrangement will result in reduced class size because you will divide the students and each teach some of them. On the other hand, you might be envisioning a situation where you and your colleague both teach the whole group with one person leading (e.g., lecturing or presenting) and the other supporting (e.g., providing individual assistance with note taking, writing key vocabulary on the board). Because these are three valid but different interpretations with very different implications for the participants, it is important to clarify specific meanings for everyone involved.

Another reason for developing shared meanings is to ensure a common understanding of resource needs. In the example just presented, if your team teacher's notion of coteaching is correct, you will probably need additional space. If your version of the relationship is agreed upon, you may need to reschedule some of your other students so that you and your team teacher will have some joint planning time.

Securing Resources for Planning

Program planning requires resources. The extent and type depend upon the scope and nature of the planning effort, but it is likely that some personnel, time, and space resources will be required. It may be possible to acquire planning resources without cost, or you may have to negotiate to obtain additional funds.

Remember that this is the first stage of resource negotiation. The discussion of resources at this stage is designed to solicit support for planning and developing the program, not implementing it. The individuals who hold the program resources may be more willing to commit them to a well-designed planning effort than to approve anticipated resource needs for the full implementation of a program not yet widely accepted.

Building Relationships

As you negotiate for planning resources you will accomplish another purpose, that of building a base of relationships. You make contacts, build support, and discover opposition for your program. Your goal should be to assess and solicit support from top administrators and from all other levels of stakeholders. This includes establishing relationships with teachers and, depending on the nature of the project, with parents, students, the teachers' union, the PTA, and community groups. As you begin to establish these relationships you can gather information about the context that may be helpful at later stages. For instance, you might gain answers to questions such as these:

- How will the organization be affected by the program?
- What are the norms of that organization?
- Who are the leaders? Who has authority or influence?
- Who has public relations ability?
- Who else has needed resources?
- How do others view the program?
- How does the organization react to innovation?

Establishing a Planning Structure

If your project is schoolwide or stands to affect many people, forming a planning team or task force is the next activity. Team membership that includes a representative group of stakeholders can ensure that diverse perspectives are considered and the program has a broad base of support. The optimal size of such a team is relatively small (5–12 people) with member selection based on an analysis of the role groups most likely to be affected by the project. In constructing a team you may include administrators, teachers from all subject and grade levels, special service providers, parents, students, and community members. A mix of veteran teachers, new teachers, different ethnic groups, and men and women may contribute to successful team composition. Of course, the team should be composed of those who have the needed knowledge and skills and who are likely to be able to work cooperatively.

Assess Needs and Set Goals

The final task in the initial program development stage is needs assessment and goal setting. This requires looking carefully at the project, whom it affects, and how they are affected. For example, consider the project described below that Martin, a middle school resource teacher, proposes to implement with his colleagues, Linda and Ken.

Linda and Ken both teach eighth-grade history using the district adopted text and following district curriculum guidelines. Linda has three students who receive learning strategies assistance from Martin in the resource room. Ken has two students in his class who also receive resource services. Linda and Ken each have an additional four to six students who consistently fail history unit tests and have many learning problems although they do not qualify for special education. Ken and Linda are good teachers with strong organizational and presentation skills. They are frustrated because they do not feel they are reaching their students. Some students cannot keep up, and others are bored by the slow pace of the group instruction. Many students are daydreaming and cutting class.

Martin is also frustrated because he knows that the five students from these classes who work with him in the resource room are falling further behind in content classes (e.g., history, literature), partly because they are scheduled for resource services during these classes and thus miss important instruction and miss their opportunity for earning Carnegie units. Martin believes that coteaching with the content area teachers is the preferred approach for serving these students as it allows them to derive maximum benefit from both programs. Although he would like to coteach in the regular classrooms of all resource students, Martin has decided to approach only Ken and Linda about coteaching in their classrooms and to treat their joint efforts as a pilot for possible expansion later.

An analysis of this project and the initially identified goals is shown in Table 10.2.

The foregoing example illustrates a needs assessment and goal setting process in a pilot activity involving a limited number of people. The same process can be used to set goals for larger projects or programs as well. Table 10.3 illustrates the application of this procedure for analyzing a schoolwide support team activity. In this example, an increased number of disciplinary contacts has resulted in the vice principal spending great amounts of time responding to the behavioral problems of individual students and in students spending considerable time out of their classrooms. The analysis of needs and the determination of goals led those involved to seriously consider developing a teacher support team where teachers could problem solve with colleagues on the team to develop interventions for students with behavior or learning problems.

Goal setting should derive from the assessment of needs. One of the most important questions to ask at this point is, "What are our outcome goals?" At first glance this question may seem too basic for consideration, but it is essential. A program that emphasizes intervention assistance to general education teachers, for example, may have as an outcome goal an overall reduction of referrals to special education, an increase of general education teacher skills for handling students with learning and behavior problems, or individualization of services for all students in a school setting. In a project that focuses on interpersonal collaboration among professionals for purposes other than making decisions about individual students (e.g., curriculum development team, peer coaching, teaching team), the goals may include improved morale, increased skills, or other elements that contribute to teacher empowerment. All those goals may be appro-

TABLE 10.2. SAMPLE NEEDS ANALYSIS AND GOAL SPECIFICATION FOR A LIMITED-SCOPE COTEACHING PROGRAM

Kind of Program	Curriculum and instruction
	Student integration
Who Is Affected	Resource teacher
	Two sections of eighth-grade history
	Two history teachers
	Five resource students
	Eight to 12 general education students
How They Are Affected	History Students
	Some unable to keep up
	Some repeating material
	Some tuning out and ditching classes
	Resource Students
	Isolated from peers
	Little access to class discussion
	No opportunity to earn Carnegie units
	Teachers
	Frustrated by barriers to student learning
	Unable to vary instruction for student needs
Evidence	Teacher observation of special education students' isolation
	Record of 6–8 students failing unit tests in each class
Goals	Improved student performance on unit tests
	Increased teacher knowledge of ways to modify instruction
	to meet student needs
	Opportunities for enrichment activities
	Improved student attitudes toward history
	Improved student attendance
	Learning assistance for resource students
	in general education classes
	Interest in coteaching on the part of teachers in other classes

priate, as might many others. The goals for any program need to be stated explicitly so that the expectations are clear.

Specifying outcomes of a program may also help avoid the potential for overuse of collaborative approaches when they are not appropriate, an issue that arises frequently. Teacher–teacher or team problem solving is not the appropriate strategy for all decisions school personnel must make in the performance of their professional responsibilities. And yet, some personnel in districts beginning collaborative efforts attempt to use these approaches even when administrative or supervisory intervention is indicated.

Stage Two: Planning for Implementation

The second stage of program development is systematically planning a course of action to achieve the desired program goals. This involves several tasks including identifying and describing in detail the desired program outcomes, matching context and resources,

TABLE 10.3. SAMPLE NEEDS ANALYSIS AND GOAL SPECIFICATION FOR A SCHOOL-
WIDE SUPPORT TEAM PROGRAM

Kind of Program	Social and behavioral Behavior management
Who Is Affected	All students Grades 1–6 Teachers Vice principal

How They Are Affected	Students
	   Environment affected by student behavior problems
	   Punitive response to student behavior problems
	   Absence of opportunities to learn appropriate behaviors
	   Instruction missed while in vice principal's office
	Teachers
	   Frustrated by escalating behavior problems
	   Do not know how to prevent or manage disruptive behaviors
	   Concerned about how lack of classroom management will
	      affect performance evaluation
	Vice Principal
	   Frustrated by amount of time spent on disciplinary matters
	   Inappropriately burdened by time spent on deportment
	      reports and record keeping

Evidence	Increased number of disciplinary contacts Record of increased amount of time students spending out of class

Goals	Teacher knowledge of how to work with colleagues
	   to develop interventions
	Teacher knowledge of effective strategies for preventing
	   and managing behavior problems in classrooms
	Appropriate student social skills
	Increased vice principal time spent on program development
	   and teacher support

designing implementation strategies derived from the program analysis, specifying program components, and establishing timelines.

Identifying and Describing the Ideal Outcome

Loucks-Horsley and Hergert (1985) present a planning process that has many similarities to the problem solving process described in Chapter 4. The beginning point in their model, as in problem solving, is problem identification and definition which then leads to delineation of a preferred solution. In discussing this stage of program development, the focus becomes describing the desired outcome rather than stating a problem. Many of the suggestions we offered for defining problems in Chapter 4 are useful strategies for completing this important task, including (1) developing criteria for the outcome, (2) applying criteria for the outcome, and (3) making a decision or selecting the ideal outcome. Because these were thoroughly discussed earlier they are not examined again here. You may wish to review relevant sections of Chapter 4 before considering the next two strategies recommended for this planning task: determining for whom the program is appropriate and establishing criteria for selecting participants.

Determining who will benefit directly from the program and for whom it is appropriate become central as you develop a concrete description of the ideal outcome. For example, if special education professionals are involved in serving students who are not eligible for their services or if services to special education students are altered in any way, some legal or procedural clarification will be required. Issues of state reimbursement for salaries, allocation of professional time, and due process rights may all be affected by new programs. Another reason for clarifying the appropriateness of the program for different students is that this information gives an indication of how many students will be served and thus assists in allocating appropriate amounts of teacher time and other resources. Similarly, knowing the categories of professionals for whom the program is appropriate assists in estimating the number of professionals that will be affected.

The final strategy for the planning and implementation task is determining the criteria for selecting participants. Because it is often advisable to start new programs on a small-scale pilot basis, the selection of initial participants may determine the ultimate success or failure of the effort. Teams should delineate criteria for selecting professionals who have the attitudes and skills needed to participate effectively, to work collaboratively with colleagues, and to help communicate about the pilot to others. In programs that serve students, the question also concerns establishing entry and exit criteria. Many times, general professional judgment has been the primary criterion used for students' entry into and exit from programs. Although this approach may have some intuitive appeal, the necessity of establishing parameters that can be documented seems self-apparent. Specifying these criteria will help to clarify communication about the program and serve as guidelines for ensuring that the most appropriate students are selected for participation.

Matching the Context and Resources

A new program cannot exist as an add-on to the already extensive responsibilities of school professionals. Establishing a new program or initiating a new project requires the careful assessment and allocation of appropriate resources and may necessitate securing some resources from outside sources or through internal reallocation from other programs.

Can you identify any more critical resource than time? Personnel involved in new programs or projects that emphasize collaboration often find that they are expected to work together, discuss students or other issues, experiment with various solutions, and develop a strong professional relationship, yet they are not given the noninstructional time to meet these expectations. For all school personnel, the problem of creating time for adult–adult interactions may be manageable with appropriate administrative support. For example, special service providers may be able to rearrange their schedules to accommodate necessary meeting times because their students already have another "home." The identification of noninstructional time in these professionals' schedules may be simply a matter of developing creative approaches to scheduling (e.g., grouping more students together for direct service, not seeing students one day per week; teaming with other special service personnel and general education teachers; employing teacher-certified aides). For general education teachers, the time issue is likely to be more cumbersome. Some districts have used a "floating sub" to help alleviate the problem of occasionally freeing general education teachers for collaborative interactions. Some have modified entire school schedules to provide an additional planning period, often called *collaboration time*, so that all teachers have some available time for working with colleagues. Others have focused on instructional grouping arrangements (e.g., cooperative learning and peer-tutoring groups) to provide teachers with some opportunities to meet during instructional time.

The time issue is not one that can readily be resolved to everyone's satisfaction, and lack of time will undoubtedly hamper collaborative endeavors. It is particularly difficult because the concept of giving professionals time during the day to meet with one another is a relatively new notion in education. Traditionally, teachers and other special service providers work with children, not other adults. That tradition changes in collaboration. And districts committed to creating these types of projects should use their creative energy to provide adequate time for collaboration.

The second critical resource is financial support. At least at the outset, collaborative endeavors should not be viewed as cost-saving measures. Although teachers, administrators, parents, and students become accustomed to the new programs, class size or caseloads should be kept as low as possible and funds should be devoted to staff training and opportunities for interaction. Once programs are well-established and operating successfully, it is reasonable to expect that personnel will become more efficient at collaborative interactions and may learn how to divide labor and coordinate efforts efficiently. At that point costs may decrease to the level of similar programs that do not emphasize collaboration.

The likelihood of achieving the ideal outcome you envision is influenced by the presence or absence of local resources that ultimately act as opportunities or constraints for your project. The information you collected earlier when establishing initial relationships can now contribute to your efforts to assess the context and identify the resources that will assist or impede the achievement of your goals. That is, you need to know what resources (e.g., time, money, administrative support) are available to assist you in achieving your goals.

Lewin's (1951) force field analysis may be helpful as you conduct analyses of the resources needed for your program. Lewin proposed that every situation and every proposal for change is subject to two opposing sets of forces. Facilitating forces are those that support and encourage changes and program implementation; restraining forces are those that mitigate against implementing new programs and act as obstacles to change. We suggest a variation of Lewin's approach and offer an example in Table 10.4 using the earlier example of Martin and his colleagues. In this variation we identify five categories of resources (time, space, administration, skills, and attitudes) and consider how each one may facilitate (an opportunity) the successful implementation of the program or impede (a barrier) its success.

Designing Implementation Strategies

Based on your analysis of current barriers and opportunities, you can begin to reconceptualize the previously specified ideal outcome and make decisions about the most feasible structural, material, and procedural parameters for your program. As you design the program and develop a plan for implementing it, you will be considering and selecting the implementation strategies that offer the most promise for achieving the

TABLE 10.4.   ANALYSIS OF BARRIERS AND OPPORTUNITIES IN A SAMPLE PROJECT

	Barriers	Opportunities
Time	Students are scheduled for resource services when the history classes meet Resource teachers' planning periods are at different times The teachers each have several preparations to do each day and need their planning periods The teachers are already overloaded with extra curricular activities and committee responsibilities	Resource teacher's schedule would allow for scheduling resource students during other periods Another resource teacher has some schedule flexibility and is supportive of the effort
Space	Other classes meet in classrooms during teachers' planning periods The teachers' lounge is used by 8–12 teachers each period The head of the history department uses the department office during the teachers' planning period	Resource students use resource room for study hall when no classes are scheduled
Administration	The district is experiencing severe budget restrictions Most attention is devoted to the college preparation program Resources are focused on advanced placement and gifted programs	Increasing school achievement scores is a goal Administrators are respected by teachers Administrators respect the professionalism of the teachers
Skills	Resource teacher is not familiar with the history curriculum or methods of large group instruction Neither resource teachers nor the other teachers have experience with collaborative planning The two history teachers are not knowledgeable about differences in learning styles	The history teachers have content expertise and large group management skills Both history teachers are organized lecturers Resource teachers work cooperatively with other special service personnel Resource teacher understands the assistance the five resource students need to benefit from the class
Attitudes	All teachers in the history department want to teach advanced sections Most teachers in the school are concerned with high academic standards and their students' scores on state competency tests Students in the resource program are rejected by other students Students in the school say the resource teacher is the teacher for kids with problems	The two history teachers and resource teacher agree that this project will benefit them and their students The students in these classes want to achieve The five resource students have confidence in their listening and comprehension skills when they use certain learning strategies Teachers in the school want additional training; they want to achieve excellence in teaching

ideal outcome in this context. This will require you and any established planning team to adapt the implementation model you originally envisioned so that it is appropriate for your particular setting. The importance of adapting programs, collaborative structures, and implementation strategies to the ecology of the school cannot be overemphasized because the sense of ownership and commitment that develops during the adaptation process is critical to the success of these endeavors (e.g., Berman & McLaughlin, 1978; Phillips et al., 1990).

An example of implementation strategy development may be derived from the analysis presented in Table 10.4. From the information presented, it is evident that joint planning time should be provided for the three involved teachers. Furthermore, the history teachers may have serious difficulty if they have to add the responsibilities associated with this project into their already overloaded schedules. Additionally, some adjustments need to be made to provide the resource teacher with unscheduled instructional time when the two history classes meet. The administration has severe budget restrictions that prohibit hiring additional aides or a part-time substitute teacher to provide the needed release time. Moreover, the administration has dedicated any flexible resources to advanced placement and gifted programs.

When the three teachers finished their context analysis they considered the various possibilities for securing the needed time. Their brainstorming resulted in the following list of possibilities:

1. Reschedule resource students into different groupings to free the team teaching period.
2. Have the other resource teacher teach the scheduled resource students during the team teaching period.
3. Have planning meetings before or after school.
4. Have the history teachers "trade" their coveted advanced placement classes for a reduction of extra after school responsibilities (e.g., study hall, club sponsorship).
5. Prepare a proposal for the administration demonstrating how the project will serve as staff development and increase professional collaboration.
6. Ask administrators to teach some classes to provide teachers with planning time.

After evaluating these and other alternatives the teachers developed a strategy that combined various elements and seemed likely to be successful in their setting. Based on their knowledge of the principal's high stature in the administration as well as her commitment to teacher professionalism, they decided to develop and present her with a proposal that framed this activity as a pilot project. The proposal described a collaborative teaching and staff development project that could be expanded to any combination of teachers addressing any teaching purpose (e.g., interdisciplinary teams, subject matter teams, peer coaching). The proposal enumerated the potential benefits of the project in ways that were consistent with the principal's and school's dominant values. And, wisely, it proposed feasible means for meeting the resource and logistical needs.

The principal became the champion of the project and assisted in its implementation by approving the transfer of the scheduled resource class to a different teacher and reducing the three teachers' noninstructional responsibilities to allow more opportunity for planning. Because of the principal's interest in *her* project, she also began attending the planning meetings and learned about the pragmatic issues in project development along with the teachers. As the pilot progressed and proved effective, the principal involved other administrators, the teachers' association, and parent advisory committees in determining how to provide more teachers with collaboration time so the project could be expanded. During the following year, with the support of the stakeholder groups, the school schedule was redesigned to shorten all periods by a few minutes, extend the school day slightly, and provide all school personnel with a common time for collaboration.

This example illustrates how implementation strategies can be designed to maximize their effectiveness in a particular situation. There are as many variations in strategies as there are different schools, personnel, and communities. The point is this: By considering all barriers and opportunities in context and deliberately fostering divergent thinking, you and your colleagues may develop creative strategies for turning barriers into opportunities. For example, you may contemplate a project that the literature and experts claim requires extensive teacher training and curriculum development time. The situation in your school may prohibit making any significant new demands for teacher time. Yet, your context analysis may reveal that funds are available in particular budget lines to purchase new materials (thus reducing or eliminating the need for teachers to develop new materials) and two previously scheduled inservice days can be used for teacher training time. In this circumstance, money may be more readily available than time, and you may be able to use it to reduce some of the time requirements.

Specifying Component Parts

Another important element in the implementation plan is the specification of the program's component parts. Once you or the planning team have decided upon the ideal outcome, analyzed the context, and designed implementation strategies, you will want to develop concrete and specific descriptions of such components as the types of services or activities involved or the procedures needed to support the program. Such specification provides guidance for carrying out the program and sets appropriate expectations for the individuals involved.

An example may assist in clarifying this concept: In one local district, a pilot project to provide teachers with assistance in developing interventions for their students with learning or behavior difficulties was undertaken at five elementary school sites. One of the first activities completed by the planning team was to establish these services as part of the project: individual assistance in developing strategies to improve student performance in classes, assistance in implementing alternative classroom grouping arrangements such as cooperative learning and peer tutoring groups, social worker and psychologist assistance for social skills training, arrangement of inservice training for teachers as requested, and development of supplemental materials for students. By creating this list, one of the most common sources of discomfort in new projects was eliminated: The intervention team members knew what they could and should do, and classroom teachers knew what services were available. In another district in which this was not done, the same questions are still occurring after two years of implementation. Some of the team members and the mentors they designated ask, "Okay, so exactly what do I *do* when I work with a classroom teacher?" The classroom teachers ask, "So there's a team that is supposed to help me with these kids. What kind of help am I supposed to be getting and what do *I* have to do to get it? Will I just get more advice about what I should do? Is someone going to take this student?"

It is beyond the scope of this text to evaluate the many types of specific services or activities (e.g., coteaching, peer coaching, peer collaboration) that might be undertaken as collaborative programs in schools. However, keeping in mind their outcome goals when making these decisions and developing concrete descriptions of the program components as a means of ensuring clear communication are essential in any type of program development.

Establishing Timelines
A timeline for program implementation and timelines for program components facilitate planning and effective implementation. The timelines should provide adequate time for preparation, development, implementation and evaluation. By developing timelines you help to further clarify goals and communicate realistic expectations for the program. An overly ambitious timeline causes frustration and stress, and so timelines should be sufficiently long to allow for inevitable delays and adaptations and demonstration of a program's success before expansion occurs.

Stage Three: Preparing for Implementation

Once an implementation plan is developed a number of other development tasks remain. These collectively represent a stage for detailed preparation. Completing them readies you and others for implementation.

Creating Awareness
When individuals are first confronted with the possibility of changing their practices or roles they are likely to have very self-oriented concerns: What is the new practice? What will it mean to me? What do I have to do about it? In their Concerns-Based Adoption Model (CBAM), Hall and Loucks (1978) describe the feelings school personnel experience as they learn about, plan for, use, and subsequently modify new practices. According to this model, only after the concerns of a self-oriented nature are resolved do individuals progress to other concerns about managing the new practice (How do I implement it effectively?) or about its impact on students (How is this affecting students?). The CBAM model suggests that preparing for implementation necessitates using strategies that respond to the levels of concerns of the persons to be affected by the change in practice.

Because the first level of concern is typically self-oriented, initial preparation of the affected professionals should focus on increasing their awareness and providing them with introductory information. This may involve sharing information in meetings or preparing brief written material. Some schools have used staff meetings, grade-level meetings, or small-group briefings to familiarize personnel with new programs. Vehicles for written information include school bulletins, faculty memos, fact sheets, school newspapers, and the like. Any of these various mechanisms may be used effectively to share necessary overview information, but the emphasis should be on brevity since personnel are not likely to want detailed information, procedures, or skill development in these beginning stages. They are more likely to want to know how they will be affected by the program.

This text is written about school-based special service providers and their collaborative activities with colleagues. Because these relationships occur most frequently in the context of coordinating general education and special education services, some of the unique concerns of these professionals should be mentioned.

The shifts in roles and responsibilities for professionals who participate in collaborative programs are likely to be significant and far reaching. For instance, special educators newly involved in service delivery programs that emphasize collaboration may fear that their professional positions are gradually being eliminated. Although discounting this as unlikely is simple for those who are removed from programs, the fear is a real one and should be addressed directly. Another concern is professional self-confidence: Many special service providers question whether or not they have valuable information to share with classroom teachers. They have specific expertise, but they wonder how it applies to students in the general education classroom context. A third fear relates specifically to programs that involve team teaching: Special service providers sometimes fear they will be used as classroom aides, a demeaning and inappropriate role shift for them. Other concerns special service providers may experience include these: ability to deal with the personalities of many other colleagues, lack of training in instructional strategies effective in mainstream settings, uncertainty about what to do in a new role, and concern that previous negative experiences in attempting to work collaboratively with colleagues will be repeated.

General education teachers, too, will have concerns about the implementation of programs that result in them collaborating with special service providers. For example, they may fear that others will be coming into their classrooms to tell them what to do, and teachers used to working autonomously are likely to resent this invasion of their "turf." Similarly, they may anticipate that special service providers will come into their classes to evaluate them. Other concerns include a conviction that many special service providers do not understand the complexities of general education classroom and the limitations on their time for implementing extensively individualized interventions; and fear that the dubious reward for participating in collaborative programs will be to get more students with disabilities in their classes.

Selecting Implementors

One strategy in the earlier task of describing ideal outcomes involved establishing criteria for selecting participants. Now, as you prepare to implement the program you apply those criteria to identify the personnel and students to be involved. Because the focus of this text is collaboration, and voluntariness a defining characteristic, we urge you to select implementors from among individuals who volunteer to participate. However, there are some drawbacks to completely voluntary implementation, particularly if the program is meant to have an eventual schoolwide effect. The distinction between implementors and nonimplementors in a voluntary project may lead to divisions in staff and may create dissension. Awareness of this potential, emphasis on the pilot nature of new programs, and communication of selection criteria may help to reduce this.

Setting Expectations

Whether your project is a pilot for a schoolwide program or a smaller one, such as voluntary peer coaching with one other colleague, the expectations for the effort and its participants should be clearly established and articulated. Administrators often play a key role in this. Even for projects involving only two or three staff, it is a good idea to ensure that administrators are aware of the program and share your expectations for its impact. For larger programs, formal administrative support and participation is strongly advocated.

Making Logistical Arrangements

Although earlier tasks included assessing and beginning to negotiate for needed resources and materials, securing these and arranging for their use is part of preparing for implementation. Logistical arrangements may involve arranging for and scheduling the needed training for staff, determining room and other space assignments, selecting and ordering materials and equipment, and otherwise arranging for the smooth implementation of the program.

One logistical arrangement that merits additional discussion here is developing reporting forms and record keeping procedures. When professionals become involved in programs that require them to interact with others, accountability for professional time sometimes becomes an issue. Especially in new programs in which effectiveness is just being demonstrated and credibility established, procedures for time accounting should be determined. A simple log is usually sufficient and you can create one that satisfies the need for accountability yet does not overburden you with trivial recordkeeping.

Another useful product to develop at this stage is a procedural guide. It may be rather detailed for complex programs, or it may be a brief checklist designed to provide a shorthand procedural prompt. Each program and set of participants will have their own reporting and record-keeping needs. For example, a teacher consultation program may require keeping records of the amount of teacher–teacher contact and planning, whereas a coteaching program will probably require records of both teacher–student and teacher–teacher contact. Regardless of the specifics, the need for some form of procedural guidance should not be overlooked.

Training Personnel

You should be aware, particularly if you are involved in a pilot project, that while implementors are receiving skill-based training, many others in the school or district probably still require awareness training and basic information. One important consideration for pilot programs is to plan for dissemination and expansion during subsequent semesters or years. This is mentioned now because it may have implications for training activities you develop during this stage. If the pilot implementors are to be involved in disseminating and expanding the project in the future it may be wise to incorporate the skills they will need for these activities into the training already planned for the implementation stage.

Designing an Evaluation Plan

Determining whether or not a collaborative endeavor is successful depends on the assessment of many variables, both those addressing the project's outcome and those considering the satisfaction of individuals affected by the project. Any evaluation plan should, of course, be based on the goals set for the program. Thus, depending upon the nature of the project, topics for evaluation might include systematic assessment of program effectiveness indicators such as student achievement data, the number of referrals for other services, the satisfaction of personnel with the services available, and parent and student satisfaction with the program. Eventually cost efficiency (time, financial resources, number of students served versus benefits for students, teachers, and parents) should be examined. Standard evaluation practices should be employed for evaluating a small-scale, pilot, or districtwide program.

One distinct concern arises in evaluating collaborative efforts involving special service professionals in schools, however. Because collaborative projects generally require special service providers and teachers to accept new role responsibilities, the procedures used for evaluating them should reflect those changes. A common complaint, especially among special education teachers, is that they are spending a significant amount of time interacting with other adults as consultants or resource personnel, yet they are evaluated primarily on their skills as direct service providers for handicapped students. This evaluation issue is not difficult to resolve, and attending to it promotes staff sense of program importance. In some schools this has been addressed by staff committees reviewing and revising evaluation procedures. In others where personnel evaluation procedures were not so easily modified, the addition of structured but informal feedback from peers and administrators served to resolve the concerns.

Stage Four: Implementing the Program

It is ironic that this section on implementation and the next should be the shortest in a chapter about program development. Everything that we hope to have occur at these points should have been planned for and anticipated in earlier stages. At this point the strategies designed earlier, the training that was provided, and the logistics that were arranged all come together for the smooth implementation of a well-planned program. The major tasks of this stage are training and evaluation.

Expanding Professional Development Activities

Training shifts at this stage to match the new level of concern of participants. The concerns of implementors, having progressed beyond their initially self-oriented concerns, now focus on management issues. They are probably most concerned with learning how to effectively participate in the new program and how to acquire the skills they need to be successful. Considerable attention should be paid to assisting professionals to develop positive communication skills. The majority of education professionals have been well-trained to work with children, but they may know surprisingly little about adult–adult interactions that drive collaboration.

Carrying Out Program Activities

This is the task that is left to you. Whether you have planned a formal program that requires major changes in professionals' roles and responsibilities, or whether you and a colleague or two are systematically trying a first step toward sharing a program, the benefits of the detailed efforts you have taken to prepare will become apparent as you carry out your program.

Evaluating the Program

The importance of evaluation has been discussed. At this point you should only have to implement the evaluation design that was developed in the last stage. Both formative and summative evaluation strategies should be used. The formative evaluation can be coupled with project progress monitoring strategies to assist you in obtaining valuable information during project implementation.

Stage Five: Maintaining the Program

Refining the Program

Reviewing your evaluation data should assist you and the planning team to review progress and identify both the problems and the strengths of program implementation. This review should provide indications of possible changes and identify the strengths that should not be modified. Based on these results and their interpretations, a team or steering group should be able to make recommendations for program refinement and continuation. Of course, these data could indicate that the program is not successful and that it should be terminated.

Planning for and Providing Support

Assuming that program refinements can be successfully designed and implemented, the next and final task is to plan for and support ongoing maintenance on the program. Ideally, planning for maintenance was built into every stage of the program development and implementation. It requires attention to all of the same issues reviewed throughout this chapter. Timelines, awareness, logistics, assessing the context, and all of the other tasks need to be reconsidered and possibly reexecuted if you are to maintain and expand a program. Administrative support that facilitated development at earlier stages becomes particularly critical at this point. Administrators or others with leadership skills should take responsibility for troubleshooting and helping to obtain needed resources to ensure program continuation.

SUMMARY

Whether you are planning a small-scale collaborative activity to implement with one or two colleagues or designing a pilot for a schoolwide program, if the project you are promoting involves collaboration among professionals, you are promoting change. When professionals in schools collaborate, they may challenge the traditional professional roles and relationships that have characterized that work setting. The development and implementation of a project that emphasizes collaboration can be viewed as progressing through five stages, each of which contains several tasks. In Stage One, establishing the program and its goals, the tasks include clarifying intent, securing resources for planning, building relationships, establishing a planning structure, assessing needs, and setting goals. The tasks of Stage Two, planning for implementation, include identifying the outcome, assessing the context and resources, designing implementation strategies, specifying components, and establishing timelines. Stage Three, preparing for implementation, involves creating awareness, selecting implementors, setting expectations, making logistical arrangements, training personnel, and designing an evaluation plan. Stage Four, implementing the program, includes expanding professional development activities, carrying out the program activities, and evaluating the program. Stage Five, maintaining the program, requires continued attention to all of the tasks described in the previous stages and refinement of the program design as needed.

ACTIVITIES AND ASSIGNMENTS

1. Based on your evaluation of a situation in your school or in a school with which you are familiar, describe a schoolwide project that emphasizes collaboration that you would like to see implemented. With a classmate or colleague develop a plan for implementing the program.

2. Apply the planning and implementation stages presented in this chapter to a current collaborative relationship you have with a colleague (e.g., a classmate, a team teacher, a consultee, another special service provider). Analyze the extent to which each stage was carried out and the impact this had on implementation success.

3. Meet with a classmate or colleague and describe a program that one or all of you would like to develop. Conduct an analysis of opportunities and constraints and brainstorm strategies for enlisting stakeholder support for the program.

4. Identify a leader in your school or in your preparation program. Interview that person about their experiences in working with colleagues. How do they view the role of teacher attitudes? Teacher skills? Inservice training? Administrative leadership?

RELATED READINGS

Brown, J. A. (1977). *Organizing and evaluating elementary school guidance services: Why, what, and how?* Belmont, CA: Brooks/Cole.

Hall, G., & Loucks, S. (1978). Teacher concerns as a basis for facilitating and personalizing staff development. *Teachers College Record, 80,* 36–53.

Loucks-Horsley, S., & Hergert, L. (1985). *An action guide to school improvement.* Washington, DC: Association of Supervision and Curriculum Development.

Reisberg, L. (1988). Developing a consulting model of service delivery in special education. In J. F. West (Ed.), *School consultation: Interdisciplinary perspectives on theory, research, training, and practice.* Austin, TX: Association of Educational and Psychological Consultants.

Reisberg, L., & Wolf, R. (1986). Developing a consulting program in special education: Implementation and interventions. *Focus on Exceptional Children, 16*(3), 1–8.

Zins, J. E., Curtis, M. J., Graden, J. L., & Ponti, C. R. (1988). *Helping students succeed in the regular classroom.* San Francisco: Jossey-Bass.

References

Abelson, M. A., & Woodman R. W. (1983). Review of research on team effectiveness: Implications for teams in schools. *School Psychology Review, 12*, 125-136.

Alpert, J. L. (1976). Conceptual bases of mental health consultation in the schools. *Professional Psychology, 7*, 619-626.

Argyle, M. (1983). *Psychology of interpersonal behavior*. Harmondsworth, Middlesex, England: Penguin.

Armer, B., & Thomas, B. K. (1978). Attitudes towards interdisciplinary collaboration in pupil personnel service teams. *Journal of School Psychology, 16*, 168-177.

Baldwin, C. (1987). A question classification scale for marriage and family therapy. *Journal of Marital and Family Therapy, 13*, 375-386.

Bauwens, J., Hourcade, J. J., & Friend, M. (1989). Cooperative teaching: A model for general and special education integration. *Remedial and Special Education, 10*(2), 17-22.

Bell, C. R., & Nadler, L. (1985). *Clients and consultants: Meeting and exceeding expectations* (2nd ed.). Houston, TX: Gulf.

Benjamin, A. (1987). *The helping interview with case illustrations*. Dallas, TX: Houghton Mifflin.

Bennis, W. G. (1969). *Organizational development: Its nature, origins, and prospects*. Reading, MA: Addison-Wesley.

Bergan, J. R. (1977). *Behavioral consultation*. Columbus, OH: Charles E. Merrill.

Bergan, J. R., & Tombari, M. L. (1975). The analysis of verbal interactions occurring during consultation. *Journal of School Psychology, 13*, 209-226.

Berman, P., & McLaughlin, M. W. (1978). *Federal programs supporting educational change: Vol. VIII. Implementing and sustaining innovations*. Santa Monica, CA: Rand.

Bogdan, R. C., & Bicklen, S. K. (1982). *Qualitative research for education: An introduction to theory and methods*. Boston: Allyn & Bacon.

Brammer, L. M. (1985). *The helping relationship* (3rd ed.). Englewood Cliffs, NJ: Prentice-Hall.

Brinkley, R. C. (1989). Getting the most from client interviews. *Performance and Instruction, 28*(4), 5-8.

Brown, D. K., Kratochwill, T. R., & Bergan, J. R. (1982). Teaching interview skills for problem identification: An analogue study. *Behavioral Assessment, 4*, 63-73.

Brown, D., Pryzwansky, W. B., & Schulte, A. C. (1987). *Psychological consultation: Introduction to theory and practice*. Boston: Allyn & Bacon.

Caplan, G. (1970). *The theory and practice of mental health consultation*. New York: Basic Books.

Chalfant, J. C., Pysh, M. V., & Moultrie, R. (1979). Teacher assistance teams: A model for within building problem solving. *Learning Disability Quarterly, 2*, 85-96.

Christie, L. S., McKenzie, H. S., & Burdett, C. S. (1972). The consulting teacher approach to special education: Inservice training for regular classroom teachers. *Focus on Exceptional Children, 4*, 1-10.

Conoley, J. C. (Ed.). (1981). *Consultation in schools: Theory, research, procedures*. New York: Academic Press.

Conoley, J. C., & Conoley, C. W. (1982). *School consultation: A guide to training and practice*. New York: Pergamon Press.

——. (1988). Useful theories in school-based consultation. *Remedial and Special Education, 9*(6), 14-20.

Cook, L., & Cavallaro, C. C. (1985). *Communication skill training for consultants: A training program* (unpublished manuscript). Northridge: California State University, Northridge.

Cook, L., & Friend, M. (1990a). *A conceptual framework for collaboration in special education*. Preconvention keynote paper presented at the 68th Annual Convention of the Council for Exceptional Children, April 22-27, Toronto, ON.

——. (1990b). Pragmatic issues in the development of special education consultation programs. *Preventing School Failure, 35*(1), 43-46.

——. (1991a). Collaboration in school services for students with disabilities. *Preventing School Failure, 35*(4), 24-27.

——. (1991b). *Preparing teachers to participate in collaborative activities*. Unpublished manuscript, Northern Illinois University, DeKalb, IL.

Cummings, A. L., Murray, H. G., & Martin, J. (1989). Protocol analysis of the social problem solving of teachers. *American Educational Research Journal, 26*, 25-43.

Danziger, K. (1976). *Interpersonal communication*. New York: Pergamon Press.

Delbeq, A. L., Van de Ven, A. H., & Gustafson, D. H. (1975). *Group techniques for program planning*. Glencoe, IL: Scott, Foresman.

DeVito, J. A. (1986). *The interpersonal communication book* (3rd ed.). New York: Harper & Row.

D'Zurilla, T. J., & Nezu, A. M. (1987). The Heppner and Krauskopf approach: A model of personal problem solving or social skills? *Counseling Psychologist, 15*, 463-470.

Evans, S. B. (1980). The consultant role of the resource teacher. *Exceptional Children, 46*, 402-404.

Feezel, J. D. (1987). The communication skills of teachers: A coherent conception. In J. L. McCaleb (Ed.), *How do teachers communicate?: A review and critique of assessment practices* (pp. 29-42). Washington, DC: American Association of Colleges for Teacher Education.

Feldman, R. S. (1985). *Social psychology: Theories, research and applications*. New York: McGraw-Hill.

Fenton, K. S., Yoshida, R. K., Maxwell, J. P., & Kaufman, M. T. (1979). Recognition of team goals: An essential step toward rational decision-making. *Exceptional Children, 45*, 638-644.

Festinger, L. (1957). *A theory of cognitive dissonance*. Stanford, CA: Stanford University Press.

Fiedler, F. E. (1967). *A theory of leadership effectiveness*. New York: McGraw-Hill.

Fleming, C. C., & Fleming, E. R. (1983). Problems in implementation of the team approach: A practitioner's perspective. *School Psychology Review, 12*, 144-149.

Friend, M. (1984). Consultation skills for resource teachers. *Learning Disability Quarterly, 7*, 246-250.

——. (1988). Putting consultation into context: Historical and contemporary perspectives. *Remedial and Special Education, 9*(6), 7-13.

Friend, M., & Cook, L. (1988). Pragmatic issues in school consultation. In J. F. West (Ed.), *School consultation: Interdisciplinary perspectives on theory, research, training, and practice.* Austin: Research and Training Project on School Consultation, University of Texas.

———. (1990). Collaboration as a predictor for success in school reform. *Journal of Educational and Psychological Consultation, 1*(1), 69–86.

Gallessich, J. (1982). *The profession and practice of consultation.* San Francisco: Jossey-Bass.

Glickman, C. D. (1985). *Supervision of instruction: A developmental approach.* Boston: Allyn & Bacon.

———. (1989). Has Sam and Samantha's time come at last? *Educational Leadership, 46*(8), 4–9.

Goodlad, J. (1984). *A place called school.* New York: McGraw-Hill.

Goodman, G. (1978). *SASHAtape user's manual.* Unpublished manuscript, Department of Psychology, UCLA, Los Angeles.

———. (1984). SASHAtapes: Expanding options for help-intended communication. In D. Larson (Ed.), *Teaching psychological skills: Models for giving psychology away* (pp. 271–286). Monterey, CA: Brooks/Cole.

Graden, J. L., Casey, A., & Bonstrom, O. (1985). Implementing a prereferral intervention system: Part II, The data. *Exceptional Children, 51*, 487–496.

Gutkin, T. B., & Curtis, M. J. (1982). School-based consultation: Theory and techniques. In C. R. Reynolds & T. B. Gutkin (Eds.), *Handbook of school psychology.* New York: Wiley.

Hall, E. T, (1959). *The silent language.* Garden City, NY: Doubleday.

———. (1966). *The hidden dimension.* Garden City, NY: Doubleday.

Hall, G. E., & Loucks, S. F. (1978). Teacher concerns as a basis for facilitating staff development. *Teachers College Record, 80*(1), 36–53.

Hargie, O., Saunders, C., & Dickson, D. (1987). *Social skills in interpersonal communication* (2nd ed.). Cambridge, MA: Brookline.

Hayek, R. A. (1987). The teacher assistance team: A prereferral support system. *Focus on Exceptional Children, 20*(1), 1–8.

Heron, T. E., & Harris, K. C. (1987). *The educational consultant: Helping professionals, parents, and mainstreamed students.* Austin, TX: PRO-ED.

Hersey, P., & Blanchard, K. H. (1988). *Management of organizational behavior* (5th ed.). Englewood Cliffs, NJ: Prentice-Hall.

Horowitz, J., & Kimpel, H. (1988). Taking control: Techniques for the group interview. *Training and Development Journal, 42*, 52–54.

Huse, E. F. (1980). *Organization development and change.* New York: West.

Idol, L., Paolucci-Whitcomb P., & Nevin, A. (1986). *Collaborative consultation.* Rockville, MD: Aspen.

Idol, L., & West, J. F. (1987). Consultation in special education (Part II): Training and practice. *Journal of Learning Disabilities, 20*(8), 474–497.

Johnson, D. W., & Johnson, F. P. (1987). *Joining together* (3rd ed.). Englewood Cliffs, NJ: Prentice-Hall.

Johnson, D. W., & Johnson, R. T. (1983). The socialization and achievement crisis: Are cooperative learning experiences the solution? In L. Bickman (Ed.), *Applied social psychology annual 4.* Beverly Hills, CA: Sage.

———. (1990). Social skills for successful group work. *Educational Leadership. 47*(4), 29–33.

Jwaideh, A. R. (1984). The principal as a facilitator of change. *Educational Horizons, 8,* 9–15.

Kaiser, S. M., & Woodman, R. W. (1985). Multidisciplinary teams and group decision-making techniques: Possible solutions to decision-making problems. *School Psychology Review, 14,* 457–470.

Karp, H. B. (1984). Working with resistance. *Training and Development Journal, 38*(3), 69–73.

Kennedy, G. C. (1980). Exploring issues in teacher education: Questions for future research. In

G. E. Hall, S. M. Hord, & G. Brown (Eds.)., *Exploring issues in teacher education: Questions for future research* (pp. 349–356). Austin: University of Texas, Research and Development Center for Teacher Education.

Kenton, S. B. (1989). Speaker credibility in persuasive business communication: A model which explains gender differences. *Journal of Business Communication, 26,* 143–157.

Kurpius, D. J., & Brubaker, J. C. (1976). *Psychoeducational consultation: Definition, functions, preparation.* Bloomington: Indiana University Press.

Lange, J. I. (1984). Seeking client resistance: Rhetorical strategy in communication consulting. *Journal of Applied Communication Research, 12*(1), 50–63.

Lewin, K. (1951). *Field theory in the social sciences.* New York: Harper & Row.

Lieberman, A. (Ed.). (1986). *Rethinking school improvement: Research, craft, and concept.* New York: Teachers College Press.

Lieberman, A., & Miller, L. (1990). Restructuring schools: What matters and what works. *Phi Delta Kappan, 71,* 759–764.

Little, J. W. (1982). Norms of collegiality and experimentation: Workplace conditions of school success. *American Educational Research Journal, 19,* 325–340.

Lortie, D. C. (1975). *School teacher: A sociological study.* Chicago: University of Chicago Press.

Loucks-Horsley, S., & Hergert, L. F. (1985). *An action guide to school improvement.* Andover, MA: ASCD The NETWORK.

McCaleb, J. G. (1987). Review of communication competencies used in statewide assessments. In J. L. McCaleb (Ed.), *How do teachers communicate?: A review and critique of assessment practices* (pp. 7–28). Washington, DC: American Association of Colleges for Teacher Education.

McClellan, E., & Wheatley, W. (1985). Project RETOOL: Collaborative consultation training for post-doctoral leadership personnel. *Teacher Education and Special Education, 8,* 159–163.

McGrath, J. E. (1984). *Groups: Interaction and performance.* Englewood Cliffs, NJ: Prentice-Hall.

MacIver, D. J. (1990). Meeting the needs of young adolescents: Advisory groups, interdisciplinary teacher teams, and school transition programs. *Phi Delta Kappan, 71,* 458–464.

McKay, M., Davis, M., & Fanning, P. (1983). *Messages: The communication skills book.* Oakland, CA: New Harbinger.

Maeroff, G. I (1988). *The empowerment of teachers: Overcoming the crisis of confidence.* New York: Teachers College Press.

Margolis, H., & McGettigan, J. (1988). Managing resistance to instructional modifications in mainstreamed environments. *Remedial and Special Education, 9*(4), 15–21.

Mehrabian, A., & Ferris, S. R. (1967). Influence of attitudes from nonverbal communication in two channels. *Journal of Consulting Psychology, 32,* 248–252.

Menlo, A. (1982). Consultant beliefs which make a significant difference in consultation. In C. L. Warger & L. Aldinger (Eds.), *Preparing special educators for teacher consultation.* Toledo, OH: Preservice Consultation Project, College of Education and Allied Professions, University of Toledo.

Menninger, W. C. (1950). Mental health in our schools. *Educational Leadership, 7,* 520.

Miller, G. R. (1980). On being persuaded: Some basic distinctions. In M. E. Roloff & G. R. Miller (Eds.), *New directions in theory and research* (pp. 16–21). Beverly Hills, CA: Sage.

Molyneaux, D., & Lane, V. W. (1982). *Effective interviewing: Techniques and analysis.* Boston: Allyn & Bacon.

Morrissey, C. T. (1986). Oral history: Tricks of the trade. *International Journal of Oral History, 89*(2), 91–94.

Newman, R. G. (1974). *Groups in schools.* New York: Simon & Schuster.

Nezu, A., & D'Zurilla, T. J. (1981). Effects of problem definition and formulation on the generation of alternatives in the social problem-solving process. *Cognitive Therapy and Research, 5,* 265-271.

Okun, B. F. (1982). *Effective helping: Interviewing and counseling techniques.* Belmont, CA: Brooks/Cole.

Parker, C. A. (Ed.). (1975). *Psychological consultation: Helping teachers meet special needs.* Minneapolis: University of Minnesota Leadership Training Institute.

Parsons, R. D., & Meyers, J. (1984). *Developing consultation skills.* San Francisco: Jossey-Bass.

Passow, A. H. (1986). Beyond the commission reports: Toward meaningful school improvement. In A. Lieberman (Ed.), *Rethinking school improvement* (pp. 206-218). New York: Teachers College Press.

Pfeiffer, S. I. (1980). The school based interprofessional team: Recurring problems and some possible solutions. *Journal of School Psychology, 18,* 388-394.

———. (1981). The problems facing multidisciplinary teams: As perceived by team members. *Psychology in the Schools, 18,* 330-333.

Phillips, V., McCullough, L., Nelson, C. M., & Walker, H. M. (1990). Teamwork among teachers: Promoting a statewide agenda for students at risk for school failure. *Special Services in the Schools.*

Piersal, W. C., & Gutkin, T. B. (1983). Resistance to school-based consultation: A behavioral analysis of the problem. *Psychology in the Schools, 20,* 311-320.

Pryzwansky, W. B. (1974). A reconsideration of the consultation model for delivery of school based psychological service. *American Journal of Orthopsychiatry, 44,* 579-583.

———. (1977). Collaboration or consultation: Is there a difference? *Journal of Special Education, 11,* 179-182.

Pryzwansky, W. B. & Rzepski, B. (1983). School-based teams: An untapped resource for consultation and technical assistance. *School Psychology Review, 12,* 174-179.

Pugach, M. C. (1988). The consulting teacher in the context of educational reform. *Exceptional Children, 55,* 273-275.

Pugach, M. C., & Johnson, J. L. (1988). Rethinking the relationship between consultation and collaborative problem solving. *Focus on Exceptional Children, 21*(4), 1-8.

Reisberg, L., & Wolf, R. (1986). Developing a consulting program in special education: Implementation and interventions. *Focus on Exceptional Children, 19*(3), 1-14.

Rettke, G. R. (1968). Psychological services: A developing model. *Journal of School Psychology, 7,* 34-39.

Reynolds, C. R., Gutkin, T. B., Elliott, S. N., & Witt, J. C. (1984). *School psychology: Essentials of theory and practice.* New York: Wiley.

Rogers, C. R. (1951). *Client-centered therapy.* Boston: Houghton-Mifflin.

Rosenfield, S. (1985). Teacher acceptance of behavioral principles. *Teacher Education and Special Education, 8,* 153-158.

Rosenfield, S. A. (1987). *Instructional consultation.* Hillsdale, NJ: Erlbaum.

Ross, J., & Ross, W. (1982). *Japanese quality circles and productivity.* Reston, VA: Reston Publishing.

Rubin, J. Z. (1989). Some wise and mistaken assumptions about conflict and negotiation. *Journal of Social Issues, 45,* 195-209.

Sarason, S. B. (1982). *The culture of the school and the problems of change* (3rd ed.). Boston: Allyn & Bacon.

Schmuck, R. A., & Runkel, P. J. (1985). *The handbook of organizational development in schools* (3rd ed.). Palo Alto, CA: Mayfield.

Scott, J. J., & Smith, S. C. (1987). *Collaborative schools* (ERIC Digest Series No. 22). Eugene, OR: ERIC Clearinghouse on Educational Management, University of Oregon. (ERIC Document Reproduction Service No. ED 290 233).

Shelby, A. N. (1986). Theoretical bases of persuasion. *Journal of Business Communication, 25,* 5–29.

Sherif, M., & Hovland, C. (1961). *Social judgment: Assimilation and contrast effects in communication and attitude change.* New Haven: Yale University Press.

Sherif, M., & Sherif, C. (1956). *An outline of social psychology.* New York: Harper & Row.

Snow, D. A., Zurcher, L. A., & Sjoberg, G. (1982). Interviewing by comment: An adjunct to the direct question. *Qualitative Sociology, 5,* 285–311.

Sparks, G., Nowakowski, M., Hall, B., Alec, R., & Imrick, J. (1985). School improvement through staff development. *Educational Leadership, 42*(6), 59–61.

Tharp, R., & Wetzel, R. (1969). *Behavior modification in the natural environment.* New York: Academic Press.

Thomas, K. W., & Kilmann R. H. (1974). *Thomas–Kilmann conflict mode instrument.* Tuxedo, NY: Xicom.

Tjosvold, D. (1987). Participation: A close look at its dynamics. *Journal of Management, 13,* 739–750.

Toffler, A. (1980). *The third wave.* New York: Morrow.

Wall, V. D., & Nolan, L. L. (1987). Small group conflict: A look at equity, satisfaction, and styles of conflict management. *Small Group Behavior, 18,* 188–211.

Waugh, R. F., & Punch, K. F. (1987). Teacher receptivity to systemwide change in the implementation stage. *Review of Educational Research, 57,* 237–254.

West, J. F. (1990). Educational collaboration in the restructuring of schools. *Journal of Educational and Psychological Consultation, 1*(1), 23–40.

Westhead, E. (1978). Interviewing: An abbreviated introduction. *Academic Therapy, 13,* 329–336.

Wilson, G. L., & Hanna, M. S. (1990). *Groups in context: Leadership and participation in small groups* (2nd ed.). New York: McGraw-Hill.

Wolf, R. (1979). *Strategies for conducting naturalistic evaluation in socio-educational settings: The naturalistic interview.* Kalamazoo, MI: Occasional Series, Evaluation Center, Western Michigan University.

Zins, J. E., Curtis, M. J., Graden, J. L., & Ponti, C. R. (1988). *Helping students succeed in the regular classroom.* San Francisco: Jossey-Bass.

Zischka, P. C., & Fox, R. (1985). Consultation as a function of school work. *Social Work in Education, 7*(2), 69–79.

Index